A History and Genealogy of the HABERSHAM FAMILY

In connection with the history, genealogy and mention of the families of Clay, Stiles, Cumming, King, Elliott, Milledge, Maxwell, Adams, Houstoun, Screvens, Owens, Demere, Footman, Ellis, Washington, Newell, deTreville, Davis, Barrington, Lewis, Warner, Cobb, Flournoy, Pratt, Nephew, Bolton, Bowers, Cuthbert, and many many other names either as having a connection to some other family or showing of the name as related or connected to some family in this work.

By Joseph Gaston Baillie Bulloch, M. D.
Of the United States Indian Service

COLUMBIA, S. C.
The R. L. Bryan Company
1901

This Work is Dedicated
to the late distinguished physician and surgeon,
my father,
Dr. William Gaston Bulloch,
and
to my mother,
Mary Eliza Adams Lewis,
his wife,
an author and poet,
and
to her friend and cousin,
Mrs. Anna Wylly Habersham,
and
her husband,
Rev. Charles Barrington King,
and
to my friend and relation,
William Neyle Habersham, Esq.

PASTE IN HABERSHAM BOOK.

ERRATA.

Page 16, line 23, read: Phoebe Waight, or Weight; not Wright.

" 19, last line, read: son of Gilbert Neyle and Miss Neville. (?)

" 25, Simkins, not Simpkins.

" 35, John Williams, not William.

" 56, David Adams was without doubt son of Nathaniel 3d.

" 63, last line, Commodore Josiah, not E. F. Tatnall.

" 81, Roswell was son of Timothy King the first.

" 99, line 4, daughters of James Gigniliat and Charlotte Pepper.

" 132, Richard Ellis must have married first Elizabeth Green, and second Miss Hogg; the last, mother of Mrs. de Treville.

Page 182, VI. Eliza Clifford, 2nd daughter of John W. Anderson, married Judge Chisholm. Her name was not Georgia Anderson.

Page 193, line 25 from bottom: Geo. W., and not S. Owens who married Harriet Parsons.

" 172, line 25: and Alice, not Mary, daughter of Col. Richard Bedon.

" 200, Benj. Williamson married Eliza Elliott.

" 206, line 20: Edward M., not C., midshipman on Alabama.

" 63, IV. Called by some, Matilda; by others, Sarah Fenwick. There may have been two of them, tho' the Jones say it was Sarah.

Page 174, Dr. Thomas F. Screven, not P., had also Richard Screven who died.

" 165, line 25: John Dennis of Brunswide, N. J., not Brunswick. He had I. Col. Richard Dennis and three daughters, Sarah C., Elizabeth and Margaret Dennis.

James Gignilliat and Charlotte Pepper had also Elizabeth who married Col. John Cooper. See pages 99 and 103.

Page 120, line 2: Lieutenant Pierre, and not St. Pierre Mercier.

" 97, Note: Ramsay, not Ramsey.

Katharine Elliott Habersham should by sign be g, not c, and be Katharine as on page 8. See pages 5 and 8. Not sure as to marriage of Margaret Lesesne to one mentioned; might be Matthewes; not sure that the son of Edward M. Habersham was Edward J., page 7.

Page 165, Judge Walter S. Chisholm who married Eliza Clifford Anderson, not Georgia Anderson.

Page 167, line 3 from bottom: and her nephew.

" 146, Eliza Screven Hart was daughter of John Hart and Mary Screven, daughter of Gen. James Screven and Mary Odingsell, son of James Screven and Mary Hyrne Smith, etc. See page 171.

The following Corrections and Explenations are made to bring the Book of The Habersham and other Southern families up to date.

Page 5 Line 15 from bottom should read daughter of John Raven Matthewes not daughter of Edward Matthewes.

Page 7 Line 6 from top of page read Richard West Habersham married Martha daughter of John Raven Matthews not Edward.

Page 7 Line 4 from bottom read Margaret Lesesne did not marry Thompson but Wm. Maner Bostick.

Page 8 Line 6 read Ella.

Page 8 Line 8 read Edward Hedden Habersham.

Page 23 read Col Wm. S. Rockwell had also a son Theodosius and two daughters Hermione and Bertha.

Page 40 Line 30 read Edmund not Edward Pendleton Rogers.

Page 49 Line 8 read Alfred Cuthburt and Sarah Jones had only one son Alfred Cuthburt who married Anna M. Davis and had as below given.

Page 63 note bottom of page read Commodore Josiah not E. F. Tattnall.

Page 74 Line 5 read Nov. 9, 1673 not 1763 and same page line 10 Ann not Elizabeth Bowers.

Page 85 read Nicholas J. son of Dr. Nicholas S. Bayard and Ann Livingston and on same page note should be Nicholas J. Bayard m. 1st Sarah daughter of Noble Glen and had I John Bayard m. Rose Howell II. Florida Bayard m. John J. Seay his 2nd wife and had: 1. Clifford Seay m. Miss Streett, 2. Florida Seay m. James J. Tracy.

Page 87 Line 23 read Edward Quintard m. Miss Shepherd daughter of Governor Shepherd of Washington, D. C.

It is now known that the ancestor of the Barringtons was Josiah. See Barrington.

Page 120 See Washington and Stanyarne, and for a more correct version consult the Strother family by Owen, and the Bulloch, Stobo book by Bulloch of these families. After line 4 page 121 the data is correct.

Page 123 and 124 See extra Sheet on Joyner by Dr. J. T. Curry where it is shown that the first Dr. Brantly m. twice. 1st to a McDonald, Sister of Gov. McDonald of Ga. issue. 2nd to Margaret Joyner issue. See also page 124 and compare with record sheet inserted.

Rev. John Brantly and Hemans and others were by McDonald marriage.

Page 125 Consult Bulloch Stobo and Irvine of Cults for a more correct history as regards the marriage and issue of James Stanyarne.

Page 132 See Ellis family by A. S. Salley in which there is a more correct history as to the first generation of marriages of Richard and Edmund and Ellis.

Page 138 and 139 require correction as to Pinckney history and marriages of Col Brewton who did not marry a Pinckney, nor do the Jones's descend from Pinckney. See Salleys History of Pinckney for correct data.

Page 139 at bottom read Robert Brewton and Mellicent Bullock not Bulloch had: Mary who married Joseph Jones, and had, Major John and Millicent Jones.

Page 158 It doesnot appear that this Moore family was the same as that of Gov. Moore of S. C.

Page 164 Line 11 read John Postell not Posey Williamson.

Page 169 and 190 read Samual Screven was the father of those given to Wm. Screven and Catherine Stoll.

Page 198 Line 8 read Wm. Patrick Johnston m. Mary Hooe not Hool,

Page 203 A more correct history of Fuller and Potter and Cuthbert will be found in the book Cuthberts of Castle Hill and their descendants in S. C. and Georgia by Bulloch.

Page 209 Line 14 read Thomas not Wm. Clifford.

Page 220 There was no Pinckney descent of Jones family but the Brewtons were related to Pinckney through a marriage of a Pinckney to Ruth Brewton.

Page 63 For a Correct account of Fenwick family see D. E. Huger Smith's article in January Number of S. C. Genealogical Magazine and an error corrected by me and acknowledged by Mr. Smith in the April number as regards the Jones desent.

J. G. B. BULLOCH, M. D.

ERRATA AND CORRECTIONS

—TO—

"A History and Genealogy of the Habersham and Other Southern Families."

BY DR. J. G. B. BULLOCK.

Page 59, "Son of Joseph Bryan and Mrs. Murray." Should be: Son of Joseph Bryan and

Page 174, "Dr. Thomas P. Screven and Adelaide V. Moore had: †1. Ellen S. Screven, married W. W. Gordon." Should be: Thomas F. Screven and Adelaide V. D. Moore had: 1. Richard Moore Screven. 2. John Screven married Mary G. Bond, daughter of Thomas P. Bond and Julia Floyd Gallie.

†Ellen Screven is the daughter of George P. Screven No. IV.

Page 199. "IX. James Bryan married (March 18, 1790,) Elizabeth, the daughter of James Langley and Elizabeth Polhill. James Bryan and Elizabeth Langley had: 1. Ann Bryan, born April 29, 1791, married. 2. Jane Bryan, born February 22, 1802, died June 1, 1881, married." This James Bryan is said to have died December 20, 1832, and his wife, Elizabeth Bryan, died May 5, 1809. A recent examination of the records in the Superior Court and Court of Ordinary in Savannah, Ga., has developd the fact that the above statement is not true when applied to James Bryan, the son of Jonathan Bryan, and the proof is shown by the following references, viz.: Superior Court, Chatham Co., Ga., Minute B'k F., May 29, 1790, in regard to "James Bryan of Brampton." Also B'k B., Feb. 12, and Aug. 14, 1795: Minute B'k C, April 6 and 18, 1796, in regard to "Joseph Bryan, nephew of James Bryan," and to "Hannah Houstoun and Mary Wylly, sisters to James Bryan." Court of Ordinary, March 27, 1797, as to appointment of "Joseph Bryan Admr. Est. of James Bryan, of Chatham Co., deceased." Superior Court, Dec. 19, 1800, "Ann Bryan vs. Jos. Bryan, et. al. in equity." Jan. 8, 1807, "David Middleton and Ann, wife of the said David (formerly Ann Bryan, wife of James Bryan, deceased), to Joseph Bryan, Hannah Houstoun and Mary Wylly, both widows," in regard to the settlement of the estate of James Bryan, deceased, and record that Ann Middleton, widow, bought a house and lot in Savannah in 1816. As will be seen by reference to the genealogy, under the head of "Bryan," published in the "History and Genealogy of the Habersham and other Southern Families." James Bryan, the son of Jonathan Bryan, was the only James Bryan, who was descended from Joseph Bryan and Janet Cochran, of South Carolina, and the above records prove that his wife was Ann Bryan (family name unknown) and not Elizabeth Langley. James Bryan, the son of Jonathan Bryan, and Ann, his only wife, left no issue.

Page 174. "4. Maj. Thomas Screven married Bessie Lawton." Should be: Maj. Thomas Screven married Emily A. Lawton.

The above corrections are made by Thomas F. Screven.

SAVANNAH, GA., April 15, 1902.

PREFACE

A race unable to narrate a true account of its progress, or to tell from whence it came is apt to be of low intellect, or wanting in energy. The Anglo-Saxon and other progressive people, as a rule, had their bards or historians, and the true historian, in order to get a satisfactory account of his people, must take cognizance of the exploit of the individual, and must consult the family munuments to get a view of the entire historical field. Genealogy gives an account of the deeds of each family, its kinsmen and friends, and no historian can give an accurate account of the deeds of his people without the study of family history, nor can form an idea of a race from an hereditary standpoint without a knowledge of its origin. So many elements enter into the make-up of the American, that without a study of the fountain-heads of the race one can form no conception of its peculiarities, nor say why in intellect, in bravery, in invention, our race surpasses all others. The wit and vivacity of the Irishman, and the manner of the Frenchman, mingled with the blood of the sturdy Scot, and the determined Englishman and the sprinkle of other races, form an individual unsurpassed in the annals of mankind.

In this history of the Habersham and other families, the author feels that he has about completed a history of most of the families of the coast country of Georgia in connection with his other works, though there are yet a good many more to write about.

In regard to the Clay family, the author is much indebted to a chart by Montgomery Cumming, Esq., and to Dr. Henry Stiles, of the North, for a good deal of the descent of the Stiles in Bermuda.

The Adams of South Carolina and Georgia could not be well done justice to without showing the connection of the family to the Ellis and DeTrevilles of South Carolina, and to the Warners, Lewis, Cobbs and others in Virginia and Georgia; and just so as in the one case so in others, the work, though ostensibly of the Habersham family, has included families related to it and genealogies of others related to those connected with the Habershams, though not actually related to the latter family.

To Major Edward Stiles Elliott, to the Virginia Magazine of History and Biography, and to other individuals and periodicals, the author is much indebted. Reference to family trees and records, etc., will verify much of the enclosed work.

The author is also much indebted to Dunwody Jones, Esq., of Atlanta, for most of the Jones line of Liberty County, Georgia, and to James Barnwell Heyward, to Mrs. Emily Verdery, and to R. A. Ellis, Mrs. Patrick Houstoun, Miss Johnston, of Savannah, Ga., Geo. J. Kollock, to Transactions of Huguenot Society of South Carolina, Historical and Genealogical Magazine, and its editor, A. S. Salley, Esq.

It must also be borne in mind that many of these individuals were known to the author or to his mother as far back as the time of Dr. J. C. Habersham, the elder; so that if dates are sometimes wanting, it must be remembered that these people were known to the author or his parents and grand-parents or his friends and their forbears.

It is with regret that the author is not able to insert the coats-of-arms of many of these families. As Mr. Dunwody Jones is positive as to the descent of James Smith, of Darien, and as the author has seen the Smith pedigree, which gives room in several places as to the descent of James Smith from the 1st Landgrave, we put it as Mr. Jones has written.

HABERSHAM

Habersham seems to be but one variety of spelling the name, and Habershon, Haversham, Habergham, Habrinchsham, all appear to have been names derived from the ancient family of Habergham or de Habrincham. The highly honorable, ancient and prominent family of Habersham of Georgia descends from James Habersham, of Beverley, Yorkshire, England, who with his wife Elizabeth lived in that country, and had the following children:

I. James Habersham, baptized February 25th, 1712; died February 26th, 1712.
II. James Habersham, baptized June or January, 26th, 1715; went to Georgia.
III. Elizabeth Habersham, married Ralph Clay.
IV. Edward Habersham.
V. George Habersham, died infant.
VI. Margaret Habersham, died infant.
VII. Joseph Habersham, went to Georgia with his brother.
VIII. Margaret Habersham.

James Habersham, died aged 61, second but eldest surviving son of James Habersham and Elizabeth his wife, who died in 1722, went to Georgia with his friend, the Rev. George Whitfield, in 1740, and with him went his brother Joseph, who seems to have died leaving no issue, and his nephew, Joseph Clay, founder of the Clay family of the coast of Georgia, and son of his sister, Elizabeth Habersham, wife of Ralph Clay, of England.

The Habershams of Georgia were among the foremost of our eminent families, furnishing to the service of the country statesmen, soldiers and professional men, merchants, planters and officers of the church; and so high were the services of this family that the State of Georgia named one of its counties Habersham, after Lieut. Col. Joseph Habersham. Let us take a glance at the various positions of honor, trust and patriotic offices held by this illustrious family, and then see if one can find anything to detract from its worth, or refuse it the high position it has so justly occupied for so long as one of the founders of Georgia.

James Habersham assisted his friend, the celebrated Whitfield, as lay reader and teacher at Bethesda Orphans' Home in 1740, near Savannah, Ga., and was President of Bethesda Orphans' Home; and so great was the appreciation of Mr. Habersham by the government, that he was made Secretary of the Province, assistant to President of the Colony to advance the culture of silk in the Colony. He then became a member of the King's Council, President of the upper House of Assembly; and so great was the confidence in him that Sir James Wright, the Royal Governor, on his departure for the old country, recommended him as a fit person to assume the position of Governor during his absence; so that Hon. James Habersham was for a stormy period the Governor of the Colony of Georgia. He with Mr. Charles Harris established the first commercial house in Georgia, and exported the first bale of cotton. Mr. Habersham, though a Royalist, deeply sympathized with the Colonists, but not sufficiently to break with a country that had showered so much honor upon him, though his sons became ardent patriots and aided the Colony to attain its independence.

His eldest son, Hon. James Habersham, was a prominent patriot and rebel financier, and subsequently Speaker of the Legislature of Georgia, and one of the Trustees of the University of Georgia; and from this eminent Georgian, the first Bishop of Georgia, Right Rev. Stephen Elliott, descends; as do the old Milledge family, a branch of the Maxwells, Footmans, Demeres, Bonds, Screvens, Lesesnes and others. Lieut. Col. Joseph Habersham, second son of Governor Habersham, was Lieutenant Colonel Continental Battalion of Georgia; on Committee to Co-operate with Colonists in strife for freedom and on Committee Friends of Liberty. Takes powder out of Royal magazine for defence of Colonists. Member Provincial Congress, 1775; member Council of Safety. Places Sir James Wright, the Governor, under arrest. Member Executive Council; on Committee to supply arms to the colonists; Speaker of General Assembly; appointed Assistant Justice of Chatham County, Ga., and subsequently appointed Postmaster General of the United States under Washington's administration. Behold him then as soldier, one of the saviors of our country, a patrot among patriots, a statesman and one of the galaxy of stars of our Commonwealth, and one of the founders of the Society of Cincinnati of Georgia, one of the highest orders in America.

John Habersham, third son of the Governor, James Habersham, was one of the foremost patriots of the day. Major in Continental Army, where he aided us as a gallant Georgian to attain our independence, and where he was appreciated as a soldier by General Wayne, and rendered that aid which his blood called upon him to perform. Later on, he was appointed Trustee of the State University; Commissioner in Boundary Disputes; Delegate to Continental Congress; Collector of the Port of Savannah, and President of the Executive Council presiding at the Land Court in Augusta. All honor to Major John Habersham, one of the three but not the least of the gallant Habersham trio—James, Joseph and John Habersham of the Revolution.

Nor are these all who have contributed to the glory of the family; for James Habersham, the rebel financier, had among others Richard Wylly Habersham, member of Congress, attache of legation to a foreign court; and his sons were Richard Wylly, the artist, Rev. Barnard Elliott, an Episcopal minister, Alexander, a naval officer, and Dr. Stephen Habersham, all contributing to the family renown.

Lieut. Col. Joseph Habersham had among others the genial Robert Habersham, an eminent merchant and high officer in the church; and among Robert's sons were Joseph Habersham; Robert, City Sheriff; William Neyle Habersham, merchant, who for years continued the rice factorage business, a commercial establishment carried on or being a continuation of the first commercial house established in Savannah. Mr. Habersham was a man of refinement, a perfect gentleman, a fine musician, great sportsman, an authority on salmon fishing, having a "fly" named after him, and, in other words, a specimen of a "Southern gentleman," a true man and husband; President of reorganized Society of Cincinnati. Two of his sons, Lieut. Joseph Clay Habersham and William Neyle, gallant Confederates, died before Atlanta, Ga., for a cause they believed to be right—all honor to these chivalrous gentlemen of the Confederate States Army.

Major John Habersham, third son of Governor Habersham, had among others Dr. Joseph Clay Habersham, a well known physician of Savannah, a lovely man, also a geologist, discovering a part of the remains of a mastodon near Savannah; and his sons were Dr. Joseph Clay Habersham, many years Health Officer of Savannah, Surgeon in the Confederate States Army, rank of Major, and an officer in Savannah Volunteer Guards. Also, John Bolton Habersham of the Guards, Mayor of city of Brunswick, Ga., and William Waring Habersham, at one time a Judge in the West. Is not this a family for Georgia to be proud of—can we give it too much honor? Long live the name of Habersham of Georgia!

Among the families descended from this most eminent one are to be found the names and branches of Elliott, Barnwell, Boone, Carmichael, Milledge, Footman, Demere, Screven, Shoup, Owens, Haskell, Coleman, Rogers and others of elder line; and Footman, Ward, Daniell, Elliott, White, Jones Simpkins, Colquitt, King, Manigault, Clark, Caperton, Jackson; and with the intermarriages and marriages of these descendents the infusion of the Habersham blood has been far-reaching, and many a one in the United States may be proud of this rich strain of the Habersham blood.

Elizabeth Habersham and Ralph Clay were the parents of Joseph Clay, Esq., the patriot; and from the Habershams, through Clay, descend many families and their branches, such as Cumming, Houstoun, Gray, Cuthbert, Stiles, Wallace, Young, etc.

Governor James Habersham married Mary Bolton, daughter of Robert Bolton, Esq., of Philadelphia, Penn., Church Warden of Christ Church, an eminent merchant, descended from the Boltons, of Bolton and Blackburn, Lancashire, England, from the Lords of Bolton, Saxon Earls of Mercia, and the Saxon Kings. Robert Bolton married Ann Clay, widow, daughter of Winlock Curtis, whose brother was John, Chief Justice of Pennsylvania, sons of John Curtis, Esq., a large landed proprietor of Kent on Delaware, Penn. Winlock Curtis married Ann Bowers, daughter of Benanuel Bowers, son of George Bowers, of Scituate, Mass., and of England, who came to Massachusetts as early as 1637, and was a land owner there whose family attained eminence. Benanuel Bowers married Elizabeth Dunster, daughter of Robert Dunster, and niece of the distinguished Henry Dunster, first President of Harvard College, sons of Henry Dunster, Esq., gentleman, of Balehout, England, in Lancashire.

Robert Bolton had a son, Robert, who married Susannah Mauve, daughter of Matthew and Jane Mauve, from Switzerland, French Huguenots, and many are the descendants from these two marriages; so that from the Boltons, Curtis, Bowers,

Dunsters and Mauves descend not only those already given, but branches of the Adams, Stiles, Footmans, Lewis, Kings, Habershams, Bullochs, Newells, Turners, Wests, Jones and many others. The Boltons also married into the Van Raenssalier, Schuyler and McClean families.

Governor James Habersham and Mary Bolton had the following children:

1. James Habersham, rebel financier, married Esther Wylly.
2. Lieut. Col. Joseph Habersham, married Isabella Rae.
3. Major John Habersham, married Ann Sarah Camber, daughter of Thomas Camber, Esq.

Hon. James Habersham and Esther Wylly (died June 25th, 1808), had the following children:

(A.) Richard Wylly Habersham, M. C., married Sarah Elliott.
(B.) John Habersham, married Ann Barnwell.
(C.) Alexander Habersham.
(D.) Mary Habersham, married James B. Maxwell.
(E.) Esther Habersham, married Stephen Elliott, LL. D., born 1771, son of William Elliott and Mary Gibbes Barnwell, of the ancient Elliott and Barnwell families of South Carolina.

Hon. Richard Wylly Habersham, M. C., married, May 18th, 1808, Sarah Hazzard, daughter of Capt. Barnard Elliott and Hazzard, and had the following children:

(a.) Richard Wylly Habersham, artist, married Martha Mathewes, daughter of Edward Mathewes, of Charleston.
(b.) Rev. Barnard Elliott Habersham, married Emma Mathewes, sister of above.
(c.) Alexander Wylly Habersham, of navy, married Jessie Steele.
(d.) Stephen Elliott Habersham, M. D., married first, Lucy Pollard, and second, Virginia Garner, of Augusta, Ga.
(e.) Sarah Georgia Habersham.
(f.) Francis Barnard Habersham, died, buried in New York City.
(g.) Catherine Elliott Habersham, married July 25th, 1836, John Milledge, son of Governor John Milledge, the ardent patriot, U. S. Senator, &c., who

married, 1812, Ann Lamar, daughter of Thomas Lamar, of Edgefield, S. C., son of John Milledge, Captain in a troup of rangers, and a prominent man in the Colony, who came to Georgia with Oglethorpe from England.

John Milledge and Catherine Habersham had:

I. Capt. John Milledge, State Librarian, married Fanny C. Robinson, of Virginia.

II. Richard H. Milledge, married Rosa Gresham.

III. Kate Milledge, artist.

IV. Gazaway Elliott Lamar Milledge, married Lillie Brassey.

MILLEDGE

This ancient Georgia family, whose ancestor came over with Oglethorpe, has contributed in many ways to the advancement of the State, and amongst members of this eminent family was, first of all, the ancestor of the family, John Milledge, who held positions of trust, civil and military, and who, on March 29th, 1742, by authority of the Crown, became Captain of a troop of rangers, his commission being signed by Oglethorpe. He was also member of Colonial Assembly, 1768. His son, Captain John Milledge, born in Savannah, Ga., 1757, died at the Sand Hills, near Augusta, Ga., February 9th, 1818. Lawyer, Captain in Revolutionary War, member of Georgia Legislature, member of Congress, 1792-5-9, Governor of Georgia, 1802, U. S. Senator, President *pro tem.* of Senate in 1809, benefactor of State University, giving it 700 acres of land, a large part of which forms the present site of Athens. Such, then, was this eminent man, whose services to country and State can scarce be eclipsed, for he was a warrior, statesman and benefactor to his native land. His son, John Milledge, born in Augusta, Ga., January 8th, 1814, died in Forsyth, Ga., May 13th, 1872—a prominent lawyer and member of the State Legislature, who married, July 25th, 1836, Catherine, daughter of Hon. Richard Wylly Habersham and Sarah Hazzard Elliott, and had, among others, *Col. John Milledge, born in Augusta, Ga., April 7th, 1837; graduated with rank of Captain, Georgia Military Insti-

*Married Fannie C., daughter of Edwin Robinson, of Virginia, July 11th, 1865; married second

tute; entered the Confederate States Army as Captain of artillery; afterwards was lawyer, police Judge, State Librarian, Colonel of State troops and Vice-President Sons of Revolution of Georgia. Milledgeville, the former capital of the State, was named after this eminent family.

(a.) Richard Wylly Habersham, Jr., married Martha, daughter of Edward Mathewes, of Charleston, S. C., and had the following children:

(1.) Edward M. Habersham, married Miss Miller.

(2.) Esther Habersham, married Edward Blake Lesesne.

(3.) Mary Habersham, married Mr. Johnson.

(4.) Mattie or Martha Habersham, married first Mr. Moffatt.

(5.) Katharine Habersham.

(1.) Edward Habersham and Miss Miller, daughter of Miller, had:

(1.) Edward J. Habersham, died.

(2.) Righton Habersham.

(3.) Habersham, died.

(2.) Esther Habersham and Edward Blake Lesesne (son of Isaac Lesesne, of an old Huguenot family, and Mary Louisa, daughter of Edward Blake and Catharine DeVeaux, son of Capt. John Blake and Margaret Mercier, daughter of Nathaniel DeVeaux and Eleanor Cursan, son of Andrew DeVeaux and Catharine Barnwell, daughter of John and Martha Barnwell,* son of John Barnwell and Ann Berners; Andrew DeVeaux was a son of Andrew DeVeaux and Hannah, daughter of Col. John Palmer and Elizabeth Bellinger, daughter of Landgrave Edmund Bellinger), had:

(I.) Marie Lesesne.

(II.) Katherine Lesesne, married Jasperson Smith.†

(III.) Mattie Lesesne, married Smith, son of Jasperson Smith.

(IV.) Margaret Lesesne, married Mr. Thompson.

(V.) Habersham Lesesne.

(VI.) Edward Lesesne.

(VII.) Richard Lesesne.

*John Barnwell married Phoebe, daughter of John Chaplain and Phoebe Jenkins.

Mattie Habersham and Moffatt had issue, Mattie Habersham, married second, and had issue.

(b.) Rev. Barnard Elliott Habersham‡ and Emma, daughter of Edward Mathewes, of Charleston, had issue:

(1.) Ella Habersham.

(2.) Robert Habersham, married

(3.) Richard Habersham, died and buried Rio Janeiro, Brazil.

(4.) Frank Habersham, married, and died in Portland, Ore.

c. Katharine Elliott Habersham, married John Milledge, son of Gov. Milledge, of Georgia, and had:

I. John Milledge, married Fannie C. Robinson, of Richmond, Va., married, second —

II. Richard Habersham Milledge, married Rosa Gresham, of Waynesboro, Ga., and had:

(1.) Katharine Elliott Milledge.

(2.) John Milledge.

(3.) Harriett Milledge.

(4.) Richard Habersham Milledge.

(5.) Rosa Milledge.

(6.) Adeline Milledge.

III. Katharine Elliott Milledge, artist, dead.

IV. Gazaway Lamar Milledge, married Lillian Bussey (or Brassey), of Texas.

(c.) Alexander Wylly Habersham, of the navy, late of Baltimore, Md., married Jessie Steele, of Annapolis, Md., grand-daughter of Francis Scott Key, and had:

(1.) Alexander Habersham.

(2.) Harry Habersham.

(3.) Edward or Edwin Habersham.

(4.) Wylly Habersham.

(5.) Nellie Habersham.

(d.) Stephen Elliott Habersham, M. D., married, first, Lucy Pollard, of Virginia, and had:

(1.) Margaret Reeves Habersham.

(2.) Richard Pollard Habersham.

(3.) Pauline Reeves Habersham.

‡In a chart the following are given also as his children: Emma, Elliott, John, Edgar, Marlquinha, Edith and Lillian.

(d.) Stephen Elliott Habersham, M. D., married, second, Katharine Virginia, only child of Dr. John Garner and Sarah Ann Urquhart,* of Augusta, Ga., and had:

(1.) Sarah Isabel Habersham.

(2.) John Garner Habersham.

(B.) John Habersham, son of Hon. James Habersham and Esther Wylly, married Tuesday evening, January 14th, 1812, Ann Middleton, daughter of Gen. John Barnwell, of Beaufort, S. C., and had:

(a.) Ann Hutson Habersham, married Rev. Stephen Elliott (first marriage), son of William Elliott and Phoebe Waight, and cousin of Bishop Elliott, of Georgia. They had issue:

I. Gen. Stephen Elliott, married Charlotte Stuart.

II. Rev. John Habersham Elliott, married first, Mary B. Fuller, and second, Rosa Stuart.

III. Ralph E. Elliott, born 1834; died June 6, 1864; Captain C. S. A., killed at Cold Harbor.

IV. Hon. William Elliott, married, first, Isabel Barnwell, and second, Sarah Stuart.

V. Maria Elliott, died 1841.

VI. Thomas M. Stuart Elliott, married Ann Stuart Rhett.

Rev. Stephen Elliott married, second, Miss Sarah Gibbes DeSaussure, and had:

I. Henry D. Elliott, married Mary Lowndes.

II. Louis DeSaussure Elliott, died young.

(D.) Mary Habersham, daughter of Hon. James

*NOTE.—John McLeod, of that ilk, had Mary McLeod, who married Sir James MacDonald, of Slate, son of Sir Donald MacDonald, Baronet, of Nova Scotia, and "Fair" Janet MacKenzie. Sir James MacDonald and Mary MacLeod had Marian MacDonald, who married Patrick MacGregor, and had James MacGregor, Major in the British Army; attainted with his clan and settled in King William County, Va., under the name of Thomas Mack Gehee, will dated 1727. His son, Edward MacGehee, married Katharine DeJarnette, daughter of David DeJarnette, son of Jean DeJarnette, and had David MacGehee, who married Jane Hodnett, daughter of John Hodnett and Katharine Brooke, daughter of Brooke and Miss Gartery, and had Katharine Brooke, Gartery McGehee, who married David Urquhart, born in Cromarty, Scotland, May 15th, 1779; died in Augusta, Ga., November 20th, 1842. From this line descends Mrs. S. E. Habersham, the Garners and Glenns.

*Her father came to Virginia in 1660, married Miss Gartery.

Habersham and Esther Wylly, married James B. Maxwell,* and had the following children:

I. Mary C. Maxwell, married Richard S. Footman.

II. Jane E. Maxwell, married Joseph Pelot, issue.

III. Susan Jefferson Maxwell,† married Raymond P., son of Raymond Demere, a descendant of an officer of Oglethorpe's Regiment, and had:

(1.) Raymond Demere, who had Raymond Demere, married first, Wylly, second, Lila Houstoun.

(2.) Frank Demere, married Maria Victoria Ferrill, and had Frank Demere.

(3.) Houstoun Demere.

IV. Elizabeth Maxwell.

I. Mary C. Maxwell and Richard S. Footman, son of Richard Footman and Elizabeth Caldwell, daughter of William Maxwell, had:

(1.) Mary White Footman, married Col. John Screven, issue.

(2.) Margaret Footman, married John Owens, issue.

(3.) Elizabeth Footman, married Wylly Woodbridge, issue.

(4.) Maria Footman.

†NOTE.—Susan Jefferson Maxwell and Raymond Demere had:
(I.) Raymond Demere, married Lila Houstoun, and had:
(1.) Edward Demere.
(2.) Raymond Demere.
(II.) Frank Demere, married Maria Victoria Ferrell, and had Frank Demere.
(III.) Mary Demere, married James Wilkins and had issue.

*Mrs. Richard S. Footman married second, Thomas P. Bond, and had:
I. Thomas P. Bond, who married Julia F. Gallie.
(1.) Mary G. Bond, married John, son of Dr. Thomas P. Screven, and had several sons and daughters (see Screven).
(2.) †Claude Bond.

‡NOTE.—His first wife was Jane, daughter of Governor Archibald Bulloch; second, Mary Habersham; third, Maria Schley.

MAXWELL 1

James Maxwell, of the ancient family of Maxwell, of Scotland, came to Georgia at an early day, and he and his brother Audley, of Liberty County, Ga., were the progenitors of the old honorable Maxwell family of Georgia.

James Maxwell married Constant Butler, and had James Maxwell, who married Mary Simmons, and had:

I. James Maxwell, married Ann, daughter of Hon. Capt. James Mackay.
II. William Maxwell, married.
III. John Maxwell.
IV. Jane Maxwell, married Joseph Gray.*
V. Elizabeth Maxwell, married Thomas Young
VI. Esther Maxwell, married Sabb.
VII. Mary Maxwell.
VIII. Constant Maxwell.

(I.) James Maxwell married Ann Mackay, daughter of Capt. James Mackay, of Strathy Hall, Ga., member of King's Council, Captain and a very prominent man, and had Mary Maxwell,† who married John Butler Maxwell, and had:

(1.) James McKay Maxwell.
(2.) Stephen Maxwell, ancestor to branch of Bakers.
(3.) John Butler Maxwell.
(4.) Simons Maxwell, married and had issue.
(5.) Ann Maxwell.
(6.) Barbara Maxwell.

(II.) William Maxwell, second son of James Maxwell and Mary Simmons, married, and had:

(1.) James Benjamin Maxwell, married first, Jane Bulloch; married second, Mary Habersham; married third, Maria Schley.
(2.) John Butler Maxwell, married Mary Maxwell, daughter of James Maxwell and Ann Mackay, daughter of Hon. James Mackay.

*Joseph Gray and Jane Maxwell had:
(1.) Adam Joseph Gray.
(2.) Dunbar Gray.

†Mary Maxwell married second, Major Lachlan McIntosh, and had Maria McIntosh, authoress.

(3.) Elisha Maxwell.
(4.) Wm. Maxwell.
(5.) Elizabeth (Caldwell) Maxwell, married Dr. Richard Footman, and had:
I. Richard Footman, married January 22d, 1779, Mary C. Maxwell, first cousin.
II. Henry Footman.
III. William Footman.
IV. Edward Footman, married first, Susan Ward, daughter of Benjamin Ward, and Ann, daughter of Major John Habersham; married second, Mary Adams.

James Benjamin Maxwell, son of William, son of James Maxwell and Mary Simmons, son of James Maxwell and Constant Butler, married first, February 23d, 1786, Jane, daughter of Governor Archibald Bulloch, and had:
(1.) William Bulloch Maxwell. He married second, Mary Habersham, daughter of Hon. James Habersham, eldest son of Governor James Habersham and Mary Bolton, and had:
I. Mary C. Maxwell, married Richard S. Footman.
II. Jane Maxwell, married Joseph Pelot.
III. John Butler Maxwell, married Mary Maxwell, his first cousin, daughter of James Maxwell and Ann Mackay, daughter of Hon. James Mackay, of Strathy Hall.
IV. Elisha Maxwell.
V. William Maxwell.
VI. Eliza Caldwell Maxwell.

James B. Maxwell, married third, Maria Schley, and had:
(1.) James Habersham Maxwell.

Simons Maxwell, son of John Butler Maxwell and Mary Maxwell, daughter of James Maxwell and Ann, daughter of Hon. James Mackay, married, and had:
(1.) James Maxwell.
(2.) Alexander Maxwell.
(3.) Mary Maxwell.
(4.) Hannah G. Maxwell.

Hon. James Mackay had also a daughter, who married Roger Kellsall, of Fairfield, Ga., and had:
I. John Kellsall.
II. Ann Kellsall.

From Hon. James Mackay descend a branch of Arnold, Appleton, Baker, etc.

Wylly Woodbridge and Elizabeth Footman had:

I. Richard Woodbridge, married Miss Cloud, issue.
II. William Woodbridge.
III. Harry Woodbridge, married Eliza Lamar, daughter of Col. C. A. L. Lamar and Caro Nicoll, daughter of Judge Nicoll and Miss Anderson, daughter of George Anderson, and had:
(1.) Wylly Woodbridge.
(2.) Lilla Woodbridge, married Mayhew Cunningham.
(3.) Caroline Woodbridge.

Elizabeth Maxwell, who married Thomas Young, was a daughter of James Maxwell and Mary Simmons. In her will, on record in Court House, Savannah, Ga., she speaks of following relatives:

Grand-niece, Mary C. Maxwell, daughter of my nephew, James B. Maxwell and Mary Habersham, and James Habersham Maxwell, son of James B. Maxwell and Maria Schley.

Nephew, Simmons Maxwell, and his children, Hannah G., James, Alexander and Mary Maxwell; grand nephew, John Maxwell, son of nephew, John Butler Maxwell; Maria McIntosh, daughter of Mary Maxwell; John Stephens Maxwell, son of nephew, Moultrie Maxwell; Susan Jefferson Maxwell, daughter of James B. and Mary Habersham.

Grand nephews: Richard, Henry, William and Edward Footman, sons of Elizabeth, late Elizabeth Caldwell; niece, Esther, or Hetty C. Maxwell; niece, Nelly Fleming; sister,

NOTE.—William Woodbridge descended from the ancient families of Woodbridge and the Governors, Bradford and Dudley, married Helen, daughter of Col. Richard Wylly and Mary Bryan Morel, widow of Hon. John Morel, and daughter of Hon. Jonathan Bryan, and had:

(I.) Wylly Woodbridge, married first, Elizabeth Footman, issue. He married second, Florence Stiles, his cousin, daughter of Joseph Stiles and Margaret V. Adams, no issue.
(II.) Grafton Woodbridge, married Charlotte Maria Thiot, his cousin, and descended from Mary, daughter of Col. Richard Wylly and Mary Bryan Morel, daughter of Hon. Jonathan Bryan and Mary Williamson.

Grafton Woodbridge and Charlotte Maria Thiot had:

1. Helen Bryan Woodbridge, married E. A. Penniman, of Brunswick and Savannah, Ga.
2. Charles Woodbridge, married in Texas; died 1901.
3. Grafton Woodbridge, died at an early age.

Charles Woodbridge left two daughters, Helen Bryan and Alice Woodbridge.

Constant; nephew, John Maxwell; nephew, Stephen Maxwell; grand niece, Jane E. Pelot, daughter of James B, Maxwell.

James Mackay, of Strathy Hall, Esq., member of King's Council, etc., speaks of his grand-son, John Kellsall; grand-daughter, Ann Kellsall; grand-children, Barbara, Ann, Simmons, John and Stephen Maxwell, children of deceased daughter, Ann Mackay, by her late husband, James Maxwell. To Mary Maxwell, wife of John Butler Maxwell, daughter of deceased daughter, Ann.

Mary Simmons, wife of James Maxwell, of St. Phillips Parish, Ga., bequeathes to sons: James, William and John Maxwell; daughters: Jane Gray, wife of Joseph Gray; Elizabeth, wife of Thomas Young; Esther, Mary and Constant Maxwell. Grand-sons: Morgan Sabb, William Maxwell, Adam Joseph Gray, Dunbar Gray, Elisha Maxwell, James Mackay Maxwell, James Benjamin Maxwell and John Butler Maxwell, certain property.

c. Mary White Footman, daughter of Richard S. Footman and Mary C. Maxwell, daughter of James B. and Mary (Habersham) Maxwell, married Col. John Screven of ancient family, and had:

I. Proctor Screven.
II. Georgia Screven.
III. Elizabeth Screven, married Thomas Arnold, and had Louise and Mary Arnold.
IV. Thomas Screven, married Emily Lawton. Superintendent of Police, Ordinary of Chatham County, Major also of S. V. Guards.

Col. Screven married second, Mary Brown, widow, daughter of Nesbitt and Martha Berrien, issue also.

John Owens, Esq., attorney at law, son of Geo. W. Owens, M. C., and Sarah Wallace, son of Owen Owens, a Welshman, and an early settler in Georgia, at one time Alderman of Savannah. Sarah A. Wallace was daughter of John Wallace, British Vice Consul, who married Mary, a sister of Geo. Anderson, one

NOTE.—John Wallace, British Consul for Georgia, died September 14th, 1804. His wife was Mary Wallace, sister of George Anderson, born July 30th, 1766; died December 31st, 1852.

James Wallace, British Vice Consul, died January 25th, 1825, age 71 years.

Jane Howard, daughter of John Wallace, age 62, died March 19th, 1845. T. E. Lloyd died September 14th, 1820, age 34.

John Wallace, Jr., died May 13th, 1816, age 24.

Mrs. D, Anderson died May 5th, 1812, age 76.

of the Aldermen of Savannah, Ga., children of Capt. George Anderson, of Berwick, Scotland, and Deborah Grant. John Owens, married Margaret Footman (daughter of Richard S. Footman and Mary C. Maxwell), daughter of James Benjamin Maxwell and Mary Habersham, daughter of James Habersham and Esther Wylly, son of Governor James Habersham and Mary Bolton, and had:

I. Mary Wallace Owens, married Paul Haskell, and had:
(1.) Charles Haskell.
(2.) Paul Haskell.
(3.) Langdon Haskell.
II. Watkins Owens, dead.

Esther Habersham, daughter of Hon. James Habersham and Esther Wylly (sister of Col. Richard Wylly, of the Revolution, Alexander Wylly, Speaker of Colonial Assembly, and of William Wylly, a very ancient family from Ireland, and son of Governor James Habersham and Mary Bolton), married Hon. Stephen Elliott, LL. D., a distinguished naturalist of South Carolina, of ancient family of Elliott of South Carolina (Esther Habersham died June 25, 1808), and had:

I. Rt. Rev. Stephen Elliott, first Bishop of Georgia; married first, Mary G. Barnwell; second, Charlotte Bull Barnwell.
II. William Elliott, married Mary O'Brien Habersham.
III. Rev. James H. Elliott, married first, Harriett Fuller; married second, Mrs. Shanklin, born Catharine A. Sadler, daughter of Henry R. Sadler and Catharine Ann McIntosh, daughter of George McIntosh, fourth son of John Mohr McIntosh, the Highland Chief of Borlum, Scotland. George McIntosh married a daughter of Sir Patrick Houstoun of Georgia, Baronet.
IV. Emma Elliott, married John G. Barnwell.
V. Phoebe Elliott, married Rt. Rev. William J. Boone.
VI. Isabel Elliott.
VII. Esther H. Elliott.
VIII. Maria B. Elliott, married William Habersham, son of Lieut. Col. Joseph and Isabella (Rae) Habersham, and had:
I. William Habersham.
II. Stephen Elliott Habersham.

III. Isabella Habersham, married, first, Henry Mongin; second, Rev. William Williams.

Right Rev. Stephen Elliott, first Bishop of Georgia, married, first, Mary Gibbes Barnwell (daughter of Hon. Robert Barnwell and Eliza Hayne Wigg), and had:

(1.) Stephen Elliott, married Mary Roberts.

(2.) Eliza Elliott, married W. P. Carmichael, and had:

I. Stephen Carmichael, married Miss Claghorn.

II. Anderson Carmichael, married M. L. Owens, daughter of Richard Owens, Esq., brother of Col. Geo. S. and John Owens, Esq.

III. Mary Carmichael.

Stephen Elliott had:

(1.) Chetwood Elliott, married Miss Pullen, issue.

(2.) Stephen Elliott, married Henrietta Hartridge, issue: Stephen and Mary.

(3.) Mary Elliott, married Major Crowther.

Bishop Elliott married, second, Charlotte Bull Barnwell, daughter of Capt. John G. Barnwell and Sarah Bull, and had:

I. Rt. Rev. R. W. B. Elliott, Bishop of Western Texas, who married Caroline, daughter of Dr. Ralph Emms Elliott, and M. C. Mackay, son of Hon. William Elliott and Phoebe Wright, and had:

(1.) Stephen Elliott, Lieutenant U. S. A., married Kate Otey, issue: Caroline and Dabney.

(2.) Phoebe Elliott, married A. Shepard, Jr., issue.

(3.) Charlotte Elliott.

(4.) Percy Elliott, dead.

(5.) Robert Elliott.

(6.) Meta Elliott.

II. Dr. John B. Elliott (son of Bishop Stephen Elliott), Professor in University of Louisiana, married Lucy Pinckney Huger, daughter of Joseph Alston Huger, M. D., and Mary Esther, daughter of Francis Kinloch Huger, descendants of the Middletons, Kinlochs, Elliotts, etc., and of ancient descent, and had:

(1.) Jno. B. Elliott, Jr., M. D., married, February 8,

NOTE.—William Elliott married Mary Barnwell, born April 11th, 1745, daughter of Nathaniel Barnwell, born March 3d, 1705, who married, April 7th, 1738, Mary Gibbes, daughter of Col. Jno. Gibbes and Mary Woodward, and grand-daughter of Governor Robert Gibbes, and from William Elliott and Mary Barnwell descended: Stephen Elliott, his son, Bishop Elliott, Bishop Boone and others.

1900, Noel Louise Forsythe, born December 25, 1876.

(2.) Esther Huger Elliott.
(3.) Joseph Huger Elliott.
(4.) Charlotte B. Elliott.
(5.) Huger Elliott.
(6.) Stephen Elliott, dead.
(7.) Susy Elliott.
(8.) Percy Elliott.

III. Habersham Elliott, son of Bishop Elliott, married Elizabeth Thompson, and had Hannah Elliott.

IV. Hester Elliott, daughter of Bishop Elliott, married Rev. F. A. Shoup, and had:

I. Francis Shoup, married Mary Howard.
II. Charlotte Shoup, married William Nichol.
III. Mary Shoup.
IV. Stephen Shoup.

V. Charlotte B. Ellott, daughter of Bishop Elliott, married C. McD. Puckette, and had:

I. Stephen Puckette.
II. Charlotte Puckette.
III. John Puckette.

VI. Sarah Barnwell Elliott, daughter of Bishop Elliott, is a well known author.

II. William Elliott, son of Hon. Stephen Elliott and Esther Habersham, married Mary O'B. Habersham, daughter of Robert Habersham and Mary O'Brien, and had:

(1.) Robert H. Elliott, married Mary S. Elliott,* daughter of Dr. Ralph Emms Elliott and M. C. Mackay, and had:

(A.) Arthur B. Elliott, married Mary White, daughter of Rev. Robb White, of Savannah, Ga.

III. Rev. James Habersham Elliott, son of Hon. Stephen Elliott, LL. D., and Esther Habersham, married, first, Harriett Fuller, and had:

(1.) James H. Elliott.

NOTE.—Mary Elliott married, second, Joseph A. Huger, and had:
(1.) Elise Huger, married Robert Harrison.
(2.) Lina Huger.
(3.) Emma Huger.
(4.) Claremont Huger.
(5.) Percy Huger.

(2.) Elizabeth Elliott.

(3.) Harriett Elliott, married Butolph.

He married, second, Mrs. Shanklin,† born Catharine A. Sadler, daughter of Henry R. Sadler and Catharine Ann McIntosh, daughter of George McIntosh and Miss Houstoun, daughter of Sir Patrick Houstoun, Baronet, and had:

(1.) Stephen Elliott.

(2.) Frank Elliott.

(3.) Elizabeth Elliott.

IV. Emma Elliott, daughter of Hon. Stephen Elliott, LL. D., and Esther Habersham, married John G. Barnwell, and had:

I. Capt. John G. Barnwell, married Catharine McIntosh Shanklin.

II. Isabel Barnwell, married Hon. William Elliott.

III. Rev. Stephen E. Barnwell, married Matilda Cushman; second, Elizabeth Cleland.

IV. Middleton Stuart Barnwell.

V. William Habersham Barnwell, married Ann S. Mazyck.

VI. Robert W. Barnwell, married Margaret Blair.

VII. Robert Habersham Barnwell, married Eliza S. Hulbert.

VIII. James E. Barnwell.

N. B.—There were two other sons, James E. and Robert E., who died young, and had brothers born afterward of same name.

V. Phoebe C. Elliott, daughter of Hon. Stephen Elliott and Esther Habersham, married Rt. Rev. William J. Boone, of China, and had:

I. Rt. Rev. William J. Boone, Bishop of China, married, first Mary C. DeSaussure; second, Henrietta Harris.

II. Rev. Thomas Boone, married, issue.

III. Dr. James Boone married twice, issue (Dr. Boone was by another marriage).

General Stephen Elliott, son of Rev. Stephen Elliott and Ann Hutson Habersham, married Charlotte Stuart, and had:

(1.) Rev. Stephen Elliott.

(2.) Charles Elliott.

(3.) Henry Elliott.

†Rev. James Shanklin married Catharine A. Sadler, and he died, when she married, the second time, Rev. James H. Elliott.

NOTE.—Thus is finished the elder line of Habersham, of Georgia, from whom descend so many families of prominence in Georgia and South Carolina, such as Barnwell, Elliott, Milledge, Boone—who have in turn married into Huger, Middleton, Rhett, Stuart, Fuller and Bull; so that these families embrace a large portion of the early blood of Carolina. It will be seen that Barnwell, Elliott, Milledge, Owens, Daniell, Screven, Maxwell and many others descend from the Boltons, Curtis, Bowers and Dunsters.

Rev. William Hutson had four daughters; one married Gen. John Barnwell, one a Hayne, one William Hazzard, and one Perroneau.

Thomas Hutson and Esther, his wife, lived and died in England. Their son, Rev. William Hutson, born in England, August 14, 1720, studied law, and came to the New World and was converted by Whitfield. He died April 18, 1761. His first wife was Mary Woodward, widow of Chardon and daughter of Richard Woodward and Sarah Stanyarne.

II. Lieutenant Colonel Joseph Habersham, born in Savannah, July 28th, 1751, Postmaster General of the United States, and second son of Gov. James Habersham and Mary Bolton, married at Brampton plantation, in Georgia, on May , 1776, Isabella, daughter of *John Rae, Esq., and their children were:

(A.) James Habersham.
(B.) John Habersham.
(C.) Mary Habersham.
(D.) Isabella Habersham.
(E.) Joseph Habersham.*
(F.) Robert Habersham, born December 25th, 1783.
(G.) *Joseph Habersham, born November 24th, 1785; died Savannah, Ga., December 14ts, 1801, age 46 years, is buried in family vault; married Susan Dorothy Habersham.
(H.) Isabella Rae Habersham.
(I.) William Habersham, born January 1, 1772; died Paris, France, 1820.
(J.) Eliza Ann Habersham.
(K.) Susan Ann Habersham.

Robert Habersham, son of Lt. Col. Joseph Habersham and Isabella Rae, was an eminent merchant, and held high office in the church. He married three times—first, December 22d, 1799, to Mary O'Brien, of Beaufort; second, Elizabeth Neyle, daughter of William Neyle, and Ville Ponteaux, (?) son of William Neyle and Miss Neyle (?) of an old Carolina family,

*The author thinks that these Josephs are the same, or may be one died and the other was named Joseph, the latter married Susan Dorothy Habersham.

related to the Carsons, Herbemonts and Brevoorts; third, to Mary Butler Habersham, his first cousin, daughter of Major John Habersham and Ann Sarah Camber; and by the last marriage had:

(a.) Robert Habersham, City Sheriff.

(b.) John Rae Habersham.

(c.) Susan Ellen Habersham, married William Coleman of Pennsylvania, and had:

I. Robert Coleman, married, first, J. Elizabeth Clarke; second, Edith Johnstone, issue.

II. Anna Caroline Coleman, married Archibald Rogers, issue.

(d.) Maria Habersham, married Rev. Rufus White, issue.

(e.) Telfair Habersham.

Robert Habersham and Mary O'Brien had:

(a.) Joseph Habersham.

(b.) Mary O'Brien Habersham, married William Elliott, brother of Bishop Stephen Elliott, sons of Hon. Stephen Elliott, LL. D., and Esther Habersham, and had:

I. Robert Habersham Elliott who married Mary S. Elliott, daughter of Dr. Ralph Emms Elliott and M. L. Mackay, and had (she married, second, J. A. Huger):

1. A. B. Elliott, married Mary C. White, daughter of Rev. Robb White, of ancient Virginia family and descent.

Robert Habersham and Elizabeth Neyle had two children:

I. William Neyle Habersham, President of the recently organized Society of the Cincinnati, and who married Josephine, daughter of Dr. Joseph Clay Habersham and Ann Wylly Adams, daughter of Nathaniel Adams and Mary Ann Wylly, daughter of Col. Richard Wylly and Mary Bryan, daughter of Joseph Bryan and Mrs. Murray, son of Joseph Bryan; the second Nathaniel Adams was son of Nathaniel Adams and

*The Rae family came to Georgia at a very early day, and we find John Rae, a Scouts boatman, and later Col. John Rae, Capt. John Rae, Col. Robert Rae. The plantation up the river was Rae's Hall. The Raes were from Ireland, and one of them married Gen. Samuel Elbert, of the Revolution, and we find Col. Rae a sterling patriot, and Robert Rae, a member of Provincial Congress.

Anne, daughter of Robert Bolton, brother of Mary Habersham, son of Robert Bolton and Ann Curtis. Dr. Joseph Clay Habersham was son of Major John Habersham, of the Revolution, brother of Lt. Col. Joseph, and son of Gov. James Habersham and Mary Bolton. William Neyle Habersham was born July 25th, 1817; died September 20th, 1899.

II. Isabella Habersham, died.

William Neyle Habersham and Josephine Habersham had:

(1.) Joseph Clay Habersham, Captain, killed in C. S. Army before Atlanta.

(2.) Anna Wylly Habersham, married G. Fenwick Jones.

(3.) William Neyle Habersham, killed battle of Atlanta.

(4.) Robert Beverly Habersham, married Margaret Schley; second, Maria Schley.

(5.) James Habersham, died young.

(6.) Lilla Neyle Habersham, married Wellborn Colquitt.

(7.) Maybelle Habersham, married W. D. Simkins.

(8.) Mary Josephine Habersham, died young.

(9.) Edward Camber Habersham.

Annie C. Coleman and Archibald Rogers had:

(I.) Archibald Rogers, died.

(II.) Edmund P. Rogers.

(III.) Robert Coleman Rogers.

(IV.) William Coleman Rogers.

(V.) Rae Habersham Rogers.

(VI.) Ellen Habersham Rogers.

(VII.) Herman Livingston Rogers.

(VIII.) Anne Pendleton Rogers.

Anna Wylly Habersham, daughter of William Neyle Habersham and Josephine Habersham, married G. Fenwick Jones, Esq., son of G. Noble Jones and Mary Nutall, widow of Col. Nutall, daughter of Thomas Savage and Mary Wallace, daughter of Hon. Jno. Wallace, British Vice Consul for Georgia, and Mary Anderson, daughter of Captain George Anderson and Deborah Grant. G. Noble Jones was son of Noble Wymberley Jones and Mary Campbell, daughter of McCartin Campbell and Sarah Fenwick, daughter of Edward Fenwick and Mary, daughter of Thomas Drayton and Elizabeth Bull, daughter of Gov. William Bull and Mary Quentyne. The Fenwicks were of the ancient family of Fenwick, of Staunton. Edward Fenwick was King's Councillor and son of John Fenwick, King's Councillor, who married Elizabeth, daughter of Robert Gibbes, of South Carolina.

Noble Jones was son of Dr. Geo. Jones, United States Senator, and Mary, daughter of William Gibbons, the ardent patriot of 1776, member of Council of Safety, etc.

Dr. Geo. Jones was son of Dr. Noble Wymberly Jones, who was so prominent as a physician, was a delegate to Continental Congress, and styled one of the "Morning Stars of Liberty;" he was son of the Hon. Noble Jones, member of King's Council, etc., and Miss Wymberley. (?)

The Jones came from Lambeth, County Surrey, England; were of Welsh descent, and came to Georgia with Oglethorpe in 1733. Thus, then, were united the prominent families of Habersham with all its connection and the Jones, of such fine descent and so eminent as a family.

G. Fenwick Jones and Anna W. Habersham had:

(I.) G. Noble Jones, J. P., attorney at law.

(II.) Josephine Noble Jones, married J. A. P. Chrisfield.

(III.) Mary Savage Jones.

ROCKWELL

This is an ancient family, dating back to the year 1595; the ancestor, William Rockwell, settling in Dorchester, Mass., in 1630, having come from Dorchester, England.

In Georgia, the most eminent of the name was Samuel Rockwell, a prominent lawyer of Milledgeville, Ga., and a Colonel in the Indian War of 1836. His son, Colonel William Spencer Rockwell, a prominent lawyer of Milledgeville, moved to Savannah, Ga., in 1857. He was Colonel and Chief of Staff to Gen. Sanford in the Indian War of 1836, and Lt. Col. of the first volunteer regiment in the war between the States. Col. Rockwell was a prominent Mason, having attained the highest degree, 33d, in the Scottish Rite, and was known all over the country as an authority on Masonry, being the author of Masonic works, held in high esteem by Masons. His sons, Captain William S. Rockwell and Lieutenant Theodosius D. Rockwell, were well known members of the military and other organizations and business.

The ancestor, William Rockwell, was born in Dorchester, England, in 1595; married at Holy Trinity, Dorchester, England, April 14th, 1624, Susanna Chapin (Capen), and removed to America in 1630, settling in Dorchester, Mass. Being one of the two deacons who led the Colony, and was one of the Selectmen elected to govern the Colony after its founding. He died in Windsor, Conn., May 15th, 1640. His elder son, John Rockwell, born Dorchester, England, July 18th, 1627, died in Windsor, Conn., September 7th, 1673; married, first, May 6, 1651, at Hartford, Conn., Sarah Ensign, died July 23d, 1659. He married, second, at Dorchester, Mass., August 18th, 1662, Deliverance Haws (Hayes).

His son (second son), Joseph Rockwell, born Windsor, Conn., July 8th, 1668, died at Middleton, Conn., October 28th, 1742; married at Middleton, Conn., February 1st, 1694, Elizabeth Foster, born Middleton, Conn., 1673; died same place August 15th, 1753; and had:

Joseph Rockwell, second son, born at Middleton, Conn., 1699; died same place, 1757; married there Susanna Yeomans, and had an elder son:

Samuel Rockwell, born Middleton, Conn., October 13th, 1720; married there, January 20th, 1763, Abagail Goodwin, widow of Daniel Johnson, born in Boston, Mass., December 19, 1731.

The eldest son, John Wilson Rockwell, born Middleton, Conn., March 21st, 1766; died Albany, N. Y., December 13th, 1826; married, first, Mary Brewster, at Albany, N. Y., 1787. He married, second, in 1802, at Albany, Mary Cowley, born March 20th, 1774, at Albany, N. Y.; died, Albany, January 8th, 1837.

His only son, Samuel Rockwell, born Greenbush, N. Y., September 14th, 1788; died at Milledgeville, Ga., August 4th, 1841; married Albany, N. Y., December 3d, 1808, Sarah Ann Spencer; born Providence, R. I., November 2d, 1788; died Milledgeville, Ga., November 5th, 1863.

Col. William Spencer Rockwell, the eldest son, born Albany, N. Y., October 12th, 1809; died Abingdon, Md., July 23d, 1870; married in Milledgeville, Ga., June 4th, 1837, Rebecca Stebbins Davies, born in Chatham Co., Ga., June 21st, 1817, daughter of Judge William Davies and Sarah Grantland, and had an elder son:

William Samuel Rockwell, born Milledgeville, Ga., July 24th,

1843; married Catharine Wilcox Campfield, in Savannah, Ga., November 17th, 1864; she was born in Savannah, Ga., March 18th, 1844.

Their son, William O'Driscoll Rockwell, born Savannah, Ga., July 2d, 1866; married at Vernonburg, Ga., January 31st, 1900, Marie Walker Habersham; born Savannah, Ga., August 28th, 1873, daughter of Robert Beverley Habersham and Margaret Schley, of the Schleys of Maryland and Georgia, and had:

William Spencer Rockwell, born Savannah, Ga., January 16th, 1901.

DAVIES

Edward Davies, of Welsh descent, went to Georgia, and married Rebecca Lloyd; he died in Savannah and was buried in the first old cemetery in Yamacraw. His eldest son, William Davies, born in Charleston, S. C., July 4th, 1776, died in Savannah, Ga., April 30th, 1829, and is buried in the Davies vault, in Colonial Park, with his first wife. He was Judge of the Supreme Court of what is now the Eastern Judicial Circuit, and was a well known gentleman. He married, first, at Sunbury, Liberty County, Ga., by Rev. William McWhir, March 6th, 1797, Anna McIntosh Baillie, daughter of Robert Baillie, of the Culter Allers family, who married Ann McIntosh, daughter of John Moore McIntosh. From this marriage springs a branch of Harris, of Georgia. He married, second, at Milledgeville, Ga., in 1815, Sarah Grantland, and had:

(I.) Rebecca Stebbins Davies, married, June 4th, 1837, Col. William Spencer Rockwell, and had issue.

WALLACE

The family of Wallace were from Scotland, and descended from Wallace, Lairds of Carsriggan.

In America they were prominent citizens; two of them, Hon. James and Hon. John Wallace, British Vice Consuls for Georgia, and another brother, Michael Wallace, who went from Virginia to Nova Scotia and became Treasurer of the Province, Acting Secretary, and frequently Acting Governor of Nova Scotia. Though extinct in male line in Georgia, the female line is represented in the families of Jones, De Renne, Clay, Howard, Owens, etc.

*Hon John Wallace married Mary, sister of George Anderson, ancestor of Andersons of Savannah, Georgia, and children of Captain Geo. Anderson, of Berwick, Scotland, and Deborah Grant, and had:

I. Mary Wallace, married Thomas Savage.
II. Jane Wallace, married Charles Howard.*
III. Sarah Wallace, married Geo. W. Owens.
IV. Eliza Wallace, married Thomas Lloyd.

Robert Beverly Habersham, son of William Neyle and Josephine Habersham, married, first, Margaret Schley, of the eminent family of Schley, of Georgia and Maryland, of whom came Gov. Schley, of Georgia, and Admiral Schley, U. S. N., and had (Robert Habersham married, second, Georgia Schley):

(I.) Marie W. Habersham, married William O'Driscoll Rockwell (son of Capt. William S. Rockwell and Miss Kate Campfield, son of Major Rockwell, and Miss Davies, daughter of Judge Davies, of Georgia), and had:
(I.) William Spencer Rockwell.

Lilla Neyle Habersham, daughter of William Neyle and Josephine Habersham, married Walter Wellborn Colquitt (brother of Senator and Gov. Colquitt, of Hon. Hugh Colquitt, sons of Walter T. Colquitt, U. S. Senator, and Miss Lane), and had:

I. Lilla Neyle Colquitt.
II. Harriett Ross Colquitt.
III. William Neyle Colquitt.
IV. Joseph Clay Habersham Colquitt.
V. Anna Habersham Colquitt.
VI. Wellborn Colquitt, Jr.
VII. Maybelle Habersham Colquitt, dead.

Maybelle Habersham, daughter of William Neyle and Josephine Habersham, married William D. Simpkins, of an old Revolutionary family of South Carolina, and had:

(I.) Neyle Simpkins.

*NOTE.—Also a son, John Wallace, Jr. Charles Howard and Jane Wallace, had:
I. Rev. Charles Wallace Howard.
II. Miss Howard, married F. H. Goulding, author of Young Marooners, and had, besides others, Mrs. Mary G. Helmer.

(II.) Annie Cole Simpkins.

Josephine Noble Jones and James Alfred Pierce Chrisfield had:

(I.) Lillie Habersham Chrisfield.

(II.) Arthur Woodland Chrisfield.

COLEMAN

The ancestor of this family was Robert Coleman, of Lancaster, Pa.—born November 4th, 1748; died August 14th, 1825; married October 4th, 1773, Ann Old—born May 31st, 1756; died October 11th, 1844. They had Thomas Bird Coleman, of Cornwall and Colbrook, Penn.—born September 4th, 1794; died September 10th, 1837; married at York, Penn., by Rev. Dr. Robert Cathcart of the Presbyterian Church, Hannah Cassatt—born October 8th, 1796; died November 19th, 1830, daughter of David Cassatt, of York, Pa., and had:

William Coleman, born at Colbrook, Pa., August 20th, 1826; died at Florence, S. C., May 24th, 1861; married at Christ Church, Savannah, Ga., by Bishop Stephen Elliott, June 12th, 1855, Susan Ellen Habersham—born at Savannah, Ga., July 25th, 1836; died at Hyde Park, N. Y., April 22d, 1892, and had:

(I.) Robert Habersham Coleman, born Savannah, Ga., March 27th, 1856; married, first, J. Elizabeth Clark, at Hartford, Conn., January 15th, 1879, who died at Paris, France, May 10th, 1880. He married, second, in Baltimore, Md., Edith Elliott Johnstone, October 1st, 1884, and had:

I. Robert Coleman, born Cornwall, Pa., August 23d, 1885.

II. William Cassatt Coleman, born December 26th, 1886.

III. Ralph Elliott Coleman, born February 26th, 1888.

IV. Neyle Habersham Coleman, born March 19th, 1889.

NOTE.—The Colquitts, besides their own descent, also descend from the Lane and McKinne families of North Carolina. Joel Lane, born 1710, married Patience McKinne, in 1730, daughter of Barnabas McKinne, Sr., and had, among others, Jesse Lane, who married Winnifred Aycock—born 1733, died 1806; and had Joseph Lane, Jr., born March 28th, 1775; married Elizabeth Hill, and had, among others, Mrs. Walter T. Colquitt.

V. Ann Caroline Coleman, born March 29th, 1890.

(II.) Ann Caroline Coleman, daughter of William Coleman and Ellen Habersham, was born Cornwall, Pa., October 27th, 1858; married Archibald Rogers, born Jersey City, February 22d, 1852; married at St. Bartholomew's Church, New York City, by Bishop Beckwith of Georgia, assisted by Dr. Cook, the Rector, May 11th, 1880, and had:

(I.) Archibald Rogers, born New York, February 23d, 1881; died Hyde Park, December 26th, 1889.

(II.) Edmund Pendleton Rogers, born Hyde Park, July 28th, 1882.

(III.) Robert Coleman Rogers, born Newport, R. I., June 26th, 1883; died Hyde Park, June 9th, 1884.

(IV.) William Coleman Rogers, born Hyde Park, February 24th, 1885.

(V.) Rae Habersham Rogers, born Hyde Park, February 15th, 1887.

(VI.) Ellen Habersham Rogers, born Hyde Park, December 9th, 1889.

(VII.) Herman Livingston Rogers, born Hyde Park, September 27th, 1891.

(VIII.) Anne Pendleton Rogers, born Hyde Park, March 12th, 1894.

NOTE.—Ann Old was daughter of David Old—born 1730, died May 1st, 1809—who married Margaretta, daughter of Gabriel Davis, of White Hall, Pa.

NOTE.—Susan Ellen Habersham was daughter of Robert Habersham—born December 25th, 1783, at Savannah; died January 30th, 1870, at Savannah; married June 10th, 1819, Mary Butler Habersham—born May 31st, 1792; died May 22d, 1875; daughter of Major John Habersham, of Savannah, Ga.—born December 28th, 1754; died November 19th, 1799; married March 19th, 1783 or '82, to Ann Sarah Camber.

Robert Habersham was son of Col. Joseph Habersham, of Savannah, Ga.; born July 28th, 1751; died November 17th, 1815; married May 19th, 1776, Isabella Rae. Major John and Lieut. Col. Joseph were sons of Governor James Habersham; born Beverly, Yorkshire, England, 1712-15; died August 28th, 1775; married December 26th, 1740, Mary Bolton—born Philadelphia, Penn., May 8th, 1724; died January 4th, 1763.

ROGERS OF NEW YORK

This family is descended from the Woolseys, Taylors, Bards, Ramsays and others of the North, and from the Pendletons, Claytons and many others of Virginia.

Edmund Pendleton Rogers was born July 31st, 1827, and died February 10th, 1895; married Virginia Dummer; and had:

(I.) Archibald Rogers, married Ann Caroline Coleman, daughter of William Coleman and Susan Ellen Habersham.

(II.) James Bulloch Rogers, U. S. N., named after his father's friend, Captain James D. Bulloch, of U. S. Navy, afterwards Confederate States Agent abroad.

Edmund Pendleton Rogers was son of Archibald Rogers, born Stamford, Conn., 1791; died Hyde Park, N. Y., February 10th, 1850; son of Moses Rogers—born 1750; died November 30th, 1825; married, 1773, Sarah Woolsey—born 1750; died July 24th, 1816; son of Samuel Rogers, of Norwitch, Conn.—born 1712; married Elizabeth Fitch, of Norwalk, Conn., daughter of Samuel Fitch—born 1700; died July 18th, 1774.

Archibald Rogers, Sr., married, May 8th, 1821, Anna Pierce Pendleton—born 1796; died Hyde Park, December 26th, 1883—daughter of Nathaniel Pendleton and Susannah Bard.

WOOLSEY

Sarah Woolsey was the daughter of Benjamin Woolsey, Jr., of Long Island, who was born February 12th, 1720; died September 9th, 1771; married, 1749, Esther Isaacs—born July 19th, 1730; died March 29th, 1756; son of Ralph Isaacs and Mary Ramsay, daughter of Benjamin Ramsay. Benjamin Woolsey was son of Rev. Benjamin Woolsey—born November 19th, 1687, and died August 17th, 1754—and Abagail Taylor—born 1695—daughter of John Taylor and Mary Whitehead, daughter of Daniel Whitehead, born 1646, and Abagail Stevenson, son of David Whitehead. Abagail Stevenson was daughter of Thomas Stevenson and Maria Bullock, widow of William Bernard. Rev. Benjamin Woolsey was son of Geo. Woolsey, of Yarmouth, England; born October 27th, 1610; died before 1698; married, December 9th, 1647, Rebecca Cornell, daughter of Thomas Cornell, born 1595, died 1655, and Rebecca Briggs. Geo. Woolsey was son of Benjamin, son of Thomas Woolsey.

PENDLETON

Nathaniel Pendleton, of Culpepper Co., Va. (born 1756, died Hyde Park, October 20th, 1821), was son of Nathaniel Pendleton, of Culpepper Co., Va.—born 1715; died 1794; married, 1740, Elizabeth Clayton, of Virginia, daughter of *Philip Clayton, son of Henry Pendleton, son of Philip Pendleton and Elizabeth Hart, son of Henry Pendleton, son of Henry Pendleton and Susan Camyn; married, September 30th, 1605, at St. Simons and St. Judes, Norwich, England; buried at St. Stephens, July 15th, 1635; son of Geo. Pendleton and Elizabeth Pettingale, buried at St. Stephens, Norwich, England, 1603; married July 29th.

BARD

Susan Bard was daughter of John Bard, born February 1st, 1716; died April 1st, 1799; married, Christ Church, Philadelphia, Penn., 1737. Susan Valleau, born February 19th, 1721, daughter of Pierre Valleau and Magdalen Fauconnier, born London, 1695; died New York after 1750; son of Pierre Valleau, born 1662 in France; died 1712 in New York; son of Esaie Valleau, born France, 1638; died New Rochelle, N. Y., 1713.

Magdalen Fauconnier was daughter of Peter Fauconnier, Collector of Port and Receiver General of Taxes, and stood high with Governors Bellomont and Cornbury. He married Magdalen Pasquereau, daughter of Louis Pasquereau and Magdalen Chardon. Peter Fauconnier was son of Fauconnier and Mademoiselle de la Fouche, daughter of Grand Pre de la Fouche.

John Bard was son of Col. Peter Bard, of France, who died Burlington, N. J., February 13th, 1734; married, 1709, Miss D. Marmion, of Leicestershire, Eng., who died Burlington, N. J., after 1760; daughter of Dr. Samuel Marmion, of Leicestershire, Eng., born 1650; died at Burlington, N. J., March 20th, 1734; married Elizabeth Parker, of England, 1670; married at Astley Abbotts, Salop, July 28th, 1692; died Burlington, N. J., September 24th, 1729.

Col. Peter Bard was son of Benoit Bard, who died in London, 1734.

*NOTE.—Philip Clayton married Mary Taylor, daughter of James Taylor and Mary Gregory.

DUMMER

Edward Pendleton Rogers married Virginia Dummer—born August 13th, 1831; died March 3d, 1857; daughter of P. C. Dummer—born 1797; died 1875; son of Stephen Dummer—born 1755; died 1835, and Eunice Cook; married June 4th, 1780; son of Matthew Dummer—born 1730; died 1813; married October 24th, 1754, Tryphena, daughter of Stephen Austin, son of Edward Dummer and Jerusha Andrew—married June 2d, 1725; died about 1744; daughter of Nathan Andrews, of New Haven, Conn.

HOLT

William Holt had Nathaniel—born 1647, died 1723; who had Nathaniel—born 1683; died 1751; who had William—born 1709; died 1769; who had William—born 1736; died 1810; who had Charles Holt—born 1772; died 1852; who married Mary Dobbs—born 1771; died 1831; and had Eliza Dobbs Holt—born 1803; married P. C. P. Dummer, and had Virginia Dummer.

William Habersham, son of Col. Joseph Habersham and Isabella Rae, married Mary B. Elliott, daughter of Hon. Stephen Elliott and Esther, daughter of Hon. James Habersham and Esther Wylly, and had:

(a.) William Habersham.
(b.) Stephen E. Habersham.
(c.) Isabella Rae Habersham, married, first, Henry Mongin; second, Rev. William Williams.

Joseph Habersham, son of Lt. Col. Joseph Habersham and Isabella Rae, married Susan Habersham, daughter of Major John Habersham, and had:

(I.) Lt. Frederick Habersham, C. S. A., who married Eliza Mackay, daughter of Dr. Ralph Emms Elliott and M. C. Mackay, and had:
(a.) Frederick Habersham, married, first, Miss Hazelhurst; second, Mrs. Randolph.
(b.) Meta Habersham, married King Couper.
(c.) Charles Habersham.

(II.) Major John Habersham, third son of Gov. James Habersham and Mary Bolton, married March 27th,

NOTE.—Joseph Habersham had also Charles and Robert Habersham.

1786, Ann Sarah Camber, daughter of Thomas Camber, Esq., and had the following children:

(A.) Ann Habersham, born December 17th, 1783; married, 1802, Benjamin Ward.

(B.) John Harris Habersham, died, aged 21, of yellow fever.

(C.) James Camber Habersham.

(D.) Joseph Clay Habersham, M. D., married Ann Wylly Adams.

(E.) John Bolton Habersham.

(F.) Mary Butler Habersham, born May, 1795, married Robt. Habersham, son of Lt. Col. Joseph Habersham.

(G.) Susan Dorthy Habersham, born March 17th, 1798; married Joseph Habersham, son of Lt. Col. Joseph Habersham.

The Cambers were allied to the Habershams; Geo. Walton, signer of Declaration of Independence; Brisbane, an early patriot; and to the Butlers and Walkers. A. Ann Habersham and Benjamin Ward, an Englishman, had:

(I.) Isabella Ward.

(II.) Susan Ward, married Edward Footman, son of Dr. Richard Footman and Elizabeth (Maxwell) Caldwell, and had:

(I.) Susan Ann Footman, married Tattnall Daniell (son of Dr. William C. Daniell, an eminent physician of an old Virginia family, descended from the Coffee family; Dr. William C. Daniell married Martha, daughter of John Screven and Hannah Proctor), and had:

(1.) Elizabeth Daniell.

(II.) Willie Daniell,* married Eldred Simpkins.

Robert Bolton was son of Robert Bolton and Ann Clay, daughter of Winlock Curtis and Ann Bowers, daughter of

NOTE.—Camber marriages: Dorthy Camber married, June 16th, 1806, Polly Camber married, Savannah, Ga., May 12th, 1775, Adam Fowler Brisbane; Ann Sarah Camber married Major John Habersham.

(D.) Dr. Joseph Clay Habersham, son of Major John Habersham and Ann Sarah Camber, married Ann Wylly Adams, daughter of Nathaniel Adams, son of Nathaniel Adams, of Georgia, and Ann Bolton, daughter of Robert Bolton and Susannah, daughter of Mathew and Jane Mauve, of Switzerland.

†Brother of William D. Simkins, who married Maybelle Habersham.

Benanuel Bowers and Elizabeth, niece of Henry Dunster, first President of Harvard, and grand-daughter of Henry Dunster, of Balehout, Lancastershire, England. Benanuel Bowers was son of Geo. Bowers, of Scituate, Mass., and of England.

Nathaniel Adams, Sr., of Georgia, was son of Nathaniel Adams, of St. Helena, S. C., and Margaret, daughter of Edmund Ellis. Nancy Adams was daughter of Nathaniel Adams and Mary Ann Wylly, daughter of *Col. Richard Wylly, of the Revolution, born 1745, died October 11th, 1801 (a prominent patriot of ancient family), and Mary Bryan, daughter of Joseph Bryan and Mary Storey, son of Joseph Bryan and Mrs. Murray, son of Joseph Bryan, of an old Carolina family, and Sarah Janet Cochrane. Dr. Joseph Clay Habersham and Ann Wylly Adams had (he died November 21st, 1833, aged 64 years and 15 days):

(A.) Mary Ann F. Habersham, married Joseph Washburn, third wife.

(B.) Josephine Habersham, married William Neyle Habersham.

(C.) John Bolton Habersham, born August 31st, 1825; died September 21st, 1881; married, Brunswick Ga., Frances E. Hazelhurst.

(D.) William Waring Habersham, married Johnanna Wade, daughter of Major Wade, U. S. A., and Miss Buchanan.

(E.) Joseph Clay Habersham, M. D., H. O. of Savannah, Ga.; born October 9th, 1829; died January 19th, 1881; married Mary Anna Stiles, daughter of Joseph Stiles and Margaret Vernon Adams.

(F.) Anna Wylly Habersham, married, Rev. Charles B. King.

(G.) Fanny Habersham, married Louis Manigault.

Josephine Clay Habersham and William Neyle Habersham had:

(a.) Josephine Habersham.

(b.) Joseph Clay Habersham.

(c.) Anna Wylly Habersham, married G. Fenwick Jones.

(d.) William Neyle Habersham.

NOTE.—Richard Wylly married, second, Mary Morel, daughter of Jonathan Bryan and Mary Williamson, and had: Helen Wylly, married William Woodbridge, and Wylly married Thiot.

(e.) James Habersham.

(f.) Lilla Neyle Habersham, married Wellborn Colquitt.

(g.) Maybelle Habersham, married William D. Simkins.

(h.) Edward Camber Habersham.

Anna Wylly Habersham married Rev. Charles Barrington King, son of Barrington King and Catharine Nephew, daughter of James Nephew and Mary Magdalene Gignilliat. Barrington King was President of Roswell Cotton Factory, and a fine specimen of a gentleman, handsome and a good, noble Christian. He was son of Roswell King, the founder of Roswell and Catharine Barrington.

The Kings of Roswell were among the first citizens. The Kings came from Yorkshire, England, settled at Berlin, Conn., the first being John King, who came to America in 1645; his descendant, Roswell King, moved to Georgia.

Died: Sarah, wife of James Nephew, January 22d, 1810.

Anna Wylly Habersham and Rev. Charles Barrington King had:

(I.) Charles Barrington King, died infant.

(II.) Catharine Anna King, married Hugh Caperton.

(III.) Habersham King, married Ann Rebecca Strobhar.

(IV.) Charles William King, married, first, Sarah C. Kollock; second, Sarah Joyce Alexander.

(V.) Mary Josephine (Daisy) King, married Reuben G. Clark.

(VI.) James Nephew King.

(VII.) Edith Barrington King, married James U. Jackson.

(VIII.) Clifford King, married Nan Gwaltney.

NOTE.—Among the early tax collectors we find P. Nephew and J. Barrington. The Nephews were an old family, allied to the Wests, etc., and the name of Barrington occurs at an early day. We find P. Nephew and Josiah Barrington holding office in Colonial times.

In early grants we find the name "Nevie," and it is said this was the original name for Nephew. We see, also, that Hampden, son of Gen. Lachlan McIntosh, married Catharine Clifford Nephew, and had sons, who died, and two daughters. Mary McIntosh married Rev. Frederick Mervyn Winston, and had: Frederick H. and Susan and Lacy Winston; and second, Maria McIntosh, who married William Mell, and had: George Mell, Mrs. Wakelee and Mrs. Falligant. The family of West descend, also, from Nephew, and Rev. Joseph Stiles married Catharine C. Nephew, half-sister of Mrs. Barrington King.

(IX.) Joseph Clay Habersham King married Ida Wyly.
(X.) Walter Roswell King, died infant.

Catharine Anna King and Hugh Caperton had:
(I.) Hugh Caperton.
(II.) Charles Barrington Caperton.
(III.) Anna Habersham Caperton.
(IV. Edwin Caperton.
(V.) Henry Caperton, died.
(VI.) Thomas Bowyer Caperton.
(VII.) Carthrae Alexander Caperton.
(VIII.) James Nephew Caperton.
(IX.) Katharine King Caperton.

Habersham King and Ann Rebecca (Rhea), daughter of Captain Strobhar and Miss Bevill, had:
(I.) Belle Vernon King.
(II.) Frances Barrington King.
(III.) Habersham King.
(IV.) Rhea King.

Charles William King and Sarah C. Kollock, had:
(I.) Sarah Hull King.

Charles William King married, second, Sarah Joyce Alexander, daughter of Col. Thomas M. Alexander and Sarah Joyce Hooper, and had:
(1.) Sarah Joyce King.
(2.) Barrington King.

Mary Josephine (Daisy) King and Capt. Reuben Grove Clark, capitalist, soldier, manufacturer, had:
(I.) Josephine Habersham Clark.
(II.) Reuben Grove Clark.
(III.) Nephew King Clark.

Joseph Clay Habersham King and Ida Wyly, had:
(1.) William Davidson King.
(2.) Wyly Barrington King.

Clifford Barrington King and Nan Gwaltney, had:
1. Clifford Barrington King.

Edith Barrington King and James U. Jackson, had:

NOTE.—Charles William King married, first, Sarah Campbell Kollock, daughter of Dr. P. M. Kollock, a well known physician of Savannah, and Sarah Hull Campbell, grand-daughter of Macartan Campbell, a patriot of the Revolution, and Miss Fenwick, of ancient family, one of whom was King's Councellor, descended from Fenwick, of Staunton. The Fenwicks, of South Carolina, married into Gibbes and Drayton families, and the Tattnalls and Jones also descend from them. Dr. Kollock was son of Dr. Lemuel Kollock and Miss Sarah Hull Campbell.

(I.) Daisy King Jackson.
(II.) Edith Barrington Jackson.
(III.) James Urquhart Jackson.
(IV.) John William Jackson.
(V.) Jackson.

BARRINGTON

Josiah Barrington died previously to or during the Revolutionary War, and left two daughters.

(I.) Eliza Barrington, married William Cook, an elegant accomplished English barrister, who had come to Savannah, Ga., on business. He was a great traveler and was considered one of the most polished gentlemen of the "Old School." His relatives in England had expected him to marry there, but the beauty of Miss Barrington captivated him. He had many papers, government grants, etc.

(II.) Katharine Barrington, married Roswell King, of Sharon, Conn., a man of sterling integrity and vigorous mind.

Mrs. Barrington, the mother of these two ladies, was Miss Williams. Her brothers were Thomas Williams, a minister, and Richard and Stephen Williams, planters, who all lived in Savannah from the earliest times, well known people and respected by all and perfect gentlemen of the "Old School."

John Lewis married, first, Susan Ann Adams, and had:

(I.) John N. Lewis, married Frances Simond Henry, and had:
(I.) John Adams Lewis.
(II.) Robert Henry Lewis.
(III.) Isabella Seton Lewis, married Jacob Spivey.
(IV.) George Lewis.
(V.) Margaret R. Lewis.

(II.) R. Adams Lewis, married Catharine Ann Barrington Cook, daughter of William Cook, Esq., and Eliza Barrington, daughter of Josiah Barrington and Miss Williams, and had:

(I.) Eliza Catharine Lewis, married *James Audley Maxwell, son of Roswell King and Miss Maxwell, of Liberty Co., Ga., and had:
(I.) Kate Maxwell King.
(II.) Julia Rebecca King.
(III.) Robert Lewis King.

(IV.) Audley Maxwell King.
(II.) Robert Lewis, Jr., married and had issue, living North.
(III.) Isabella Margaret (Meta) Lewis, married James Roswell King, his second wife.
(IV.) Anna Barrington Lewis.
(V.) William Clarence Lewis, married Augusta E. Pawling, and had:
(1.) Sophie Lewis.
(2.) Alice Catharine Lewis.
(3.) Clarence Lewis.
(4.) Walter Lewis.
(VI.) Frances Barrington Lewis, married Ardena Whitsitt, of Kansas City, Mo.

MANIGAULT

Fanny Habersham married Louis Manigault, of Charleston, S. C., son of Charles Izard Manigault and Miss Heyward, daughter of Nathaniel Heyward. The descent of the Manigaults is as follows: Jean Manigault, member of the Commune of La Rochelle, France, 1558-1567. His son, Francois Sieur de Limouillet, was succeeded by his son, Gabriel Manigault, Governor of St. Bartholomew, 1593, Deputy to confer with Henry IV., in 1602, also member of governing body. He was succeeded by his son, Gabriel Manigault, styled also Sieur des Ormeaux, and he was father of the two refugees to America, one of whom was Peter, who married, 1699, Judith Giton, a widow, and had: Gabriel Manigault, merchant, married, 1730, Ann Ashby, daughter of Jno. Ashby, and had: Peter Manigault, Speaker of Assembly, who married Elizabeth, daughter of Joseph Wragg, and had: Gabriel, married Margaret, daughter of Ralph Izard and Alice DeLancy, and had: Charles Izard Manigault, married Margaret Heyward, who had Louis, married Fanny Habersham, and had:
(I.) Louis Manigault, married Miss Taylor, a cousin.
(II.) Josephine Manigault, married Hawkins Jenkins.
(III.) Charles Manigault, married Elizabeth, second daughter of Christian Daniel Eberhardt and Mary Elizabeth Blankenstein, of Germany, and had:

*The Kings, of Darien, of Roswell, of Liberty County, Ga., are all descended from Roswell King and Katharine Barrington.

(I.) Charles Eberhardt Manigault.
(II.) Daughter, Manigault.

NOTE.—Manigault: This ancient family of South Carolina was unquestionably of noble descent, and were landowners and prominent citizens of France, bearing the prefix of Sieur and at least belonging to the lesser noblesse. In Carolina they descended from the noted family of Izard, who descended from Governor Robert Johnson and from the noble family of Chastagnier and others, whose alliances were of the best. The Manigault family also descended from Ashby, one of whom was a Carolina Cacique of the nobility of the Province. Also from the eminent families of Wragg, DeLancey and Heyward; and this family itself has contributed men of worth and eminence in commerce, war and various walks of life, and well should the descendants be proud of the name of Manigault.

The Manigaults were allied to the Izards, Draytons, Ashbys, Heywards, Wraggs, Middletons and others, and were a fine family and rendered services of untold worth during the Revolutionary War. They seem to have been a noble French family, and came to South Carolina at an early day. See sketch of family in vol. 4, Transactions of South Carolina Huguenot Society, 1897. We only give eldest line.

CLAY

Elizabeth Habersham and Ralph Clay, of Yorkshire, England, had: Hon. Joseph Clay, member of the Council of Safety, member of Provincial Congress, member of Executive Council, Trustee of State College, and in every way a man of eminence and founder of the Clay family of the coast of Georgia. From the Clays descend the Cumming family, whose ancestor came to Georgia at an early day, and through them a branch of the Houstouns, so eminent in the annals of Georgia. We find, also, intermarriages between the Clays with Cuthbert, Wallace, Young and Stiles, and so we see all descendants of Clay have the Habersham blood.

Hon. Joseph Clay and Ann Legardere, daughter of Elias Legardere and Parnell Wilson, of Ireland, had the following children:

(I.) Hon. Joseph Clay, married Mary Ann Savage.
(II.) Elizabeth Clay, married Dr. James Box Young.
(III.) Sarah Clay, married January 13th, 1791, William Wallace.
(IV.) Catharine Clay, married, 1793, Joseph Stiles.
(V.) Mary or Polly Clay, married, February 14th, 1785, Seth John Cuthbert, and had:
(I.) Alfred Cuthbert, married Sarah Jones.
(II.) John Cuthbert, married Laura C. Croft.

Alfred Cuthbert, U. S. Senator, and Sarah Jones, daughter of Dr. Geo. Jones, U. S. Senator, and Mary Gibbons, daughter of Hon. William Gibbons, the prominent patriot of 1776, had:

(I.) Alfred Cuthbert, married Ella Shebbard.
(II.) Mary Cuthbert.

Dr. George Jones, married, February 1st, 1783, Mary Gibbons. He married, second, Eliza Smith, and had: George Wymberley Jones De Renne.

Hon. Joseph Clay married Ann Legardere, daughter of Elias Legardere and Parnell Wilson, of Ireland, and had the following children:

(I.) Hon. Joseph Clay, married Mary Ann Savage.
(II.) James Clay.
(III.) William LeConte Clay.
(IV.) Parnell Clay.
(V.) Ralph Clay, married Mary Jeane Melanie Picot de Boisfeuillet.
(VI.) Catharine Clay, married, 1793, Joseph Stiles (see Stiles).
(VII.) Sarah Clay, married, January 13th, 1791, William Wallace.
(VIII.) Mary Clay, married, February 14th, 1785, Seth John Cuthbert.
(IX.) Elizabeth Clay, married Dr. James Box Young.
(X.) James Clay.
(XI.) Ann Clay, married Thomas Cumming, and had:
(I.) William Cumming.
(II.) Joseph Cumming, married, first, Matilda Ann Poe; married, second, Caroline Auze; married, third, Mrs. Susan Jones Maxwell.
(III.) Thomas Cumming.
(IV.) Robert Cumming.
(V.) John Habersham Cumming.
(VI.) Mary Cuthbert Cumming, married Samuel S. Davis.
(VII.) Henry Harford Cumming, married Julia Bryan.
(VIII.) Alfred Cumming, married Elizabeth Randall.
(IX.) Ann Elizabeth Cumming, married Peter Smith.
(X.) Sarah Wallace Cumming.

(II.) Joseph Cumming and Matilda Ann Poe had:
(1.) Thomas Cumming.
(2.) Frances Ann Cumming.
(3.) William H. Cumming, married Elizabeth Reed McDowal.
(4.) Mary Cuthbert Cumming, married Thomas C. Nisbet.
(5.) Montgomery Cumming, married Rosalie Wade.
(6.) Wallace Cumming, married Harriet, daughter of Adam Alexander, and had:
(1.) Charles Maxwell Cumming.
(2.) Sarah Gilbert Cumming, married Dr. J. P. S. *Houstoun (of the ancient Georgia family of Houstoun, descended from Sir George Houstoun and Ann Moodie, daughter of Moodie, a Colonial officer, and from Sir Patrick Houstoun, Baronet, member of King's Council), and had:
(I.) James P. Houstoun.
(II.) Edward Houstoun.
(III.) Harriet Houstoun.
(IV.) Mary C. Houstoun.
(V.) Claude Houstoun.
(3.) Mary Cumming.
(4.) Wallace Cumming.
(5.) Joseph Cumming.

Children of Wallace Cumming and Harriet Alexander. William H. Cumming and Elizabeth Reed McDowal, had:
(1.) Edward H. Delevan Cumming.
(2.) Montgomery Cumming.
(3.) Ann Clay Cumming.
(4.) Wallace Cumming.
(5. Susan Stewart Cumming.
(6.) William H. Cumming.
(7.) Charles S. Cumming.
(8.) R. Alexander Reid Cumming.
(9.) Elizabeth Reid Cumming.
(10.) Mary Nisbit Cumming.

Mary Cuthbert Cumming and F. C. Nisbet had:
(I.) Joseph C. Nisbet.
(II.) Eliza C. Nisbet.

*Adam Alexander was son of Dr. Alexander, surgeon in Revolutionary War.
†Son of Edward Houstoun and Claudia Bond.

(III.) Harriet Nisbet married Edward D. Latta, and had:
(I.) Maria Nisbet Latta.
(II.) Edward D. Latta.
(III.) Janet Acton Latta.
(IV.) Thomas Cooper Nisbet.
Montgomery Cumming and Rosalie Wade, had:
(I.) Montgomery Cumming.
Mary Cuthbert Cumming and Samuel Davis had:
(I.) Thomas C. Davis, married Fanny Kinser, and had Fanny.
(II.) Ann M. Davis, married Alfred Cuthbert (see Cuthbert).
(III.) Caroline Davis, married Joseph Jones (see Jones).
(IV.) Sarah N. Davis, married Alfred Cumming.
(V.) Julia Davis, married Paul H. Langdon.
Caroline Davis and Joseph Jones had:
(I.) Stanhope Jones, married Minna Bayne, and had:
1. Stanhope Jones.
2. Marian Gayle Jones.
3. Thomas Boyne Jones.
(II.) Charles C. Jones.
(III.) Mary Cuthbert Jones.
Julia Davis and Paul H. Langdon, had:
(I.) Samuel D. Langdon, married Minnie Rowland.
(II.) Paul D. Langdon.
(III.) Annie C. Langdon.
(IV.) Mary C. Langdon.

Henry Harford Cumming and Julia Bryan had eight children.
(1.) Ann Cumming, married Charles Hall, and had:
(I.) Bryan Hall.
(2.) Alfred Cumming, married Sarah Ann Davis, his cousin, and had:
(A.) Julian Cumming, married Georgia Freeman, and had:
(a) Mary Cumming.
(B.) Caroline Bryan Cumming.
(C.) Henry Harford Cumming.
(3.) Julian Cumming.
(4.) Thomas Cumming, married Mary Hazen, and had:

(a.) Henry Harford Cumming, married Caroline Palmer, and had:
1. Carolyn Cumming.
(b.) Mary Hazen Cumming.
(5.) Emily Cumming, married Harry Hammond, and had:
(I.) Julia Hammond.
(II.) Katharine F. Hammond.
(III.) Henry Cumming Hammond.
(IV.) Christopher C. F. Hammond.
(V.) Alfred Hammond.
(6.) Joseph Bryan Cumming, married Katharine Hubbell, and had:
(a.) Bryan Cumming, married Mary G. Smith.
(b.) Jane Cumming, married James Verdery.
(c.) Emily H. Cumming.

Bryan Cumming and Mary G. Smith had:
(a.) Mary S. Cumming.
(b.) Joseph B. Cumming.
(7.) Harford M. Cumming.
(8.) Marian Cumming, married Hall De Rosset Lamar, of that most eminent family, and had:
(I.) Henry C. Lamar.
(II.) Paul Cazenove Lamar.
(III.) Mary Lamar, married Frank Miller, and had:
(I.) Cazenove L. Miller.
(II.) Julian K. Miller.

Jane Cumming and James Verdery had:
(I.) Catharine Verdery.
(II.) Pauline Verdery.

VERDERY

In the reign of Charles V., Emperor of Germany and Spain, etc., Charles De La Verdere was a Belgian Knight and noble of the Court; and later on we find the ancestor of the American family to have been Le Sieur Maturin Mareschal de Verdery, youngest son of the Sieur Jacques de Verdery, who was the King's Councillor (Councilleur due roi au Parliaments de Guienne, France) in the Assembly and Courts of Guienne, France, and a member of the noblesse, and a landlord and a land owner in Guienne, and in the capital city, Bordeaux, were situated the estate and chateau of the family.

Monsieur Maturin Mareschael de Verdery, the youngest son of the Sieur (lord) Jacques de Verdery, settled first in St. Domingo, where he owned sugar and coffee plantations and 1,000 slaves, and there with the rest of the earlier settlers remained until the French revolution and massacre of the whites by the negroes took place, where, as is well known, many of the opulent planters lost all and had to flee from the island for their lives, thus adding to our population some of the finest blood of France, useful and intelligent citizens. With other refugees, he fled to America, landing in Charleston in 1793-94, and there married, in 1794, Mademoiselle Pavagean, finally making his home near Augusta, Ga.

The issue of this marriage were as follows:

(I.) Benjamin Francis Verdery.

(II.) Mandos Pierre Verdery.

(III.) Auguste Nicola Verdery.

(IV.) Eugene Francois Verdery.

(V.) Clio Francois Verdery, married, first, Charles M. Hill, of New Jersey, second, Pleasant Stovall, of Augusta, Ga., and died without issue; the rest marrying and having issue.

Auguste Nicola de Verdery, son of Monsieur Maturin Mareschal de Verdery, and grand-son of Le Sieur Jacques de Verdery, married Susan Hampton Burton, and had the following children:

(1.) William Mathurin Verdery, married Miss Cornelia Skinner, of Columbia County, Ga., and had eight children: Auguste, William, Jere, Marc, Carlos, Oriana, Marie, Byrd.

(2.) Emily Ann Verdery, married Dr. George Battey. Has no children; now living at Robinson Springs, Ala.

(3.) Thomas Jefferson Verdery, killed at the battle of Fredericksburg. Unmarried.

(4.) Mary Frances Verdery, married Warren Akin, of Cass County, Ga. Six children: Warren, John, William, Mary, Sarah, Paul.

(5.) Augustus Freeman Verdery, married Miss Mary Beall, of Warren County, Ga. Lives in Winchester, Tex. Five children: Virginia, Mary, Freeman, etc.

(6.) Virginia Adele Verdery, married Dr. Hezekiah Witcher, of Cedartown, Ga. Two sons: Warren, Hezekiah.

(7.) George Theodore Verdery, died from wounds received at the battle of Gettysburg. Unmarried.

(8.) Susan Hampton Verdery, married John S. Prather, of Chambers County, Ala. Four daughters.

(9.) Orianna Louisa Verdery, married Azmon A. Murphey, of Barnesville, Ga. Two daughters.

(10.) Adelaide Anna Verdery, married Dr. Dudley Robinson, of Robinson Springs, Lowndes County, Ala. No children.

(11.) Pleasant Stovall Verdery, married Miss Charity Conn, of Savannah, Ga. Four children: Adelaide, Marcia, Bertha, Pleasant.

(12.) John Eve Verdery, died in childhood.

The Verderys were a large, tall, handsome race of blondes, and have served their country—two having lost their lives in the late war. Auguste Nicolas de Verdery was born in Languedoc, though the family lived in Guienne, France.

Hon. Joseph Clay (eldest son of Hon. Joseph Clay and Ann *Legardiere), married Mary Ann Savage, daughter of Thomas

NOTE.—William B. Burton and Thomas J. Burton, brothers, came to Georgia from Henrico County, Va., in 1800. William Burton married Anne Hughes and settled in Clark County; Thomas Burton married and settled in Baldwin or Hancock County.

William Burton and Anne Hughes had the following children:

(I.) Isaac Burton—served under Sam Houston in the Mexican War, was one of the heroes of San Jacinto. Is said to have died unmarried, leaving to the children of Anne Hughes* a league of land in Texas, called "The Burton League of land."

(II.) Susan Hampton Burton—married (1822) to Auguste Nicholas de Verdery, of Augusta, Ga. Had twelve children.

(III.) Thomas Jefferson Burton—married a Miss Byrd. Their only child, Byrd Burton, was killed before Richmond during the Civil War. He married a Miss Martha after the death of his first wife, by whom he had six children.

(IV.) Virginia Burton—married a Mr. Watson, of Cuthbert, and after his death, a Mr. Mercer, of Dougherty County. Several Watson children.

(V.) Louise Burton—married a Mr. Thomas White, of Macon, Ga. One child, Thomas White, of Macon.

(VI.) America Burton—married a Mr. McLendon, of Rome, Ga. Two children: first died unmarried, second is Mrs. Tharpe, of Albany, Ga.

*Anne Hughes was the daughter of Peter Hughes and Sarah Grant, of Henrico County, Ga.

*Pronounced Lego-Deer.

Savage, Esq., planter, and Mary Elliott Butler, daughter of Hon. Capt. William Butler and Elizabeth, daughter of William Elliott and Elizabeth Emms, daughter of Dr. Ralph Emms, all of South Carolina.

Hon. Joseph Clay and Mary Ann Savage had issue:

(I.) Thomas Savage Clay, married Matilda W. McAllister, daughter of Col. McAllister and Miss Bowman.

(II.) Mary Clay, married W. R. Gray.

(III.) Ann Clay.

(IV.) Elizabeth Caroline Clay.

Thomas Savage Clay and Matilda W. McAllister had:

(1.) Joseph Clay, married Mary Herndon, of Virginia.

(2.) Thomas Carolin Clay, married Caroline Law.

(3.) W. G. McAllister Clay.

(4.) Ann Clay, married Ingersoll Washburn.

(5.) Emma J. Clay.

(6.) Robert Habersham Clay, married Evelyn Mills.

Joseph and Mary Herndon Clay, daughter of Dr. Herndon, a relative of the celebrated Commodore Maury, had:

(A.) Thomas S. Clay.

(B.) Mary Clay.

(C.) Elizabeth Clay.

Thomas Savage and Mary Elliott Butler had:

(I.) Elizabeth Savage, married Judge Thomas Heyward.

(II.) Mary Ann Savage, married Hon. Joseph Clay.

(III.) Susannah Parsons Savage, married Ralph Elliott.

(IV.) Thomas Savage, married Mary Wallace, daughter of Hon. John Wallace and Mary Anderson, daughter of Capt. George Anderson, of Berwick, Scotland.

By this marriage the Jones, Nutalls, and DeRennes descend, and the Andersons, Lloyds, Owens, Haskells, branch of Screven, Haynes, Shotter and all become related.

Thomas Carolin Clay and Caroline, daughter of the eminent jurist, Judge Law, of Liberty County, Ga., had:

(A.) William Law Clay.

(B.) Thomas S. Clay, married Ann Burroughs, descended of the Harden and Burroughs families, and had:

(a.) Ellen Clay.
(b.) Caroline Law Clay.
(C.) James Stark Clay.
(D.) Elizabeth C. Clay.
(E.) Samuel Law Clay.
(F.) Ellen Clay.
(G.) Ralph E. Clay.
(H.) Caroline M. Clay.

Ann Clay and Ingersoll Washburn, of Savannah, Ga., descended from an ancient family of Massachusetts, had:

(I.) Ingersoll Washburn.
(II.) Emma H. Washburn.
(III.) Edward E. Washburn.
(IV.) Willis McAllister Washburn.
(V.) Matilda Washburn.

Ralph Clay, fifth son of Hon. Joseph Clay and Ann Legardiere, married Mary Jane Melanie Picot de Boisfeuillet, and had the following issue:

(I.) James Clay.
(II.) William Clay.
(III.) Mary Ann Clay, married Edward A. Strong, and had:
(I.) Robert W. Strong, married Caroline Neville.
(II.) Josephine C. Strong, married J. N. Strong.
(III.) Melaine Strong.
(IV.) Joseph Clay.
(V.) Edward Clay.
(VI.) Henry Clay.
(VII.) Elizabeth Clay.
(VIII.) Ralph Clay, married Lucy Ann Gassaway, and had:
(1.) Henry de Boisfeuillet Clay, married Hattie Field, and had:
(A.) Ralph Clay.
(B.) Ethel Clay.
(2.) John Kenneth Clay.
(3.) William Clay.
(4.) Nicholas Clay.
(5.) Lucy Clay, married Francis S. Brown, and had:
(I.) Lawrence Clay Brown.
(II.) Wallace Brown.
(6.) Melanie de Boisfeuillet Clay, married Charles A. Brown, and had:

(I.) Lucy Brown.
(II.) Lois Wood Brown.

Sarah Clay, daughter of Hon. Joseph Clay and Ann Legardiere, married William Wallace, and had:

(I.) Ann Clay Wallace.
(II.) Robert Wallace.
(III.) Sarah Wallace.
(IV.) William Campbell Wallace, married Henrietta Riggs, and had:
(1.) William Wallace.
(2.) Sarah Wallace.
(3.) Mary Wallace, married Richard H. Allen.
(4.) William Wallace.
(V.) Mary Wallace.
(VI.) Charles Joseph Wallace.
(VII.) Elizabeth Young Wallace.
(VIII.) Catharine Stiles Wallace.

Mary Clay, daughter of Hon. Joseph Clay and Mary Ann Savage, married W. R. Gray, and had:

(I.) William Gray, married Sarah F. Loring.
(II.) Francis H. Gray, married Regina H. Shober.
(III.) Frederick Gray.
(IV.) Mary Gray.
(V.) Ann Gray.
(VI.) George Gray.
(VII.) Ellen Gray.

William Gray and Sarah F. Loring had:

(1.) Mary Gray.
(2.) William Gray, married Catharine Cunningham.
(3.) Frank Gray.
(4.) Isa Gray.
(5.) Frances Gray, married William Stewart.
(6.) Ann Gray.
(7.) Lawrence Gray.
(8.) Edward Gray, married Elizabeth Story, and had:
(A.) Edward Gray.
(B.) Marguerite Gray.
(C.) Howard Gray.

William and Catharine Cunningham Gray had:

(A.) Catharine Gray, married Dudley Fay.
(B.) William Gray, married Sarah Newman, and had:
(a.) Francis Gray.

(C.) Howard Gray.
(D.) Marion Gray, married George Lewis, and had:
(I.) Marian Lewis.
(II.) George Lewis.
(E.) Sarah Gray, married George Salstonstall Silsbee, and had:
(I.) George Silsbee.
(II.) Elizabeth Silsbee.

Catharine Gray and Dudley Fay had:
(I.) Elizabeth Bowditch Fay.
(II.) Alice Fay.
(III.) Ethel Fay.
(IV.) Rosamond Fay.
(V.) Richard D. Fay.

Francis H. Gray and Regina H. Shober had:
(1.) Francis C. Gray.
(2.) Mary C. Gray.
(3.) Samuel P. Gray, married Caroline B. Weld, and had:
(A.) Ralph Gray.
(B.) Pope Gray.
(C.) Stephen Gray.
(4.) Reginald Gray, married Rose Lee, and had Reginald Gray.
(5.) Maurice Gray, married Flora Grant, and had:
(A.) Maurice Gray.
(B.) Elizabeth Gray.
(C.) Frances Gray.

Frances Gray and William Stewart had:
(I.) Francis Stewart.
(II.) William Stewart.
(III.) Mary Stewart.
(IV.) Violet Stewart.

Mary Clay, daughter of Hon. Joseph Clay and Ann Legardiere, was married, February 14th, 1785, to Hon. Seth John Cuthbert, Secretary of the Council of Safety, member of the Provincial Congress, 1775, member of Executive Council and chosen President *pro tem.*, Saturday, July 24th, 1779, of the Supreme Executive Council of Georgia.

There were two families of Cuthbert who went to Georgia—"Cuthbert of Drakies, Scotland," and Cuthbert of Castle Hill, near Inverness, and Hon. Seth John must have been one of these. Mary Clay and the Hon. Seth John Cuthbert had two sons:

(I.) Alfred Cuthbert, married Sarah Jones.
(II.) John A. Cuthbert, married Louisa Eugenia Croft, and had:
(1.) Cornelia Margaret Cuthbert, married William H. Platt, and had:
(I.) Charles W. Platt.
(II.) Edward C. Platt, married Margaret Hunter, and had:
(1.) Edward C. Platt.
(2.) A. Hunter Platt.
(3.) Edith H. Platt
(4.) Horace G. Platt.
(III.) Horace Garvin Platt.
(IV.) Ella Platt.
(2.) John Croft Cuthbert, married Ada Eugenia Davis, and had:
(A.) John A. Cuthbert.
(B.) Eloise Gouldin Cuthbert.
(C.) William H. Platt Cuthbert.
(D.) Walter Douglas Cuthbert.
(E.) Lee Davis Cuthbert.
(F.) Mary Medora Cuthbert.
(G.) Kate Clay Cuthbert.
(H.) Zaidee Vivian Cuthbert.

John A. Cuthbert and Louisa Eugenia Croft had also:

(3.) Margaret Louisa Cuthbert.
(4.) Thomas Gaulding Cuthbert.
(5.) Joseph Stiles Cuthbert.
(6.) Ann Clark Cuthbert.
(7.) George Washington Cuthbert.
(8.) Eugenia Louisa Cuthbert.
(9.) Octavia Lydia Cuthbert.
(10.) Octavius Cuthbert.
(11.) Van Brugh Livingston Cuthbert.

Hon. Alfred Cuthbert, U. S. Senator, eldest son of Hon. Seth John Cuthbert and Mary Clay, married Sarah Jones, daughter of Dr. George Jones, U. S. Senator, who married Mary Gibbons, February 1st, 1783, daughter of the eminent patriot, Hon. William Gibbons, descended from an officer in Cromwell's army. Dr. George Jones was a son of Dr. Noble

Wymberley Jones, one of the Morning Stars of Liberty, son of Hon. Noble Jones, of Lambeth County, Surrey, England, and Miss Wymberly. (?) Drakies plantation in Georgia was owned by George Cuthbert, 1797.

Hon. Wm. Gibbons was one of the foremost patriots of 1776. Dr. George Jones married, second, Mrs. Mary Gibbons; and third, Eliza Smith, and had George Wymberly Jones De Renne.

Alfred Cuthbert and Sarah Jones had one son and one daughter:

(1.) Alfred Cuthbert, married Ella Shebbard.

(2.) Mary Cuthbert.

Alfred Cuthbert and Ella Shebbard had:

(A.) Alfred Cuthbert.

(B.) George Cuthbert.

Thus do we see the blood of the Habershams running through Elliott, Clay, Cuthbert, Wallace, Gray, Cumming, Houstoun, Washburn and many others, as will be seen by perusal of these pages

CUTHBERT OF CASTLE HILL, AND OF DRAKIES

In a treaty with the Creek Indians, 1739, and Gen. Oglethorpe, as witnesses occur among others: John Cuthbert of Drakies, and George Cuthbert of Inverness. Dr. James Cuthbert, who went to South Carolina, had his pedigree attested to by the members of the Scotch Parliament. He was the son of Lord John Cuthbert, of Castle Hill, Inverness, of a very ancient family, who married Jeane, daughter of Rev. William Hay, Bishop of Moray.

George Cuthbert, commander of the forces in the battle of Harlaw, against Donald of the Isles, had William Cuthbert, 1478, who had George Cuthbert of 1548, who had John Cuthbert of 1593, who had George Cuthbert, 1611, who had William Cuthbert, who married Jane McKenzie, and had: John Cuthbert, who married Mary, daughter of George Cuthbert, of Drakies, and had: George Cuthbert, who married Magdalen, daughter of Sir James Fraser, of Brae. From Cuthbert, of Castle Hill, descend a branch of Heyward, Guerard, Roach, Barnwell and others. George Cuthbert owned Drakie's plantation, on Savannah, River, in 1797. Now we see that John Cuthbert, of Drakies, and George Cuthbert, of Inverness, in

Georgia in 1739, and a John Cuthbert and a Seth John, member of Provincial Congress of 1775; so this line of Georgia must descend from either John of Drakies or John of Inverness, and also Castle Hill, perhaps brother of Dr. James Cuthbert. The Cuthberts of Castle Hill, in Georgia, represent the family, so says Rev. Sigourlay Cuthbert, of Scotland.

STILES

This ancient Georgia family of Stiles, who have contributed toward the history of the State in various ways, is descended from John Stiles, of Bermuda, where the family were of note and were of the class entitled to bear arms. John Stiles had a son, Daniel Stiles, who married Deborah, daughter of Thomas Gibbes and Sarah Durham, grand-daughter of Frances, daughter of Thomas Grinsdith, of Hazelmere, Surrey, England. Frances Grinsdith married Richard Hunt, of London, England, and came to Bermuda, 1635; her mother was Jane, sister of Sir Nathaniel and Robert Rich, close relations of the Earl of Warwick. Daniel Stiles and Deborah Gibbs had a son, Daniel Stiles, member of Bermuda Assembly, 1723, and Warden of Port Royal Church, 1725. He married Mary Durham, grand-daughter of Richard and Frances Hunt. Her mother, Judith Hunt Lang, married Henry Durham, and again we see the same connection with the noted Rich family of England, descended from Lord Rich.

Daniel Stiles and Mary Durham had, among others, Capt. Samuel Stiles, who married Frances Lightburn, and who went to Georgia, 1765, and aided the Colonists to obtain powder for the use against the British in the Revolutionary War. Capt. Samuel Stiles had, among others, the following children:

(I.) Joseph Stiles, married, first, Catharine Clay, daughter of Hon. Joseph Clay, and had:

(I.) Benjamin E. Stiles, married Mary Ann Mackay.

(II.) Joseph Clay Stiles, married, first, Caroline Peck; second, Caroline Clifford Nephew.

(III.) Samuel Stiles.

(IV.) William Henry Stiles, married Eliza Mackay.

(V.) Ann Stiles.

Joseph Stiles married, second, Margaret Vernon Adams, daughter of Nathaniel Adams and Mary Ann Wylly, daughter of Col. Richard Wylly, and had:

(I.) George Stiles, Captain C. S. A.
(II.) Samuel Stiles, married Caroline Rogers. (See Jones.)
(III.) Clifford A. Stiles, M. D., married, first, Ann Adams; second, Katharine Livingston Hutchinson.
(IV.) Mary Anna Stiles, married Dr. Joseph Clay Habersham.
(V.) Florence V. Stiles, married Wylly Woodbridge, her cousin.

Benjamin E. Stiles and Mary Mackay had:
(1.) Joseph Stiles.
(2.) John McQueen Stiles.
(3.) Eliza Mackay Stiles.
(4.) Katharine Clay Stiles.
(5.) William Wallace Stiles.
(6.) Benjamin Edward Stiles, married Clelia Peronneau.
(7.) Sidney Stiles, married William H. Elliott, M. D., a well known surgeon of Savannah (son of Dr. Ralph E. Elliott, by Margaret, daughter of Robert Mackay and Eliza McQueen, daughter of Capt. John McQueen), and had:
(I.) William H. Elliott.
(II.) Edward S. Elliott, attorney at law, Major, etc.
(III.) Clelia Peronneau Elliott, married Clifford Carleton, and had:
(I.) Sidney Carleton.
(IV.) Wallace McQueen Elliott.
(V.) Phoebe Herbert Elliott.
(VI.) William Mackay Elliott.
(VII.) Katharine Vernon Elliott.

Rev. Joseph Clay Stiles, the noted evangelist and famous preacher, married, second, *Caroline Clifford Nephew, daughter of James Nephew and Sarah Gignilliat, daughter of Francis Pelot and widow of James Gignilliat, and had:
(1.) Catharine Ann Stiles, married Prof. H. Newton.
(2.) Josephine Clifford Stiles.
(3.) Robert Augustus Stiles, married Lelia Caperton.
(4.) Randolph Railey Stiles.
(5.) Mary Evelyn Stiles.

*Half-sister of Catharine Margaret Nephew, who married Barrington King.

(6.) Eugene West Stiles, married, first, Caroline D. Anderson; second, Rosabel Bowley.

(7.) Rosa Anderson Stiles, married, first, R. H. Christian; second, Hon. William Gaston Caperton.

Hon. William Henry Stiles, ex-Minister to Austria, and an eminent man of his day, was the son of Joseph Stiles and Catharine Clay, and consequently descended from the Habersham family. He married Eliza Mackay, daughter of Robert Mackay, son of Robert Mackay, of Wicks Caithness, Scotland, son of Rev. Robert Mackay. Robert Mackay married Eliza McQueen, daughter of Capt. John McQueen, Special Envoy from Washington to LaFayette, and son of John McQueen and Ann Dallas.

Hon. William Stiles and Eliza Mackay had the following children:

(1.) Mary Cowper Stiles, married Andrew Low.

(2.) William Henry Stiles, married Eliza C. Gordon.

(3.) Robert Mackay Stiles, married Margaret Wylly Couper.

Mary Cowper Stiles and Andrew Low had the following children:

(I.) Catharine Mackay Low.

(II.) Mary Low, married Major Guthrie, and had James, Caroline and David Guthrie.

(III.) William Mackay Low, married Daisy Gordon, daughter of Gen. W. W. Gordon.

(IV.) Jesse Low, married Hugh Graham, and had:

(I.) Ronand Andrew Hugh Graham.

(II.) Harriett Sybil Hermonie Graham.

(III.) Muriel Mary Graham.

Eugene West Stiles and Caroline D. Anderson had:

(I.) Eugenia Douglas Stiles.

By Rosabel Bowley he had:

(1.) William Henry Stiles.

(2.) Clifford Rosabel Stiles.

(3.) Joseph Clay Stiles.

(4.) Homer Randolph Stiles.

(5.) Anna Newton Stiles.

(6.) Herbert Newton Stiles.

(7.) Wallace Stiles.

(8.) Ellen Virginia Stiles.

Major Robert Stiles, attorney at law, Major C. S. A., elder

brother of Eugene W. Stiles, married Lelia, daughter of Hon. Allen Caperton, U. S. Senator, and had:

(1.) Joseph Clay Stiles.
(2.) Mary Evelyn Stiles.

Capt. William Henry Stiles, son of Hon. William Henry Stiles, married Eliza C., daughter of Hon. W. W. Gordon and Sarah Anderson Stites, and had:

(1.) William H. Stiles, married Elizabeth Chadwick.
(2.) Gulielma Clifford Stiles.
(3.) William Gordon Stiles, married Elizabeth Bowles.
(4.) Mary Cowper Stiles, married Edward J. Swann.
(5.) Alfred Stiles.
(6.) Ellen Beirne Stiles.
(7.) Ethel Gordon Stiles.
(8.) Robert Mackay Stiles.
(9.) George Gordon Stiles.

William H. Stiles and Elizabeth Chadwick had the following:

(1.) Hugh Stiles.
(2.) William Henry Stiles.
(3.) John Chadwick Stiles.
(4.) Hugh Grenville Stiles.
(5.) Dorothy Frances Stiles.
(6.) Gulielma Stiles.
(7.) Eliza Gordon Stiles.

William Gordon Stiles and Elizabeth Bowles had:

(1.) Delaine Stiles.

Capt. Robert Mackay Stiles married Margaret Wylly Couper, daughter of James Hamilton Couper and Caroline Wylly, and had:

(1.) Robert Mackay Stiles.
(2.) Caroline Couper Stiles, married William S. Lovell, Jr.
(3.) Hamilton Couper Stiles.
(4.) John Couper Stiles, married Edith Mary duBignon, and had:
  (1.) Kate Mackay Stiles.
  (2.) Mary duBignon Stiles.
(5.) *Elizabeth Mackay Stiles, married Alfred E. Mills, and had:
  (1.) Charles F. Mills.

*She married, second, Screven.

(6.) Margaret Couper Stiles.
(7.) Catharine Mackay Stiles, married Robert L. Mercer.
(8.) Isabel Cowper Stiles.

CUMMING

The ancestor of this well known Georgia family, who have shed additional lustre on the pages of her history, was William Cumming, who was born near Inverness, about 1725, took the part of Prince Charlie, was captured at Culloden in 1746, and was either sent or went to Maryland soon afterward; became a land owner, between 1751 and 1763, of nearly 2,000 acres of farm land in the Linganore Hills, in Frederick County, Md., some fifteen miles east of Frederick City. Of his sons, two became eminent, and well may Georgia be proud of the Cumming name; for in 1785, or about that time, Robert and Thomas Cumming went to Savannah, Ga., and entered into business. Thomas Cumming eventually moved to Augusta, where he became the first Mayor or Intendant, in about 1786, and was evidently one of the foremost citizens of the town, for he was called the "Father of Augusta." The other brother, Robert, returned to Frederick County, Md., and was with his father when the latter died, in 1793, on his farm in the Linganore Hills. He became a prominent citizen of Maryland, dying in 1825, as Major General of the first division of Maryland militia. Another of this eminent family was Colonel William Clay Cumming, a graduate of Princeton, and one of the foremost citizens of our State, evidenced by the number of positions offered him, most of which he declined. He was one of the ten Adjutant Generals at the close of the War of 1812; one of the authors of Infantry Tactics (1815); appointed, in 1818, Quartermaster General with rank of Brigadier, which he declined; offered the U. S. Senatorship by the Georgia Legislature; appointed Major General by Polk, in 1846—all of which he declined—and with John Forsyth kept Georgia from joining in the South Carolina Nullification Act. This brilliant and eminent Georgian deserves a niche in the Georgia Hall of Fame, should one ever be erected.

Besides these prominent men, we may mention Alfred Cumming, appointed by Buchanan Governor of Utah; Dr. Wm. Henry Cumming, Montgomery Cumming, Wallace Cumming,

Gen. Alfred Cumming, Major Joseph B. Cumming, and others of the name who have kept up the prestige of this honored name.

William Cumming, the first of the name, married Sarah Coppage, of Maryland, and had seven children:

1. Anna Cumming, married John Campbell.
2. Elizabeth Cumming, married Nicholas Hobbs.
3. Robert Cumming, married Mrs. Mary Allen Coates.
4. Sarah Cumming, married Edward Dorsey.
5. Jane Cumming, married John McElfresh.
6. Catharine Cumming, married Richard Simpson, Jr.
7. Thomas Cumming, born May 30th, 1765, died March, 1834, in Augusta; married Ann, daughter of Hon. Joseph Clay, born, London, England, son of Ralph Clay and Elizabeth, sister of Hon. Governor James Habersham.

ADAMS

The latest information of this family shows it to be one of the most ancient families in America, and its alliances with and relationshp to many of the foremost families of this country shows that its descendants have in their veins some of the best blood of the land. The following families or branches of them descend from the Adams, or are connected to them by blood or marriage: Habersham, Stiles, King, Bulloch, Lewis, Newell, Footman, Colquitt, Clarke, Caperton, De Treville and many others; and branches of the family are descended from the Bolton, Cochran, Bryan, Wylly, Capers, Ellis, Flournoy, Cobb, Lewis, of Warner Hall, Va., and Warner families; and through these connected to the Washingtons, Lees and many others. The ancestor of the family was Henry Adams, of England, who, in 1635, with six sons, went to Massachusetts, and one of his sons, Matthew Adams, was the progenitor of the Southern family. His descendant, William Adams, went to Charleston, S. C., in 1698, and the family came from Charlestown, Mass.

The men of this family have been steady, reliable and brave, and some have occupied the professions of soldiers and lawyers with ability. Among those contributing to the honor of the family are Nathaniel Adams, who, in 1770, gave £70 toward the erection of an Episcopal Church upon Edisto Island, and member of the Edisto company for defense of the Colony; also John Adams, Ensign of Old Military Company, and David Adams, a member of the Volunteer Company; also Capt. Nathaniel Adams, of the Revolution; Gen. David L. Adams; Wylly Adams, Captain 3d Artillery, Mexican War; Rev. Habersham Adams; Newell Sayre Adams, killed in War with Mexico; Robert Watkins Adams, graduate State University, Captain 5th Georgia Regiment, Percy's Brigade, member Senate and House of Representatives of Florida Legislature; Flournoy Woodbridge Adams, for twelve years a member of the Georgia Legislature, and others who at all times were ever to the front when duty called them—a family good, tried and true, whose descendants are numerous in America.

William Adams, who went to Charleston, S. C., in 1698, had:

I. David Adams, married *Elizabeth Capers, daughter of Richard Capers, Esq., planter, of South Carolina, and Mary, his wife (Richard Capers died in 1694).

II. †William Adams, married (supposed to be brother of David), and had:

1. William Adams.
2. John Adams.
3. Jane Adams.
4. Lydia Adams.
5. Elizabeth Adams, married Thomas Grimball.

The will of "William Adams of Charles Town, in the said Province of South Carolina, Glover," made June 1, 1707, recorded July 22, 1707, mentions his children, William, John, Jane and Lydia Adams, and "Elizabeth Grimball, wife of Mr. Thos. Grimball;" Peter Guerard and William Elliott, executors: William Sadler, John Child, Timothy Bellamy and Thomas Skipworth, witnesses (Probate Court Records, C. C., Book 1687-1710, p. 133). The will of "William Adams, of Edisto Island, St. John Parish, Colleton County," dated March 5, 1756, proved April 9, 1756, mentions wife, sons, William,

*Married, March 17, 1792, Ann, daughter of Nathaniel Adams, deceased, to Leighton Wilson, at residence of John Jenkins, South Edisto.

†"Know all men by these presents that we, David Adams and Elizabeth, his wife, one of the daughters of Richard Capers, of this Province, Planter, deceased * * * twentieth day of February, Anno Dom. 1710-11." Extract from a conveyance of Probate Court Records, Charleston County, Book 1716-21, p. 82. It is said that David Adams married, first, Julia Elliott; second, Miss Grimball; but it appears by record that he married only Elizabeth Capers. It would seem that William Adams was also a son of first William.

Joseph, Thomas, Isaac and John; daughter, Ann Adams, wife of David Adams, and daughters, Martha and Mary Adams (P. C. R., C. C., Book 1752-56, p. 471).

David Adams and Elizabeth Capers had:

I. Nathaniel Adams, married, first, by Rev. Jones, August 14, 1740, Mary, daughter of Richard and Rebecca Capers. He married, second, by Rev. Jones, September 16, 1744, Margaret (daughter of *Edmund Ellis), born October 10, 1727, baptized by Rev. Dyson, November 19, 1727, and had as sureties Rev. Lewis Jones and Anna and Margaret Watt. *(Edmund Ellis was buried by Rev. Dyson, 31st March, 1738.)

NOTE.—It is tradition that the Adams were descended from Henry Adams, whose descendant, Mathew, was ancestor of William, father of David Adams; but recent information from George Augustus Gordon, Esq., of N. E. Historic Genealogical Society of Boston, Mass., and its Recording Secretary, to whom many thanks are due, gives the following: "Very early in New England history, was a Nathaniel Adams—at Newport, at Weymouth, at Boston, where he died 1675, and his will is on record. He had a wife, Sarah. He had a son, Nathaniel Adams, born 1630, died 1690. His will is also on record. His widow, Mary, died 1707. That one's son, Nathaniel (3) Adams, born at Boston, 1653, died at Charlestown, Mass., 1710, had a wife, Hannah, who died 1699. They had Nathaniel (4) Adams, born 1681, and David Adams, born 1682—who are probably the brothers for whom you inquire." Now, through the able efforts of Mr. A. S. Salley, of the S. C. Hist. Soc., we have positively found that David and Nathaniel Adams are on record as having come from Charlestown, Mass. Mr. Salley gives the following reasons as to parentage of Nathaniel (5) Adams (son of David Adams), who married Margaret Ellis as his second wife: "It appears to me that Nathaniel Adams was the son of David Adams and Elizabeth Capers, daughter of Richard Capers, and his wife, Mary; Richard Capers died in 1694." I base my belief on Nathaniel Adams being a son of David on the following facts: "David had a brother, Nathaniel Adams. Two other Adams, contemporaries of David's, lived in Charleston, and neither of them mention a son Nathaniel. William Adams names his children in his will and John Adams deeds all of his property in Charlestown, S. C., to his mother, Mrs. Avis Adams. His father was John Adams. The deed of John Adams, and another by Nathaniel Adams, brother of David, show that they were originally of Charlestown, Mass." Mr. Salley considers the Nathaniel Adams who married Margaret Ellis, the son of David; and as Nathaniel Adams and Edmund, David and Richard Adams are mentioned in St. Helena Records in South Carolina as sons of Nathaniel Adams and Margaret Ellis, the record seems to be clearly made out as to ancient descent of this family. Nathaniel Adams and Edmund went to Georgia, from South Carolina, the latter having a son, David; and Mrs. Bulloch remembers her mother speaking of the peculiar manner in which her father, Nathaniel Adams, pronounced St. Helena. He was of South Carolina, and went to Georgia, became a planter, married Ann Bolton of the ancient English family of Bolton, and died in 1806. He was J. P., and lived at Vernonburgh or White Bluff, on Vernon River, near Savannah, Ga. The line, then, would run: Nathaniel 1, Nathaniel 2, Nathaniel 3, his sons; Nathaniel 4, and David, of Charlestown, Mass., who went to Charleston, S. C.; Nathaniel 5, who married Margaret Ellis, and Nathaniel 6 Adams, who went to Georgia, and married Anne Bolton, and was progenitor of the Adams family of Georgia.

Nathaniel Adams and Margaret Ellis had the following:

I. Nathaniel Adams,* born December 20, 1747; died March 7, 1806; went to Georgia and married Anne Bolton, daughter of Robert Bolton† and Susannah, daughter of Mathew Mauve, of Berne, and Jane Mauve, of Vevay, Switzerland, who came to Georgia before 1740.

II. David Adams, born September 2, 1745; married Elizabeth Ellis.

III. Edmund Adams, born 28, 1749; went to Georgia and married Jane Stultz, and became the progenitor of a branch of the Williams family, who descend from the Smiths, Bourkes, Glens, &c.; also, ancestor of Judge A. Pratt Adams, S. B. Adams, attorney at law, and David Adams, William B. Adams and others.

IV. Richard Adams, born July 2, 1752; baptized September 26, 1752.

V. Ann Adams, (?) married Leighton Wilson.

VI. Jane Adams (?).

Nathaniel Adams, Esq., of White Bluff, Ga., second son of Nathaniel Adams, of St. Helena, S. C., was born December 20, 1747, on St. Helena Island, S. C., went to Georgia, was a palnter, owning the old Adams place, at White Bluff, near Savannah; a gentleman of the "Old School," a Tory, preferring to adhere to the Crown, and dying in 1806, after holding the position of Justice of the Peace, a position then of honor. He married Anne Bolton, daughter of Robert Bolton, of Savannah, who held many public positions in Savannah, and was the first Postmaster in Georgia. He went to Georgia in 1740 with his sisters, one of whom (Mary Bolton), married Hon. James Habersham, Governor of Georgia. Robert Bolton married Susannah, daughter of Mathew Mauve, a merchant of Savannah, Ga., who held office under the Crown. These Mauves were of Huguenot descent, and reputed wealthy and of honorable descent. Robert Bolton was son of Robert Bolton, of

*Nathaniel, the sixth of name, dating from first ancestor.
†Brother of Mrs. James Habersham.

Philadelphia, Penn., and Ann Curtis, widow Clay, a descendant of the Curtis of Kent County, England, of the Bowers and the Dunsters of New and Old England. (Mathew Mauve died June 28, 1775; Jane Mauve died September 20, 1775.)

Nathaniel Adams and Anne Bolton had the following children (he died March 7, 1806):

A. Nathaniel Adams, married Mary Ann Wylly, daughter of Col. Richard Wylly and Mary Bryan, daughter of Joseph Bryan and Mary Storey; son of Joseph Bryan and Mrs. Murray; brother of Hon. Jonathan Bryan, sons of Joseph Bryan, of South Carolina, and Janet Cochrane, of Carolina. Richard Wylly married, second, Mary, daughter of Hon. Jonathan Bryan, and widow of *John Morel, President of Georgia, and was by this marriage progenitor of the Woodbridge, Thiot, Cunningham, &c., families. Hugh Bryan married Catharine Barnwell, daughter of John Barnwell and Ann Berners.

NOTE.—Wylly family: The first account we have of this family dates to an early period, for we find Edward Wylly had a grant of land as far back as 1666, of the lands of Bonnecally and Dowan, Barony of Ouna and Ana, County Tipperary, Ireland. Of this family the Georgia Wylly line descend, one of whom was the noted Revolutionary patriot, Col. Richard Wylly, Col. Thomas Wylly and Alexander Wylly, Speaker of the House.

B. Susan Ann Adams, married, December 11, 1809, *John Lewis, Esq., and had:

I. John Lewis.

II. John N. Lewis, married Frances Simond Henry.

III. R. Adams Lewis, married Katharine Ann Barrington Cook.

IV. Margaret Lewis, married Noble A. Hardee.

V. Susan Ann Lewis, died 1845.

VI. Joseph Lewis, died.

C. Margaret Adams, married, November 8, 1809, first, Joseph King, by Rev. Kollock, and had:

I. Margaret Emily Adams King, who died; she married, second, by Rev. Henry Kollock, John Lewis, on June 13, 1826, son of Joseph Lewis and Susan-

*From whom descend a branch of Wylly family.
*John Lewis, born about 1785; died 1867, age 82.

nah Baker, son of Isaac Lewis and Susan Kirkland, son of Samuel Lewis and Mary, and had:

I. Mary Eliza Adams Lewis, born January 1, 1828, married by Rev. Nathaniel Pratt, Dr. William Gaston Bulloch, on November 6, 1851 (he was born August 3, 1815; died June 23, 1885).

D. Thomas Adams, married Mary Young, and had:

a. Katharine Adams.

b. Robert Adams, married twice, and had by first:

1. Joseph Adams.

2. Mary Adams.

E. Ann Adams, married John Bolton, Mayor of Savannah, after whom Bolton street was named.

A. Nathaniel (3d) Alexander Adams, born 1797, died 1849, son of Nathaniel Adams and Anne Bolton, married Mary Ann Wylly, and had:

a. Ann Wylly Adams, born July 31, 18—, died September 12, 1896, married Dr. Joseph Clay Habersham, son of Major John Habersham and Ann Sarah Camber.

b. Nathaniel (4th) Alexander Adams, married, July 26, 1820-21 (who died August 28, 1849), Mary Mildred Flournoy, daughter of Robert W. Flournoy and Mary Willis Cobb.

c. William Evans Adams, born 1813, died 1846-47.

d. Mary Bryan Adams, born May 19, 1803, died April 17, 1899, married Edward Footman, son of Richard Footman and Elizabeth Maxwell, daughter of William Maxwell and Constant Butler, son of James Maxwell and Mary Simmons, and had:

I. Robert Footman, married Ann Davis, issue.

II. Maxwell Footman.

III. Joseph Footman, married Miss Gould, issue.

IV. Thomas Footman, married Eliza Williams, issue.

V. George Footman, married Mrs. Footman, issue.

I. Robert Footman, married Ann Davis, and had:

1. Mary Footman, married Champion McAlpin.

2. Virginia Footman, married R. Davant.

3. George Footman, married Elizabeth Hunter.

4. Susie Footman, married Lawrence Arden.

II. Maxwell Footman.

III. Joseph Footman, married Miss Gould, and had:

1. Marion Footman.
2. Bessie Gould Footman.

IV. Thomas Footman, married Eliza Williams, and had:
1. Rosa Footman, married Mr. Bibb.
2. Helen Footman.

V. Edward Footman.

VI. George Footman, married, first, Mrs. Footman, and had:
1. Julia Footman.
2. Thomas Footman.

e. Margaret Vernon Adams, born October 2, 1805, died September 30, 1892, married Joseph Stiles, son of Samuel Stiles, and had:

I. Samuel V. Stiles, married Caroline Rogers.
II. Florence Vernon Stiles, married her cousin, Wylly Woodbridge.
III. George Stiles, Captain S. V. G.
IV. Mary Anna Stiles, married her cousin, Dr. Joseph Clay Habersham, Jr.
V. Dr. Clifford A. Stiles, married, first, Anna Wylly Adams, and had issue:
1. George Floyd Stiles, married.
2. Clifford Alonzo Stiles.
3. Mary Joe Stiles.
4. Habersham Stiles.
5. Margaret Vernon Stiles.

I. Samuel V. Stiles and Caroline Rogers had:

I. S. W. Stiles, married Georgia Jacob, and had:
1. Samuel Vernon Stiles.
2. Agnes Stiles.

Dr. Clifford A. Stiles, married, second, Katharine Livingston Hutchinson, and had:
1. Florence Woodbridge Stiles.
2. Esther Wylly Stiles.
3. Clifford Allen Stiles.

f. Hester R. Adams, married Capt. Thomas Newell, son of Thomas Newell and Rebecca Bolton, and had:

I. Roberta Newell.
II. Helen Thomasine Newell, married L. Y. Gibbs.
III. Nannette H. Newell, married Capt. Jas B. West, of Ireland.

IV. Mary Newell, married Lewis Tattnall Turner, son of Lewis Tattnall Turner, of Whitmarsh Island, who married Miss Mills, son of Lewis Turner and Miss Tebeau, son of Richard Turner and Elizabeth Barnard, daughter Col. John Barnard and Jane Bradley, married in London in 1743. The Turners came to Georgia very early, were planters and the Barnards were of the family of Sir John Barnard.

V. Thomas Newell, married Josephine Turner, and had:

I. Thomas Newell, dead.

II. Josephine Newell.

g. Helen G. Adams, born December 10, 1809, died October 12, 1898, married Charles Sydney Stewart, son of Charles Stewart, of Scotland, and Miss Pritchard, of South Carolina, and had:

I. Charles Stewart.

II. Seymour C. Stewart.

NOTE.—Turner family: We find very early mention of the Turner name in the Colony of Georgia, and this family have followed the occupation of planters for generations.

Richard Turner, Esq., planter, married Elizabeth Barnard (daughter of Col. John Barnard, a Captain of the King's Rangers in the Colony of Georgia), who married Jane Bradley in London in 1743. Col. Barnard was the son of Sir John Barnard, Lord Mayor of London. (For arms of Barnard, see Burke's General Armory.)

h. Richard Wylly Adams, born October 11, 1811, married, first, Emma Guerard; second, Susette, daughter of Commodore Thomas Newell and Rebecca, daughter of Gamaliel Newell and Rebecca Foster. Capt. Newell was her double cousin; Gamaliel Newell was a brother of Thomas Newell, who married Rebecca Bolton, daughter of Robert Bolton, and had Capt. Thomas Newell, who married, first, Rebecca Newell, and had:

I. Susette Newell, married Richard Wylly Adams, and had:

1. Richard Wylly Adams.
2. Nathaniel Adams, died.
3. Hester Adams.
4. Susette Adams.
5. William James Bulloch Adams, married Mary Fenwick Neufville, daughter of Edward F. Neufville and Miss Tattnall, and had:

A. Edward Neufville Adams.
B. Richard Bulloch Adams.

Mary F. Neufville was daughter of Edward F. Neufville, son of Rev. Edward Neufville and Mary Fenwick Kollock, daughter of Dr. Lemuel Kollock and Maria, daughter of Macartan Campbell and Matilda Fenwick. Edward F. Neufville married Miss Tattnall, daughter of Commodore Tattnall, and Miss Jackson, son of Governor Tattnall and descended from the Mullrynes, Barnwells, Fenwicks, Draytons and Bulls of South Carolina. Rev. Edward Neufville married, first, Mary, daughter of Hon. William B. Bulloch, and had Mary Neufville, who died.

FENWICK

Edward Fenwick, of Staunton, married Sarah Nevill, of Cheat, Yorkshire, and had:

I. Roger Fenwick, Colonel of Horse, killed 1658, siege of Dunkirk.

II. Robert Fenwick, third son, married Ann Culcbeth, of Northumberland, and had:

1. John Fenwick, King's Councillor, died London, 1747; married Elizabeth, daughter of Governor Robert Gibbes, of South Carolina, and had: Edward Fenwick, married, first, Martha, daughter of Ralph Izard (second, Magdalen Chastagnier), and had Edward Fenwick, King's Councillor, born January 22, 1720, died July 8, 1775, married Mary, daughter of Thomas Drayton and Elizabeth Bull, daughter of Governor William Bull and Mary, daughter of Richard Quintyne and Elizabeth Edward. They had:

I. Edward Fenwick, married Stuart.
II. Harriet Fenwick, married Governor Josiah Tattnall.
III. Charlotte Fenwick, married Pierce.
IV. Matilda Fenwick, married Macartan Campbell.
V. Gen. John Fenwick.

NOTE.—Thomas Tattnall married Elizabeth Barnwell, daughter of Col. John Barnwell, and had: Josiah Tattnall, who married daughter of Col. John Mulbryne, and had: Josiah Tattnall, Governor of Georgia, who married daughter of Edward Fenwicke, of South Carolina, of ancient family of Fenwick, of Staunton, and had: Commodore E. F.

Tattnall, who married his cousin, Miss Jackson, daughter of Ebenezer Jackson, of Connecticut, and of the Revolution, who married a Fenwick of South Carolina (Lemuel Kollock married Maria Campbell).

Nannette Habersham Newell and Capt. James B. West had:

I. James Bolton West, married Mary Ella Shivers.

II. Thomas Newell West, Lieutenant Spanish-American War, U. S. V.

III. Stella West.

Mary Newell and Lewis T. Turner had:

I. Mary Ella Turner.

II. Lewis Newell Turner.

III. Francis Muir Turner.

IV. Gibson Turner.

NOTE.—Thomas Newell married Rebecca Bolton, and had:

1. Thomas Newell.
2. Robert Newell.

Gamaliel Newell was a brother of Thomas, who married Rebecca Bolton, and married Rebecca Foster, the issue being one daughter, who married Capt. Thomas Newell, her cousin, son of Thomas and Rebecca Bolton. Capt. Thomas Newell married, secondly, Hester R. Adams. By the first marriage to Rebecca Newell (daughter of Gamaliel and Rebecca Foster), he had Susette, who married her cousin, Richard Wylly Adams (the seventh child of Nathaniel Adams, Jr., and Mary Ann Wylly). The Newells were from Connecticut.

Nathaniel Alexander Adams, son of Nathaniel Adams and Mary Ann Wylly, married, July 26, 1820, Mary Mildred Flournoy, born June 18, 1805, daughter of Robert W. Flournoy, born Prince Edward County, Va., 1763, and Mary Willis Cobb, born May 9, 1794 (son of Mathews Flournoy, born June 21, 1732), and Elizabeth, widow of Charles Smith and daughter of William Pryor, married about 1755, son of Jean Jacques Flournoy and Elizabeth, daughter of James Williams, of Wales, lawyer, and Elizabeth Buckner, son of Jacques Flournoy and Julia Eyraud, son of Jacques Flournoy and Judith Pueray, son of Jean Flournoy and Frances, son of Laurent Flournoy, the emigrant of a noble French family (see Virginia Gazette), and had the following children:

I. Wylly Cobb Adams, Captain 3d Artillery in Mexican War; died without issue.

II. Rev. Habersham Adams, married, first, Mary Virginia White; married, second, daughter of Dr. Benjamin White and Jane Eleanor Clancy, and had:

1. Mary, married Cobb Lampkin.
2. Florence Adams.

3. Mettie Adams.
4. Caro J., married T. E. White.
5. John Porter Adams.

III. Newell Sayre Adams, killed Mexican War.

IV. Robert Watkins Adams, graduate Athens, Ga.; Captain 5th Georgia; in Senate and House of Florida Legislature; married Sophia Broward, and had:

1. Frank Adams.
2. Nathaniel Adams.
3. Robert Watkins Adams.
4. Julia Adams, married Rev. Saunders, of Florida.
5. Minnie Adams.

V. Flournoy Woodbridge Adams, of Athens, Ga., twelve years member of the Georgia Legislature, removed to New York City, November 4, 1874. He married Emma W. Nowland, and had, besides others dead:

1. Maxcey Adams, one of Commercial Editors New York *Tribune*.
2. Dora Adams, married, first, Alexander S. Hopkins, son of Judge John Livingston Hopkins, and had a daughter:
   I. Flournoy Adams Hopkins.

Dora Adams married, second, William Willoughby Sharp, of Norfolk, Va., descended from the Sharps, Willoughbys and Newtons, who settled in Princess Anne County, Va., 1631, and had:

I. W. Willoughby Sharp, Jr.

3. Mary Adams, married Fowler, of Los Angeles, Cal.

VI. America Flournoy Adams, married Major T. M. Lampkin, and had:

I. William H. Lampkin, of Mt. Vernon, N. Y.

II. Mildred Lampkin, married Nathaniel Barrett, of West New Brighton, N. Y., and had:
   I. Alinene Barrett.
   II. William Barrett.

VII. Mary Willis Adams, married Capt. Bulloch Jackson, son of Col. Joseph Webber Jackson, son of Governor James Jackson (of the distinguished Jackson family of Georgia, and of one tracing way back to England), and Mary Young, daughter of William Young. Issue:

I. Joseph W. Jackson, married Jones.
II. Nathaniel A. Jackson, married, first, second, Smith.
III. Mary V. Jackson, married Richard Wylly Thiot, of ancient French family, and descended from the Charltons, Bryans, Col. Richard Wylly, and had:

NOTE.—Grafton Woodbridge married Charlotte Maria Thiot. They had three children: Helen Bryan, Charles and Grafton. Grafton died at an early age, two or three years. Helen Bryan married E. A. Penniman, of Brunswick; she has no children. Charles married in Texas; he died early in this year, 1901, leaving two daughters, Helen Bryan and Alice. Richard Wylly Thiot's father was Charles Henry Thiot, and he was the great-great-grand-son of Col. Richard Wylly.

I. Richard W. Thiot.
II. Florence King Thiot.
III. Edith Flournoy Thiot.
IV. Daughter Thiot.

IV. Sarah Cobb Jackson, married Polk Stewart, of Macon, Ga.

IX. Elizabeth Julia Adams, died, age 18 years.
X. Julia Mildred Adams, married Thomas Walker, of Green County, Ala.; killed battle of Kennesaw Mountain, 1864, and had:

I. Herbert Walker, married and had issue.
II. Harry Walker, married Elise Woodbury, issue Julia Mildred Walker. Julia Mildred Adams, married, second, Edmund Bryan Adams, and had Cobb Adams, went West.

XI. Ann Adams, married Dr. Clifford A. Stiles, her first cousin (see Stiles).
XII. Margaret Helen Rebecca Adams, married George Clements, 1868, of Gainesville, Ga., no issue.

This line of Adams descend from many of the best Virginia families as well as from Georgia lines, and has an immense connection with the Lewis, Washingtons, Lees, Warners, &c.; for Mary Willis Cobbs, who married Robert W. Flournoy, was the daughter of John Cobbs and Mildred Lewis, son of John Cobbs, son of Robert Cobbs, son of Robert Cobbs, Justice and High Sheriff of Virginia, York County, 1681, son of Ambrose Cobbs, who came to York County, Va., about 1613.

"READE"

Andrew Reade, October 6, 1619, of Manor of Faccombe, married Miss Cooke, of Kent, and had Robert Reade, who married Mildred, daughter of Sir Thomas Windebanke, by Francis, daughter of Sir Edward Dymoke, hereditary Champion of England, and had Col. George Reade, 1637, member of the Council, who married a daughter of Monsieur Martian, and had Mildred Reade, who married Augustine Warner, born October 20, 1643, member of Council, son of Col. Augustine Warner and Mary. Col. Augustine Warner had also Sarah Warner, who married Lawrence Townley, and through the Grimes was ancestor of Gen. R. E. Lee. Augustine Warner and Mildred Reade had:

I. Augustine Warner.
II. George Warner.
III. Mildred Warner, married Lawrence Washington.
IV. Mary Warner, married John Smith.
V. Elizabeth Warner, born November 24, 1672; married Col. John Lewis, of Warner Hall, Gloucester County, born 1669, died 1725; member of Council; son of Major John Lewis and Isabella Warner, son of Robert Lewis, who came to Virginia, 1635; son of Robert Lewis, of Brecon, Wales; son of Sir Edward Lewis, of Van and Edgington, Wiltshire, who married Ann, daughter of Earl of Talbot.

Col. John Lewis and Elizabeth Warner had:

I. John Lewis, 1694, of the Council, married Frances Fielding, and had Fielding Lewis, who married Elizabeth Washington.
II. Robert Lewis.
III. Charles Lewis (of the Bird), born 1696, died 1799; married Mary, daughter of John Howell, and had: Howell Lewis, who married Mary, daughter of Col. Henry Willis, founder of Fredericksburg, and Mildred Howell, widow Brown, son of Francis Willis; son of Henry Willis; died before 1689; son of John Willis, born 1587; son of Francis Willis, died 1596, of Oxford England.

Howell Lewis and Mary Willis had Mildred Lewis, married John Cobb, and besides others had: Mary Willis Cobb, married May 9, 1794, Robert W. Flournoy, born Prince Edward County, Va., 1763, and had besides others Mary Mildred Flournoy, married Nathaniel Adams, and had issue.

All the Cobbs of Georgia descend from this line, and a branch of Garrard, Glenn, Olive, Smith, Jackson, Prince and many others; and we see then that the Lees, Washingtons, Warners, Reades, Martians, Smiths, Howells, Lewis, Willis, Cobbs, Adams, Jacksons, Flournoys and many others of Georgia and Virginia are all connected and related to each other, including, also, Ball, Taliaferro, Grimes, etc.; and that many of these descend from the Magna Charta Barons and from the Royal House of England.

c JACKSON

The descent of the distinguished family of Jackson of Georgia is thus: Clement and Honor Jackson, of Moreton Hampsted, Devon, England, had Abraham Jackson, born August 8, 1678; married Rebecca, and had Jabez Jackson, born October 2, 1700, buried at Moreton; married Sarah Waldron, and had James Jackson, born September 1, 1730, died May 15, 1782; married, August 30, 1755, to Mary Webber; born April 2, 1734, died at Teiginn, July 5, 1785. They had:

I. James Jackson, born Moreton, England, September 21, 1757; went to America, April 13, 1772; died March 19, 1806, Washington, D. C.; married Mary C. Young, who died July 5, 1795, daughter of William Young, the ardent patriot.

II. Abraham Jackson, married Ann Agnes Yonge, daughter of Hon. Henry Yonge, member of his Majesty's Council.

III. Dr. Henry Jackson, father of Hon. Gen. Henry R. Jackson.

Governor James Jackson and Mary Young had:

1. William Henry Jackson, State Senator, born June 3, 1786; died August, 1875; married, 1808, Mildred Lewis Cobb; ancestor of Grants of Atlanta, Ga.
2. James Jackson, professor University of Georgia.
3. Jabez Young Jackson, born July, 1790; member Congress.
4. Joseph Webber Jackson, born December 6, 1796; member of Congress; married, and had A. Bulloch

Jackson (Captain), married Mary Willis, daughter of Nathaniel Adams and Mary Mildred Flournoy.

William B. Adams married Laleah Pratt, daughter of Alexander J. Pratt, born 1800, died 1838, son of Alexander Pratt, who went to Savannah from Nassau, Bahamas, in 1800 or 1804. Alexander J. Pratt married Margaret Phillips, of St. Marys, Camden County, Ga., on September 17, 1829 (they were married by Rev. Horace S. Pratt, who married Miss Wood, and whose daughter, Laleah George Wood Pratt, married Rev. J. B. Dunwody, of Walterboro, S. C.) Margaret Phillips was the adopted daughter and relative, it is thought, of Hon. John Wood, of St. Mary's, Ga., who was a brother of Baron George Wood, of the British Exchequer, and his wife was Laleah Johnston, daughter or sister of Sir William Johnston, Governor of the Bermudas; and it is said the Pratts, who belong to the family of Earl of Camden, were instrumental in getting Sir William Johnston appointed Governor of Bermuda. The Pratts were connected to the Johnston and Wood families. Camden County, Ga., was named after the Earl of Camden.

William B. Adams and Laleah Pratt had:

I. A. Pratt Adams (Judge), married Sarah Olmstead, and had Charles Olmstead Adams.

II. Hon. Samuel B. Adams, City Attorney, married Annie Wynn, and had:

1. Alexander Pratt Adams.
2. Laleah Pratt Adams.
3. Minnie Wynn Adams.
4. Deborah Adams.

III. Laleah Pratt Adams, died.

IV. William B. Adams, never married.

William B. Adams, married, second, Rachel Gammon, daughter of Benjamin Gammon and Deborah Pratt, and had:

I. Florence Adams.

II. Lavinia Adams, married *Hon. Wm. Gammell Cann.

W. G. Cann and Lavinia Adams had:

I. Wm. G. Cann.

II. Sam'l Adams Cann.

III. Florence Adams Cann.

III. Mary Barnard Adams, married F. D. M. Strachan, of Brunswick, Ga.

*Cashier of Savannah Bank and Trust Company at the time of his death, and also an Alderman of the city of Savannah.

William B. Adams was son of Samuel Adams, a planter of Skidaway, Ga., who married Mary Louisa Barnard, and the latter was son of Edmund Adams, a brother of Nathaniel Adams and possibly of Jane Adams, who administered on Edmund's estate, who died December 9, 1796. About this time a plantation of 120 acres was sold at White Bluff.

It will now be of interest to look into the descent of the Hon. Samuel B. Adams' wife, Annie Winn, who was the daughter of Rev. A. M. Winn, D. D., and Maria Howard, daughter of Gen. Nicholas Howard, a very wealthy planter of middle Georgia, and Judith Campbell, daughter of John Campbell, of Virginia, an officer in the Revolutionary War, who belonged to the Scotch family of the name. The Howards are of same family as the Duke of Norfolk, and the original ancestor, John, went to Virginia in 1620. He was born in 1600, died in 1661, and member of House of Burgesses of Virginia in 1640. The first of the Winns was Thomas Wynne, who went from Wales to Virginia in 1683, and his great-grand-son went to Georgia about 1800.

Thomas Wynn, of Lunenburg County, Va., and his descendant or great-grand-son, Lemuel Wynn, who went to Georgia, and who married Miss Posey, had Rev. Thomas Lemuel Wynn, who married Miss McFarland, and had Rev. Alexander M. Wynn, D. D., who married Miss Howard, and had Annie Wynn, who married Hon. Samuel B. Adams. Thus we see this talented branch of the Adams descended from as ancient and honorable families as can be desired—from the Howards, Wynnes, Campbells, Pratts, Barnards and others.

THE BARNARD FAMILY

Sir John Barnard was an English Baronet, was at one time Lord Mayor of London, was prominent in the House of Commons, and had a distinguished judicial career. His son, Col. John Barnard, married Jane Bradley, in London, England, December 13, 1743.

This Jane Bradley was the daughter of William Bradley, of Lee Street, Red Lyon Square, County of Middlesex, Gentleman. The will of William Bradley, made in 1766, names William Bradley, Jr., as executor, and disposes of land in Georgia, South Carolina, and Spanish bonds of over a million dollars

(£240,000). The will mentions the testator's daughters, Jane (wife of Col. John Barnard), and Martha (wife of Isaac Young), both then living on Wilmington Island. Two copies of the will were found—one in possession of Mrs. Turner, a descendant of Martha Young, and the other of Major John Barnard. This William Bradley, Jr., was killed at sea, and devoured by a starving crew, so one of his survivors told his sister, Jane Barnard. The descendants of Richard Bradley, a younger son of William Bradley, Sr., live in Canada.

Col. Barnard settled his family on Wilmington Island, which had been granted to him by George II. Soon after his marriage he was ordered to Savannah, in command of a regiment called the Rangers, and it was after this that he settled Wilmington Island. He held his commission to the period of his death, after which event the command was given to his brother, Edward Barnard, who died about the commencement of the Revolutionary War between Great Britain and her American Colonies.

The children of Col. Barnard and Jane Bradley were the following: (1) A daughter (born October 18, 1744); (2) Timothy Barnard (born November 3, 1745); (3) William Barnard (born November 2, 1747); (4) John Barnard (born November 12, 1750); (5) Elizabeth Barnard (born July 14, 1753), married Richard Turner, of Whitmarsh; (6) Jane Barnard (born August 19, 1755), married Mr. Winn; (7) Robert Barnard (born January 10, 1757).

Timothy Barnard, the eldest son of Col. John Barnard, married a Creek girl and lived for a number of years, and died a member of the tribe, leaving a large estate. He had a number of half-breed children, who moved out West with their tribe. There is a deed on record in the office of the Clerk of the Superior Court of Chatham County by two of these children, namely, Pheloga and Timpouchchee, made to their cousin, William Barnard, January 4, 1825. At that time the Barnard family owned a large estate in Manchester, England. The grantee of this deed started to make efforts to recover the property, but died in New York City on his way to England, and the matter was then dropped.

William Barnard, the second son of Col. John Barnard, as far as I know, had but two children. One of them, William, who I think never married, bought out the interests of his half-breed cousins; and the other, Mary Louisa Barnard, who lived on Wilmington Island, and married Samuel Adams, a planter of Skidaway Island. The only child of the union who grew up to manhood was William B. Adams, who married Laleah Pratt (daughter of Alexander J. Pratt and Margaret Philipps, and grand-daughter of Alexander Pratt), and had Judge A. P. Adams, married Sarah Olmstead, Hon. Samuel B. Adams, married Annie Wynn, Laleah Pratt Adams and W. B. Adams, Jr.

John Barnard, the third son of Col. Barnard, was a Major in the American Army during the Revolutionary War, was active and prominent in that war, and was a member of the Provincial Congress that assembled in Savannah, July 4, 1775. He had the following children: Timothy Barnard (born November 2, 1775); Lucy W. Barnard (born August 13, 1777); Mary E. Barnard (born January 17, 1780); John W. Barnard (born December 23, 1783); James Barnard (born December 20, 1785), and Henrietta Barnard (born October 31, 1789). Mary never married; Lucy married, first, a Rev. C. B. Jones and afterwards Charles O. Screven; Henrietta married Stephen Williams.

Timothy Barnard (the son of Major John Barnard and grand-son of Col. Barnard), had the following children: Mrs. John T. Rowland, Mrs. William W. Wash, Mrs. Chisolm (mother of the late Judge Chisolm), John B. Barnard, Timothy Guerard Barnard, Saul S. Barnard, Caroline C. Barnard, and Mrs. Virginia M. Pritchard.

John W. Barnard, the second son of Major Barnard, was the father of the late Mrs. Mary Ann Barstow.

James Barnard (the third son of Major John Barnard), had the following children: Ann C., Virginia C. (Mrs. Demere), William (dead, no children), Vernon R., Margaret L. (Mrs. Hardee), Campbell J., Julia P. (Mrs. Quarterman), Isabelle D., Clifford V., Fuller A. and Florence (Fulton).

NOTE.—Timothy Barnard married Amelia Guerard, and his brother, James Barnard, married Catharine Guerard, and Ann Guerard married Steel White. These were daughters of Godin Guerard, son of John Guerard and Miss Godin.

ADAMS

On Edisto Island, October 2, 1775, we find a company of volunteers formed for defence of the Colony, under command of Joseph Jenkins, and among the members occur the names of Nathaniel Adams, John Adams and David Adams, Jr.; and for the Edisto Island old militia company, Mr. John Adams was chosen Ensign.

Extracts from St. Helena Register:

32—David W. Adams, married by Rev. Peasley, February 1, 1750, Catharine Grimball.

51—John Adams, baptized by Rev. Mr. Lewis, and married December 6, 1787, Mary Williamson.

William Adams, son William and Catharine, married by Rev. Jones, December 29, 1739, Elizabeth Fendin, who probably married, second, Daniel John Greene.—*S. C. Gazette.*

2—Martha Adams, daughter of William and Elizabeth, born September 24, 1740; baptized January 19, 1741; died 1741.

3—William Adams, son of William and Elizabeth Fenden; born December 9, 1743; baptized May 28, 1744.

4—Nathaniel Adams, born St. Helena; married by Rev. Jones, August 14, 1740, Mary Capers.

Nathaniel Adams, married by Rev. Jones, September 6, 1744, Margaret Ellis.

David Adams, son Nathaniel and Margaret Ellis, born September 2, 1745; married Elizabeth Ellis.

Nathaniel Adams, son of Nathaniel and Margaret Ellis, born December 20, 1747.

Edmund Adams, son of Nathaniel and Margaret Ellis; born December 28, 1749.

Thomas Adams, son of William Adams, Sr., and Martha, born December 19, 1742; baptized June 13, 1743.

Elizabeth Adams, daughter William and Elizabeth, born December 20, 1749; baptized July 7, 1751.

Richard Adams, son Nathaniel and Margaret Ellis, born July 2, 1752; baptized September 26, 1752.

Elizabeth Adams, daughter William, born May 22, 1769.

Jane Adams, daughter William, Jr., and Elizabeth, born September 23, 1770; baptized by Mr. Pierce January 27, 1771.

William Adams, son William; baptized August 13, 1789, by Rev. Mr. Lewis.

"BOWERS"

George Bowers, of Scituate, Mass., 1637; Plymouth, 1639; Cambridge, Mass.; land owner; died 1656; married Barbarine , who died March 25, 1644; and had, among others, Benanuel Bowers, who owned twenty acres in Charlestown, Mass.; married, November 9, 1763, Elizabeth Dunster, who came to Massachusetts about 1640-45; daughter Robert Dunster, born 1605; and niece of the celebrated Henry Dunster, first President of Harvard College; sons of Henrye Dunster, Gentleman, of Balehout, 1640, of Lancashire, Eng. Benanual Bowers had, among others, Elizabeth Bowers, who married Winlock, son of John Curtis on Kent, Delaware, Penn., a landed proprietor of ancient English descent, and had Ann Curtis; married, first, R. Clay, and second, Robert Bolton, and had, among others:

I. Robert Bolton, of Georgia, married Susannah Mauve.

II. Mary Bolton, married Governor James Habersham.

CURTIS

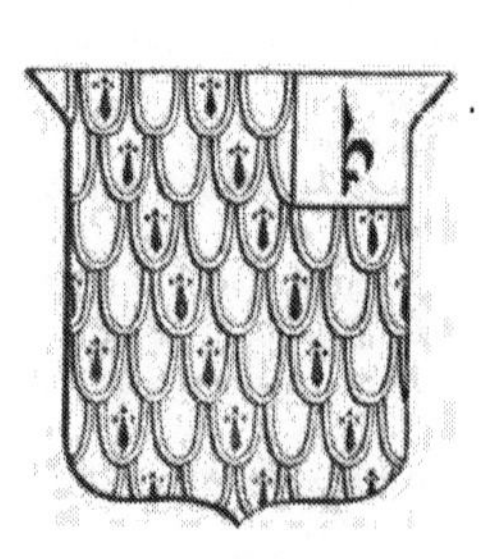

MAUVE

BOLTON

BOLTON OF BOLTON

This ancient family, according to Dugdale, descend from the Saxon Earls of Mercia, who descended from the Saxon Kings. We find the Boltons settled at the Brookhouse, Blackburn, Lancashire, where, says Fuller, the family had continued in good repute.

John Bolton, of Brookhouse, born 1570, had Robert Bolton, baptized at Blackburn; died 1609. His son, John Bolton, died 1632, had John Bolton; died Sheffield, County York, in 1700. His son, *Robert, of Sheffield, County York, removed to Philadelphia, Penn., 1719; married February 19, 1720, Ann Curtis, widow Clay; born November 15, 1690; died May 5, 1747. They had, besides others:

I. Robert Bolton, who moved to Savannah, Ga., about 1740; born January 1, 1722; died May 4, 1789; married Susannah Mauve, born 1729; died 1762; and had, besides others, Anne Bolton, born May 2, 1752; died April 27, 1818; married Nathaniel Adams, of South Carolina.

II. Mary Bolton, married Hon. James Habersham.

Habrincham or Habergham (now Habershon and Habersham), of Habergham Eaves Burnley, Lancashire. From Whitaker's History of Nally, and from chart by Reginald Bolton, Esq., C. E., along with other charts looked over by the late Neyle Habersham, Esq., and kindly sent me by G. Noble Jones, Esq., his grand-son. Also a chart of the Haberjam family,

*Robert Bolton, born July 26, 1688; died June 25, 1742; buried in Philadelphia.

copied August, 1840, from the Register of Handsworth Church, which commences in the year 1558, and is of the family of Haberjam and Habershon, of Handsworth, Yorkshire, and shows them not only to be an ancient but very large family. The record goes down to Edmund Osborne Haberjam, who died in 1874, and back to Edward Haberjam, buried November 12, 1584; and it is very evident from these two charts, based upon records in England, that Habrincham, Habergham, Habershon, Haberjam, are but one variety of the name Habersham, and one versed in the change of names can easily see how Habersham could have developed from Habrincham, &c.; and Reginald Bolton, Esq., is of the same opinion, and believes the Habershams of Georgia descend from the family whose pedigree and that of Bolton, compiled by himself and sent to Wm. Neyle Habersham, Esq., is now given:

Peter de Habringham, Adam de Habringham, Geoffrey de Habringham, Mathew de Habringham, Adam de Habringham.

Henry held lands in Habringham, living 1310, the gift of Henry de Lacy, William Habringham.

Adam de Habringham, living in 1310, had John de Habringham, who witnessed a grant, July 3, 1342. He married Margery, living as his widow in 1358. His sons were: John de Habringham, died Habergham, in 1365, and Elias de Habringham, who was Chaplain of Burnley in 1369. Richard de Habringham, son of John de Habringham, living in 1403-4, married Cicely, and had John Habringham, who settled the Manor of Habringham on his wife (1469), Elizabeth, daughter of Godfrey Fielding. They had:

I. Hugh Habringham, married Margaret.
II. Robert Habringham.

Hugh and Margaret Habringham had:

1. William Habergham, living 1509-10 (name changes here).
2. Robert Habergham, probably ancestor of the Haberjams of Handsworth (see chart alluded to).
3. John Habergham.

William Habergham, married Jennet, daughter of Mr. Thomas Parker; she married, second, James Catterall; issue: A. Lawrence Habergham, married, first, Grace Townley, widow of Sir R. Heskett (only survived her marriage a month); he married, second, Margaret Townley (half-sister to Grace), widow of William Houghton, who was Dean to Henry VIII., 1516.

B. Edward of Handsworth (?)

a. Richard Habergham, son of Lawrence and Margaret Townley; buried February 24, 1590; married Margaret Hancock, who was buried December 15, 1604.

b. Alexander Habergham.

Richard Habergham and Margaret Hancock had:

1. Lawrence Habergham, born December 8, 1556; drowned March 26, 1615; married Anna, daughter of E. Hopwood, Esq.
2. Margaret Habergham, married Edward Gellibrand.
3. Elizabeth Habergham, married Mr. Burdet.
4. Anne Habergham, married Mr. Tomkins.

Lawrence and Anne Hopwood had John Habergham, who married, first, Anne Bancroft; buried 1677, and had:

I. Lawrence Habergham, born 1617.
II. Richard Habergham, died 1667; married Helen Hammerton.
III. John Habergham, married, about 1642, Elizabeth Clay, of Clayhouse, Halifax.
IV. Lawrence Habergham.
V. Jane Habergham, married John Halsted.
VI. Anne Habergham.
VII. Elizabeth Habergham.
VIII. Mathew Habergham.

And Isabel, Mary, Catharine and Jennet.

He married, second, Anne Pollard, and had:

I. Helen Habergham, married Edmund Townley.
II. Martha Habergham, married William Dubury.

John Habergham and Elizabeth Clay had:

1. John Habergham,* born 1650; alive 1725, but was not buried at Padigam or Burnley; married Fleetwood, daughter of Nicholas Townley, who died 1703, and was buried at Padigam. He dissipated his estate and died without issue. His brother, Clay Habergham, of Norland Park, Halifax, Yorks, probably born about 1660, married perhaps, 1685. His son, John Habergham, made ineffectual efforts to recover his uncle John's estate in 1759.

*The sisters were Mary, Elizabeth, Ann, Helen, Margaret and Priscilla Habersham.

And in this generation, James Habersham was born about 1690, at Beverley, Yorkshire, England, and married about 1710; and unquestionably was of the same line and family as this Manorial one of Habergham.

Richard Habergham and Anne Hopwood had also:

2. Mathew Habergham, born 1558; entered University College, Oxford, January 30, 1606, aged 18.
3. Richard Habergham.
4. Catharine Habergham, married Thomas Duckworth.
5. Margaret Habergham, married R. Halstead.
6. Mary Habergham, married Mr. Green.

The following is the direct line of Bolton, the whole having been published by Rev. Robert, Dr. H. Carrington and Reginald Bolton, Esq.

Robert Bolton, 1487, married Ann Rushton, and had William Bolton, of Little Boulton, 1550, and of Blackburn, 1523; died 1553. His son, Adam Bolton, 1539, had Richard Bolton, of Brookhouse and of Ramsgreave Lanes, 1537, had Adam Bolton, of Brookhouse, born 1547; died 1593; married Elizabeth, died 1600; had Gyles Bolton, of Brookhouse, in 1625; died 1642, and had John Bolton, born 1616, Parish Clerk of Blackburn; died 1688, and had John Bolton, Esq., of Wales, York, born at Brookhouse, Blackburn; baptized St. Mary's Church, March 6, 1658; died about 1693-4; married Ann, who died about 1694, and had Robert Bolton, Esq., born Wales, Yorkshire, July 26, 1688; emigrated 1718; buried at Philadelphia, Penn., June 25, 1742; married Ann, widow of Robert Clay, of Sheffield, Yorkshire, daughter of Winlock Curtis, Esq., of Kent County, Del., and had:

I. Robert Bolton, who went to Savannah, Ga., 1740; married, first, Susannah Mauve; second, widow of Stirk. Ancestor of branches of families of Adams, Habersham, Lewis, Newell, Stiles, Footman, King, Bulloch, &c.

II. Ann Bolton, married, first, Wood; second, John Mercer.

III. Mary Bolton, born April 5, 1724; married, December 26, 1740 (died January 4, 1763), Hon. James Habersham, Governor of Georgia, 1771; born Beverley, Yorkshire, 1715; went to Georgia, 1736; died

1775; son of James Habersham, of Beverley, Yorkshire, England.

According to Dugdale and Bolton, &c., the Boltons descend from the Saxon Kings, through the Earls of Mercia, were Lords of Bolton and prominent citizens and Governors of Blackburn School. In America, they were citizens of prominence and connected to many of the best people North and South, and were early settlers in Pennsylvania and Georgia; in the latter State eminent citizens, &c.

c KING

This ancient American family, of Yorkshire, England, was represented in America by John King, who at the age of sixteen left England, in 1645, and went to Connecticut. He died in 1703, aged 74. He married Miss Holton, and had the following children:

I. John King.
II. William King.
III. Thomas King.
IV. Samuel King.
V. Eleazer King.
VI. Sarah King.
VII. Joseph King.
VIII. Benjamin King.
IX. David King.
X. Thankful King.
XI. Jonathan King.

Thomas King had a son, Thomas King. Jonathan King, his brother, had the following children:

1. Jonathan King, born 1712.
2. Abagail King, born 1713.
3. Charles King, born 1716.
4. Mary King, born 1718.
5. Benia King, born 1721.
6. Seth King, born 1723.
7. Oliver King, born 1726.
8. Gideon King, born 1729.

Thomas King had:

1. Zebulon King, who had Alexander King, born 1749; died 1851.

2. Timothy King, born 1727; died 1812; married Miss Fitch, and had:
    1. George King, born 1745; died 1831.
    2. Timothy King, born 1755; died 1755.
    3. Reuben King, born 1758; died 1777.
    4. Sarah King, born 1760; married Bates.
    5. Timothy King, born 1763; died 1765.
    6. Roswell King, born 1765; died 1844.
    7. Mirriam King, born 1767; died 1816.
    8. Thomas King, born 1770.
    9. Nabby King, born 1773; married Hunt.
    10. Timothy King, born 1775; died 1800.
    11. Reuben King, born 1778; married Austin.

Alexander King, son of Zebulon, born 1749; died 1851, and had:

1. Theron King, born 1801; died 1821.
2. Benoni King, born 1799.
3. Celia King, born 1795.
4. Emma King, born 1793.
5. Roderic King, born 1790.
6. Harriet King, born 1788.
7. Leonard King, born 1786.
8. William King, born 1784.
9. Alexander King, born 1782.
10. Harry King, born 1795.

Oliver King had:

1. Francis King, born 1783.
2. Oliver King, born 1787.
3. Joel King, born 1789.

Seth King had the following children:

1. Oliver King, born 1748.
2. Rhoda King, born 1750.
3. Joel King, born 1752.
4. Seth King, born 1754.
5. Ruth King, born 1756.
6. Francis King, born 1759.
7. Russell King, born 1761.

George King had the following children:

1. George King, born 1777.
2. Trefenia King, born 1779.
3. Aurelia King, born 1781.
4. Harriet King.

5. Chesterfield King, born 1786.
6. Roswell King, born 1789.
7. William King, born 1792.
8. Charles King, born 1796.
9. Timothy King, born 1800.

Roswell King, son of Timothy King, came to Georgia at an early day (about 1788-9), and moved with a colony from the coast of Georgia to Cobb County, and there founded the town of Roswell, a most delightful summer resort and settled by a genial, cultivated set of people; the Kings, Dunwodys, Bullochs, Pratts, Smiths, Mintons, Rees and others. This town was a manufacturing centre and there were to be found the cotton mills established by Roswell King, who was also a land owner. His grand-sons were well known, and among his descendants were men who gallantly went into battle for the "Lost Cause," and there distinguished themselves. His children married into the Maxwells, Bayards, Hands, Gibbs, of North Carolina, Nephews, Pratts, McLeods; and his grandchildren among the Princes, Habershams and others.

Roswell King, married Catharine Barrington, of an old family, and had:

I. Rufus King, born 1793; died 1801.
II. Roswell King, born 1795; married Julia Maxwell.
III. Barrington King, born 1798; married Catharine Margaret Nephew.
IV. Catharine King, born 1799; died 1800.
V. Ralph King, born 1801; married Isabella Gibbs, of North Carolina, and second, Mildred, of Virginia.
VI. Thomas King, born 1803; married Bryde.
VII. William King, born 1804; married Elizabeth McLeod.
VIII. P. Butler King, born 1806.
IX. Eliza B. King, born 1808; married, first, Bayard Hand; second, Nicholas J. Bayard.
X. Catharine B. King, born 1810; married Rev. Nathaniel A. Pratt (see Pratt for issue).

Thomas King, brother of Roswell, had:

1. Harriet King, married.
2. George King.
3. Thomas King.

Reuben King, brother of Thomas King, had:

1. Amanda King, married Walker.

2. Elizabeth King, married Hopkins, and had:
   I. Abagail Hopkins.
   II. Octavius Hopkins.
   III. Helen K. Hopkins.
   IV. Albert H. Hopkins.
   V. Reuben K. Hopkins.

Amanda King and Mr. Walker had:
   I. Charles Walker.
   II. Reuben Walker, married Quarterman.
   III. James Walker, married Bealer.
   IV. Isabel Walker.
   V. Joseph Walker, married Fairies.

Roderic King had:
1. Harriet King, born 1814.
2. Henry M. King, born 1816.
3. Edward King, born 1818.
4. Harriet E. King, born 1820.
5. John N. King, born 1822.
6. Emily P. King, born 1824.
7. Elizabeth King, born 1827.
8. Sarah King, born 1833.

Alexander King had:
1. Caroline King, born 1809.
2. Susan King, born 1812.
3. Abagail King, born 1814.
4. Edwin King, born 1816.
5. Alexander King, born 1818.
6. Clarissa King, born 1820.
7. Sarah King, born 1822.
8. Harriet King, born 1824.
9. Theodore King, born 1827.

George King had:
1. Frederick King, born 1803.
2. George King, born 1808.
3. Elizabeth King, born 1811.
4. Henry King, born 1806.
5. Catharine King, born 1814.

Chesterfield King had:
1. William King.
2. Helen King.

Roswell King had:
1. Trefenia King.

2. William King.

William King had:

1. Augusta King.
2. Florence King.
3. William King.
4. George King.
5. Robert King.
6. Dwight King.

Roswell King married *Miss Julia Maxwell (son of Roswell King and Catharine Barrington), and had the following children:

1. Mary E. King, born 1827; died 1871; married Dr. Welles.
2. James Audley Maxwell King, born 1820; married Kate Lewis, daughter of R. Adams Lewis and Catharine Cook.
3. George Frederick King, born 1831.
4. William H. King, born 1833; died 1865.
5. James Edward King, born 1835; died 1835.
6. Roswell King, born 1836; married Ashmead.
7. John C. King, born 1840; died 1840.
8. Isabella C. King, born 1842; married M. F. Tunno.
9. J. Clarence King, born 1844; married Miss Anderson, grand-daughter of Bayard and Eliza B. Hand.
10. Bayard H. King, born 1846.
11. John B. King, born 1848; married Mary Battey, daughter of the celebrated Dr. Battey, of Rome, Ga.

Barrington King, of Roswell and Barrington Hall, Georgia, and Catharine Margaret Nephew (son of Roswell King and Catharine Barrington), had the following children:*

1. Charles Barrington King, born 1823; married Anna W. Habersham.
2. William Nephew King, born 1825; married, first, Virginia Way, of Liberty County; second, Fanny De Camp.
3. James R. King, born 1827; married, first, Fanny Prince, daughter of U. S. Senator Oliver Prince; second, Isabel (Meta) Lewis, daughter R. Adams Lewis and Catharine Cook.
4. Thomas Edward King, Captain C. S. A., born 1829; married Marie Clemons.

*Three died in childhood: Nephew, Susan and Mary King.

5. Barrington S. King, born 1833; married Bessie McLeod.
6. Ralph King, born 1835; married Florence Stillwell, of New York.
7. Evelyn King, born 1837; married Rev. W. E. Baker, of Liberty County, Ga.
8. Joseph H. King, born 1839; married Ellen P. Stubbs.
9. Clifford A. King (Captain), born 1843; married Mary Eliza *Hardee, and had:

NOTE.—Mary Eliza Hardee was the daughter of Noble Andrew Hardee, attorney at law, an opulent merchant of Savannah, Ga., whose brother was Lieut. Gen. W. J. Hardee, C. S. A., formerly commandant at West Point. Noble A. Hardee married Margaret Lewis, daughter of John Lewis, Esq., and Ann Susan Adams. He was son of John Hardee, of Rural Felicity, and Sarah Ellis, both of Camden County, Ga., son of John Hardee, near Owen's Ferry, Camden County, Ga., and Caroline T. Aldrich, of Barnwell County, S. C.; son of Noble Worthington Hardee, near New Bern, N. C., and Mary Emily Parker, near James River, Va.; son of Anthony Hardee and Evelyn Dulverton, Devonshire, England.

1. Clifford A. King, married.
2. John H. King.
3. William H. King.
4. Barrington King.
5. Charles N. King.
6. Marie Hardee King.
7. Noble Hardee King.

NOTE.—This branch of the King family through Gignilliat is related to the Heywards and others, and through the Le Serruriers to the Le Nobles, de St. Juliens, Mazycks, Taylors, Marions, De Veauxs, DuBoses, McDuffies, Ravenels, Chastaigners, Izards, &c. See No. 4, Transactions of Huguenot Society, Rev. Robert Wilson.

Absalom Gignilliat married Mary De Ville, of Vevay, Switzerland, and had Jean Francis de Gignilliat, who received a grant of 3,000 acres, being among the first of the Huguenot settlers. He married Susanne Le Serrurier, daughter of Jacques Le Serrurier and Elizabeth Leger, son of Jacques Le Serrurier and Marie Le Compte.

Ralph King and Isabella Gibbs, son of Roswell King, had:

1. George Gibbs King, born 1829; died 1853.
2. Florida King, born 1839; married Whistler.

Thomas King, son of Roswell King, had:

1. Francis King, born 1838.
2. Thomas King, born 1841.

William King and Elizabeth McLeod, son of Roswell King, had:

1. McLeod King, born 1828; married Julia Kay or Cay, of Liberty County, Ga.
2. *William King, M. D., born 1830; married Elizabeth Clayton, of Augusta, Ga.
3. Frank King, born 1833; married Miss Morrell, of Savannah, Ga.
4. Anna King, born 1835; married William Norwood, of North Carolina.
5. Mary King, born 1837; married Bowman.
6. Roswell King, born 1840; married Clayton.
7. Elizabeth King, born 1843; married Rev. Wharey, of Virginia.
8. Barrington King, born 1847; died without issue.

Eliza B. King, daughter of Roswell King, married, first, Bayard Hand, and had:

I. Eliza Catharine Hand, born 1826; married Dr. Quintard, Bishop of Tennessee.
II. Bayard Hand, born 1830.
III. Julia J. or E. Hand, born 1832; married Dr. Anderson, of Maryland.

Eliza B. King, married, second, *Nicholas J. Bayard, and had:

I. Nicholas Bayard, married Battey.
II. Anna or Olivia Livingston Bayard, married J. A. Atwood, of Darien, Ga.

Henry M. King, son of Roderic King, had:

1. Charles H. King, born 1848.
2. George Edwin King, born 1850.

John N. King, son of Roderic King, had:

*Dr. William King and Elizabeth Clayton had:
1. Wm. C. King.
2. Mrs. Wm. M. Howard.
3. Mrs. H. W. Grady.
H. W. Grady and Miss King had:
I. H. W. Grady, Jr., married.
II. Gussie Grady, married Eugene R. Black.

*Dr. Bayard was one of the incorporators of the Georgia Medical Society, founded in 1804.

NOTE.—Nicholas Bayard married, first, Sarah, daughter of Noble Glen, and had:
I. John Bayard.
II. Florida Bayard, married John S. Seay, and had:
I. Laura Seay, married Watson.
II. Florida Seay.
III. Seay.

*Son of John Glen and Sarah, daughter of N. W. Jones.

1. Isaac W. King, born 1849.

Edwin King, son of Alexander King, had:

1. Lucy King, born 1827.
2. Sarah King, born 1833.

Alexander King had:

1. George King.
2. Onnan King.
3. Henry King.

Frederick King, son of George King, had:

1. Elizabeth King, born 1830.
2. George King, born 1835.
3. Francis King, born 1838.

Henry King had:

1. Frederick King, born 1843.
2. George King, born 1845.
3. Margaret King, born 1846.
4. Thomas King, born 1848.
5. Kate King, born 1851.

James Audley Maxwell King (son of Roswell King and Julia Maxwell, of the ancient and eminent family of Maxwell, of Liberty County, Ga.), married Kate Lewis, daughter of R. Adams Lewis, son of John Lewis and Ann Susan Adams, daughter of Nathaniel Adams and Anne Bolton, and had:

1. Katharine M. King.
2. Julia R. King.
3. Robert Lewis King.
4. Audley Maxwell King.

Roswell King, son of Roswell and Julia Maxwell, married Ashmead, and had:

1. Frederick W. King, born 1861; married De Le Gal or Delegal, of the ancient family of the name.
2. Charlton H. King.
3. William C. King.
4. Georgia R. King, married Bruice.
5. Roswell King, married Toler.
6. Bayard King.

Isabella C. King, daughter of Roswell King and Julia Maxwell, married M. F. Tunno, of an old Carolina family, related to the ancient family of Fuller, of South Carolina, and had:

I. Robert G. Tunno.
II. Julia R. Tunno.
III. William H. Tunno.

IV. Champneys Tunno.
V. Matthews H. Tunno.
VI. Elizabeth M. Tunno.

J. Clarence King, son of Roswell and Julia Maxwell King, married Miss Anderson, his cousin, and had:

1. Daisy A. King, born 1882.
2. Isabel M. King, born 1884.

John B. King, son of Roswell King and Julia Maxwell, married Miss Battey, daughter of the celebrated Dr. Battey, of Rome, Ga., and had:

1. Mary B. King, born 1877; married Hendry, and had Bard L. Hendry.
2. Robert R. King, born 1878.
3. John C. King, born 1880; died 1881.
4. Carrie W. King, born 1884.
5. Battey King, born 1886.
6. Martha M. King, born 1891.

Right Rev. Bishop Quintard, of Tennessee, married Eliza Catharine Hand, daughter of Bayard Hand and Eliza B. King, daughter of Roswell King and Catharine Barrington, and had:

I. Clara Quintard, married Wiggins.
II. George Quintard.
III. Edward Quintard, married Shepard.

Julia J. Hand, sister of above, married Dr. Anderson, of Maryland, and had:

I. Georgia B. Anderson, married J. Clarence King, her cousin, and son of Roswell King and Julia Maxwell (see J. Clarence King).
II. Julia Anderson, married McRae.
III. Rose Anderson, married DuBose.

Nicholas B. Bayard (son of Nicholas J. Bayard and Eliza B. King, her second marriage, daughter of Roswell King and Catharine Barrington,) married Miss Battey, and had:

I. Emma H. Bayard, born 1871; died 1881.
II. Julia B. Bayard, born 1874; married Holland.
III. Robert B. Bayard, born 1876; died 1878.
IV. Nicholas R. Bayard, born 1884.

Anna Livingston Bayard, daughter of Nicholas J. Bayard and Eliza B. King, married J. A. Atwood, of Darien, Ga., and had:

I. Eliza B. Atwood.
II. Alfred L. Atwood.

III. John B. McIntosh Atwood.
IV. Isabell Q. Atwood.
V. Ruth Atwood.
VI. Rosalie Atwood.
VII. Alice Atwood.

McLeod King had:

1. Lila King, married Root.
2. Julia King, married Winn.

BARRINGTON

Josiah Barrington held a Colonial office in America, and died during or before the Revolutionary War. He married Miss Williams, whose brothers were: Rev. Thomas Williams, Richard and Stephen Williams, planters, who all lived in Savannah from the earliest times, well known people, respected by all and gentlemen of the "Old School." Josiah (?) Barrington and Miss Williams had two daughters:

I. Eliza Barrington, married Wm. Cook, an elegant, accomplished English barrister, who had gone to Savannah, Ga., on important business, a great traveler and entertaining gentleman. His relatives in England had expected him to marry there, but the beauty of Miss Barrington captivated him. He had many papers, government grants, &c.

II. Katharine Barrington, married Roswell King, of Sharon, Connecticut, a man of sterling integrity and vigorous mind.

NOTE.—William Cook, Esq., and Eliza Barrington had Catharine Anna Barrington Cook, who married R. Adams Lewis, son of John Lewis and Susan Ann Adams, and had:

I. Eliza Catharine Lewis, married James Audley Maxwell King, and had:
   I. Kate Maxwell King.
   II. Julia Rebecca King.
   III. Robert Lewis King.
   IV. Audley Maxwell King, Jr.
II. Robert Lewis, Jr., married and had issue.
III. Isabella Margaret (Meta) Lewis, married James Roswell King, his second wife; he married, first, Frances Prince.
IV. Anna Barrington Lewis.
V. William Clarence Lewis, married Augusta E. Pawling, and had:
   1. Sophie Lewis.
   2. Alice Catharine Lewis.
   3. Clarence Lewis.
   4. Walter Lewis.
VI. Francis Lewis, married Tuesday, October 9, 1884, Ardena Whitsitt, of Kansas, Mo.

Rev. Charles Barrington King, graduate of Princeton, and in charge of churches in Columbus, Ga., and near Savannah, Ga., was the eldest son of Barrington King, cotton manufacturer and planter, and his wife, Catharine Nephew, of Roswell, Cobb Co., Ga.; son of Roswell King and Catharine Barrington. Rev. Charles B. King was married in Savannah, Ga., on Thursdan, 25th May, 1848, by Rev. W. W. Preston, D. D., to Anna Wylly, third daughter of Dr. Joseph Clay Habersham and Anna Wylly Adams, of Savannah, Ga., and had the following children:

1. Charles Barrington King, born March 1, 1849.
2. Catherine Anna King, born October 16, 1850.
3. Habersham King, born January 14, 1852.
4. Charles William King, born August 4, 1853.
5. Mary Josephine King, born March 2, 1857.
6. James Nephew King, born June 20, 1859.
7. Joseph Clay Habersham King, born April 25, 1861.
8. Clifford Barrington King, born October 27, 1862.
9. Edith Barrington King, born May 25, 1865.
10. Walter Roswell King, born March 1, 1868.

Rev. Charles Barrington King was born July 4th, 1824, and died in Savannah, Ga., November 24th, 1880, aged 57 years, 4 months, 20 days.

1. Charles Barrington, Jr., died May 5, 1850, aged 14 months.
2. Catherine Anna King, married in Savannah, Ga., July 8, 1875, by her father, Rev. Charles Barrington King, to Hugh Caperton, Esq., of Union, Monroe Co., West Virginia, and had issue:

I. Hugh Caperton, born April 24, 1876.
II. Charles Barrington Caperton, born September 20, 1877.
III. Anna Habersham Caperton, born November 11, 1879.
IV. Edwin Caperton, born December 6, 1882.
V. Henry Caperton, born December 27, 1884; died aged 3 1-2 months.
VI. Thomas Bowyer Caperton, born July 29, 1886.
VII. Carthrae Alexander Caperton, born May 27, 1888.
VIII. James Nephew Caperton, born March 1, 1891.

IX. Katharine King Caperton, born September 19, 1893.

3. Habersham King, married November 17, 1878, in Brevard Co., Florida, Ann Rebecca, third daughter of Capt. Henry J. and Henrietta E. Strobhar, of Effingham Co., Georgia, and had issue:
   1. Belle Vernon King, born January 5, 1881.
   2. Francis Barrington King, born June 24, 1883.
   3. Habersham King, Jr., born November 16, 1886.
   4. Rhea King, born December 18, 1892.

4. Charles William King, married, first, in Savannah, Ga., at the family residence of the Kollocks, on June 24th, 1880, by Rev. Charles Barrington King and Rev. Thomas Boone, Sarah Campbell, daughter of Dr. P. M. and Sarah Hull Campbell Kollock, of Savannah, Ga., she died on June 12, 1886, leaving Sarah Hull, born May 30th, 1881. Charles William, married, second, in Rome, Ga., at residence of Alexander family, June 14, 1894, by Rev. George T. Goetchius, *Sarah Joyce, third daughter of Col. Thomas M. and Sarah Joyce Hooper Alexander, of Rome, Ga., and had issue:
   1. Sarah Joyce King, born October 13, 1895.
   2. Barrington King, born January 22, 1898.

5. Mary Josephine King, married in Rome, Ga., in Presbyterian Church, by Rev. George T. Goetchius, January 9th, 1894, Capt. Reuben Grove Clark, of Rome, Ga. (who died March 28th, 1900), and had issue:
   I. Josephine Habersham Clark, born April 18, 1895.
   II. Reuben Grove Clark, born June 10, 1896.
   III. Nephew King Clark, born January 15, 1898.

6. James Nephew King, unmarried.

7. Joseph Clay Habersham King, married in Jacksonville, Ala., July 2, 1890, Ida, third daughter of Ben-

*NOTE.—Sarah Joyce Alexander, wife of Charles William King, is the daughter of Col. Thomas Williamson Alexander and his wife, Sarah Joyce Hooper. Through her father's family, Mrs. Sarah Joyce King is descended from the Alexanders, Pedens, Williamsons and Walkers, of Scotland, Ireland, England, Pennsylvania, North and South Carolina. Through her mother's family, she is descended from the Hoopers, Words, Adams, and Allens, of England, Wales, New England, Virginia, North and South Carolina.

jamin Cleveland and Elsie (Snow) Wyly,* and had issue:

1. William Murray Davidson King, born August 1, 1891.
2. Wyly Barrington King, born June 1, 1898.
3. Lavinia King, born December 1, 1900.

8. Clifford Barrington King, married in Athens, Ga., on November 3, 1892, Nannie Lancaster, fourth daughter of Rev. Luther Rice and Sophia Bonham Lipscomb Gwaltney, of Edgefield, S. C., and had issue:

1. Clifford Barrington King, Jr., born September 21, 1893.

9. Edith Barrington King, married in Savannah, Ga., by Rev. Dr. Deems, of New York City, and the pastor, Rev. Dr. I. S. K. Axson, at the Independent Presbyterian Church, on March 19th, 1889, James Urquhart Jackson, Esq., of Augusta, Ga., and had:

1. Daisy King Jackson, born June 18, 1890.
2. Edith Barrington Jackson, born May 17, 1893.
3. James Urquhart Jackson, Jr., born July 23, 1895.
4. John Williams Jackson, born May 9, 1900.

10. Walter Roswell King, died June 29, 1868, aged four months.

Dr. Wm. Nephew King, a well known physician of Roswell, Ga., and Savannah, second son of Barrington King and Catharine M. Nephew, married, first, Virginia Way, daughter of Wm. I. Way, of an old Liberty County, Ga., family, and had:

A. Mary Harford King, married Lieut. Drake, U. S. N.
B. Wm. Nephew King, of Navy.

Dr. Wm. N. King, married, second, Fanny DeCamp, of New York, and had two children.

James Roswell King, manufacturer, &c., married, first, Frances Prince, daughter of Oliver Prince,* U. S. Senator (he married, second, Meta, daughter of R. Adams Lewis, and Kate Cook), and had:

A. Hattie King.
B. Barrington James King, married Ada Prather.

*No relation; our family writes the name Wylly—two l's.

*Oliver Prince had Oliver, married Miss Jackson; and a daughter, married Dr. Green, of Macon, Ga.

C. Oliver Prince King, married Fanny, daughter of Rev. Henry Rees and Miss Bartow, sister of Gen. Francis Bartow, son of Judge Rees.
D. Charles King.
E. Frances Prince King, married Henry Jemison Pratt, her cousin.
F. Estelle King, married Harris Simpson, of Rome, Ga., and had Estelle Simpson.
G. Marion King.

Barrington J. King and Ada Prather, daughter of Col. Prather, of Roswell, Ga., had:
a. Prather King.
b. Hattie King, married.
c. James Barrington King.
d. Janie Bizzell King.
e. Mamie King, died infancy.
f. Norman Prince King.
g. Walter Blake King.

Evelyn King, daughter of Barrington King and Catharine M. Nephew, married Rev. W. E. Baker, of an old family in Liberty Co., Ga, and had:
I. Kate Baker, married Dr. C. A. Simpson.
II. Eva Baker, married W. H. Irvine.
III. Elliott Baker, married.
IV. Thomas Baker, married, first, Annie Nelson; second, Willie Pastlewaite.
V. Frances Baker, married N. P. Pratt, her cousin.
VI. Clifford Baker, married Rev. Ralph E. Lawson.
VII. Roswell Baker, married Roberta Bates, and had:
1. Roswell Baker, Jr.
2. Robert Baker.

Kate Baker, married Dr. C. D. Simpson, and had:
I. Carolus Simpson.
II. Elliott Simpson.
III. Evelyn Simpson.
IV. Janie Simpson.
V. Katharine Simpson.
VI. Frances Simpson.

Eva Baker, married W. H. Irvine, and had:
I. Harris Irvine.
II. Clifford Irvine.
III. Dickson Irvine.

Thomas Baker and Annie Nelson had Catharine Baker.

Thomas and Willie Pastlethwaite had:

1. Thomas Baker, Jr.
2. Albert Baker.
3. Edward Baker.

Frances Baker and N. P. Pratt had:

I. Palmer Pratt.
II. Evelyn Pratt.
III. Julia Pratt.
IV. Nathaniel Pratt.

Thomas King, a gallant Confederate Captain, killed in battle fighting for the "Lost Cause," was son of Barrington King and Catharine M. Nephew, and married Maria Clemens, and had:

A. John R. King.
B. Thomas E. King.
C. Evelyn King.

Barrington King, son of Barrington King and Catharine M. Nephew, married Bessie McLeod, and had:

A. Harris King, married Miss Baker, of Marietta, Ga.
B. Barrington King, died.
C. Margaret King, died in childhood.

Joseph Henry King, son of Barrington and Catharine M. Nephew King, married Ellen Palmer Stubbs, and had:

1. Joseph King, died in childhood.
2. Edwin Thomas King, married Clifford.
3. Ralph King, married Puckett.
4. Graham, married King.
5. Richard Nicholas King.
6. Margaret Esther King, married Bedar.
7. Theodore Dwight King.

Edwin Thomas King married Clifford Fox, of Fort Lauderdale, and had:

1. Bird King.
2. Louise King.
3. Wallace King.
4. A daughter.

Ralph King and Miss Puckett had two sons.

Margaret E. King, married William Bedar, and had one child.

"Alexander-Peden-Williamson-Walker Ancestry."

August 15th, 1899, "at 'Old Fairview' Church, in Greenville Co., S. C., more than one thousand descendants of John Peden and his wife, Margaret McDill, gathered to unveil a monument in memory of these venerated ancestors, who, with their children and grand-children, had founded this church more than a century before. Prior to 1750, John and Margaret Peden resided in North Ireland, near Carrickfergus, being honored members of the Scotch Presbyterian Church there located, of which John Peden was Ruling Elder. They had seven sons and three daughters. The eldest daughter married James Alexander, a scion of the noble Scotch family of that name.

In search of greater civil and religious liberty than his church or people could claim under the dominant Church of England Party, James Alexander determined to remove to America, and was accompanied, on his departure, by several kinsmen of his name, by almost the entire Peden family, and by numerous friends, notable among these being the Caldwell family, from whom was descended John Caldwell Calhoun. Landing first in Pennsylvania, this company of relatives and friends remained there for some time, then removed to the Carolinas. Several of James Alexander's kinsmen settled in Mecklenburg Co., N. C., where they later signed and assisted in promulgating the Mecklenburg Declaration of Independence. But James cast in his lot with his wife's family, and located in Spartanburg District, S. C., where they secured large tracts of land by grant from George II., the old titles bearing date of 1768. Here they assisted in building and establishing Nazareth and Fairview Presbyterian Churches. Through their superior education and intelligence they soon became prominent, not only in church but civil and military affairs.

John Alexander, the oldest son of James and Mary Peden Alexander, was early inured to danger by the frequent Indian raids, which he assisted in repulsing. During the Revolutionary War he served successively as Lieutenant, Captain and Major; first under Sumter and Marion; later with the gallant Col. Williams at King's Mountain. By his side fought his father-in-law, the patriotic Chaplain of his troops, Rev. Thomas Williamson, the father also of Rev. William Williamson, destined to play so important a part in the history of the Presbyterian Church in South Carolina and Ohio.

The eldest son of Maj. John Alexander and his wife, *nee* Williamson, named, in honor of his maternal grand-father, Thomas Williamson Alexander, received a liberal education, qualifying him for the practice of medicine, married Miss Martha Walker, daughter of William Walker, of Pendleton, and removed to the newly opened county of Gwinnett, in Georgia, where he soon became prominent as a physician and citizen. Here he reared a family which has furnished members of distinction to the legal and medical professions of the State. Judge Ramsey Alexander, of Thomasville, and Dr. James Alexander, of Atlanta, both recently deceased, were examples, as is their only surviving brother, Col. Thomas Williamson Alexander, of Rome, an honored Confederate veteran, widely known and appreciated for his legal knowledge, ability and probity. Col. Alexander was married in 1857 to Miss Sarah Joyce Hooper, daughter of Judge John Word Hooper, a distinguished member of the Georgia Judiciary, who decided many complicated legal questions arising between the representatives of the Federal Government and the State, while the Indians still held their lands in the Cherokee section of North Georgia, over which Judge Hooper was first to hold jurisdiction. To Col. Thomas Williamson Alexander and his wife, Sarah Joyce Hooper, were born five children, four of whom still live. The only son, Hooper Alexander, is a lawyer of note and influence in Atlanta, Ga. The oldest daughter, Martha Lamar Alexander, married Samuel F. Pegues, a representative of an old Huguenot family of Alabama, and now resides in Chicago. Hallie Miller Alexander, the second daughter, also married a representative of an old Huguenot family, James A. Rounsaville, and resides in Rome. Here, also, resides the youngest daughter, Sarah Joyce Alexander, wife of Charles William King, of the honored Savannah family, whose record is found elsewhere in this volume. Two children have blessed this union—the eldest, a daughter, Sarah Joyce, bears the name of her mother, grand-mother and two great-grand-mothers, in direct line—a name loved and honored by five generations of the Hooper-Word families. The second child, a son, Barrington, bears a name equally honored by several generations of the King family.

"Hooper-Word-Adams-Allen Ancestry."

Early in the 18th century Charles Word I., the progenitor of an extensive family, came from Llandaff, Glamorganshire, Wales, and settled in Virginia. He is recorded as "a recognized patriot." His five sons, Charles II., Thomas, John, Peter and Cuthbert, were all soldiers in the Revolutionary War, noted among their comrades for bravery. (Mrs. King is descended from both Charles and Thomas, through intermarriage of their families.)

Charles Word II. was born 1738 in Virginia. While a mere youth of seventeen he volunteered, and went out with the "Virginia Blues," under command of George Washington (then a Colonel), to guard the frontier against the French. Taking part soon after in the battle near Fort Duquesue, where Gen. Braddock was defeated, he was one of that gallant band of Colonials who, under Washington, covered the retreat of Braddock and his Regulars, thus saving them from complete destruction. Of the "Virginia Blues" only thirty escaped alive. Later Charles Word II. married Elizabeth Adams, a relative of John and Samuel Adams, and about the time the Revolutionary War began, moved to North Carolina. When his youngest child, Elizabeth Adams Word, was one year old, he was killed in the battle of King's Mountain, October, 1780. This daughter married Matthew Brooks Hooper, a young kinsman of William Hooper, Representative of North Carolina in the Colonial Congress and signer of the Declaration of Independence. Both came from the New England Hoopers and by family tradition were descendants of Bishop John Hooper, of England—who, rather than recant, was burned at the stake, in 1555, by Queen Mary. John Word Hooper, the second son of Matthew Brooks Hooper and his wife, Elizabeth Adams Word, enjoyed exceptional educational advantages, and grew up to a manhood of usefulness and honor in his adopted State, Georgia. While still quite young, he became noted as a lawyer, and was made a member of the State Judiciary, serving as the first Judge of Cherokee County, which then included nearly the whole of Northwest Georgia, probably the largest Judicial Circuit in the State (see Alexander record for further information). The wife of Judge Hooper was his second cousin, Sarah Allen Word, the grand-daughter of Thomas Word, of the Revolutionary Army. Her mother, Sarah Allen, was a relative of Ethan Allen, and also of President Madison's wife, by whom she was much beloved. The youngest daughter of Judge Hooper and his wife, Sarah Allen Word, was Sarah Joyce Hooper, later the wife of Col. Thomas Williamson Alexander (see Alexander record) and mother of Mrs. Sarah Joyce King. Educated, intelligent and accustomed from childhood to contact with the brighest minds, Mrs. Alexander was a potent factor for good in her community and entire section, honored and loved by high and low. During the war between the States she gave time, substance and tender care to the sick and suffering. Soon after the war she was made President of the Ladies' Memorial Association of Rome, serving in this position until her death, a quarter of a century later, during which time she was chiefly instrumental in erecting the Confederate monument and marble headstones above the several hundred Confederate dead there buried. Of her four living children (see Alexander record), the youngest, Sarah Joyce Alexander, like to her mother in mind and heart, as well as name, is the wife of Charles William King (see King record) and the mother of two children, Sarah Joyce and Barrington King (see Alexander record).

The eldest daughter of Col. Thomas Williamson Alexander and Sarah Joyce Hooper, Hallie Miller, who married James A. Rounsaville, has been recently honored by being elected President of the United Daughters of the Confederacy, thus adding to the lustre of all these old families.

NOTE.—Authority for above records is found in family Bibles, manuscripts, tombstones, and in various histories—Ramsey's "South Carolina," Howe's "Presbyterian Church in South Carolina," Saye's "MS. Records," Massachusetts, Virginia, Carolina and Georgia State Records, and Historical Society Records, White's "Statistics of Georgia," Foote's "Sketches," and various other volumes.

McLEOD

The McLeods, who went to Georgia, had a farm in Scotland called Flashadder in 1738, which was occupied by Alexander McLeod, son of Norman McLeod, whom he succeeded as "tacksman" tenant of that place. They were a branch of the Dunvegan family of McLeod, of McLeod. Four nephews of Alexander McLeod went to East Indies and two to North America. The wife of Norman McLeod and mother of John and Alexander McLeod, was named Nicolson.

Kate Pratt and Jno. N. Webb had:

I. Kate Webb.
II. Henry Webb.
III. Katharine Webb.
IV. Margaret Webb.

NEPHEW

The Nephew family is an old one in Georgia, and by some is said to be of Huguenot origin and called Nevie—indeed, we find a Nevie one of the early land grantees of Colonial Georgia; but Peter Nephew, the first of the name, arrived in St. John's Parish with one servant in 1754, and later received a grant of land of 100 acres in Little Ogeechee. We find, also, that he became one of the officers of the Crown, and with J. Barrington was one of the Commissioners of Roads in the Colony and tax assessors. He married Mrs. John Cooper, widow of Col. John Cooper, of Revolutionary stock, and her name was Merriam,* probably daughter of John Merriam, who went to Georgia with Whitfield in 1739. The issue was James Nephew, Esq., a rice planter, who married, first, Mary M. Gignilliat; second, Mrs. James Gignilliat, born Pelot. By the Gignilliat marriage this family and their descendants become related to the Heywards, LeSerruriers, LeNobles, de St. Juliens, Ravenels, Chastaigners, Mazycks, Taylors, Marions, Izards, DeVeauxs and many others of South Carolina, and they also descend from the Peppers and Sir John Evelyn, and like a great many of our families are connected to a large proportion of all the best people of South Carolina and Georgia, and to the McIntoshes, Wests, Kings, Stiles, Bartows and others.

Peter Nephew and Mrs. Cooper had one son, James Nephew,

*David Anderson, a nephew of Capt. Joseph Jones, married Hannah, a grand-daughter of James Nephew; she died 1837.

NOTE.—The Journal of Georgia Plantations at the Capitol, Atlanta, Ga., has registered a grant of 100 acres to Peter Nephew on Little Ogeechee.

*By Col. John Cooper she had:

I. Mary Cooper, married Capt. Joseph Jones.
II. John Cooper, married Elizabeth Gignilliat.

Mrs. Cooper was grand-mother of Sarah Anderson, who married, as his second wife, Capt. Joseph Jones, and mother of Rev. John Jones and Mary Jones, who married her cousin, Rev. C. C. Jones. David Anderson, a nephew of Capt. Joseph Jones, married Hannah, a grand-daughter of James Nephew, and he died 1839.

Esq., a cotton planter and owner of two plantations, Manchester and Ceylon. He married Mary M. Gignilliat, sister of Elizabeth Gignilliat, who married John Cooper, Jr., daughter of James Gignilliat and Caroline Pepper, daughter of an Englishman, Dr. Pepper, who married Sarah Evelyn, daughter of Sir John Evelyn.

James Nephew and Mary M. Gignilliat had the following children:

I. *Sarah Evelyn Nephew, married †Dr. Charles West, died 1835.

II. *Charlotte Nephew, married Hampden McIntosh.

III. Susan Nephew, married Wm. Dunham.

IV. James Nephew, died without issue.

V. Eliza Nephew, married Leonard Bartow, brother of Gen. Bartow, and of Wilhelmina Bartow, who married Rev. H. K. Rees.

VI. Catharine M. Nephew, married Barrington King (see King).

James Nephew married, second, Mrs. Gignilliat, born Pelot, and had:

I. Caroline Clifford Nephew, married Rev. Joseph Clay Stiles, D. D. (see Stiles).

NOTE.—James Nephew began life with very small means, but his honesty and energy commended him to an Englishman by the name of Leavette, one of the first planters of sea island cotton in America. He settled a place which to this day is known as Julianton plantation, on Harris' Neck, McIntosh County, Ga., and got James Nephew to manage it for him and to attend to his business, at the same time allowing Mr. Nephew to plant for himself a small crop, and with his cotton crop ship the products of each to England. After this James Nephew settled his own plantation, called Manchester, in same county, near Baisden's Bluff; and later on another fine plantation on which he raised rice, near Darien, Ga., on Cat Head Creek, which he called Ceylon, afterward owned by Dr. Charles West. He died in 1827, and left by will $2,000 to the Darien Presbyterian Church and endowed a scholarship in the Columbia, S. C., Presbyterian Seminary.

Samuel West, an Englishman, went to South Carolina in 1669, in the ship Carolina, one of a fleet of three vessels sent out by the King and commanded by Joseph West, afterward Governor of the Colony. They landed at Port Royal, and held the first election on Carolina soil. Samuel West was chosen one of a council of five and afterward member of first Parliament under Locke's Constitution, and a member from the

†Both buried at Rose Hill Cemetery, Macon, Ga.
*Called Catharine Clifford Nephew by the Winstons.

Commons of the Grand Council, and one of the few who had a grant of land in New Town, Charlestown.

On the Register of old St. Philips is the following: "To Samuel West and Sarah his wife, a son, Charles West, May, 1720."

This Charles West and Esther, his wife, emigrated to St. John's Parish (afterward a part of Liberty Co., Ga.), in 1748. He became an officer in the Colonial Army, and died in 1762. His will on record in Atlanta (Capitol) shows him to have been a man of considerable property. He left four children:

I. Elizabeth West,* married Simon Munro, born 1774, in Inverness, Scotland, and had, among others:

1. Annie Munro, who married Dr. Charles Rogers, of Bryan Co., Ga., whose eldest son, Rev. Charles Rogers, married Caroline Woodford, of Hartford, Conn., and had:

I. Anna Munro Rogers, married Dr. Joseph Jones West.

II. Caroline Rogers, married Samuel V. Stiles.

III. Georgia Rogers, married, first, Peyton Wade; second, H. Fraser Grant.

IV. Charles West Rogers, died without issue.

II. Samuel West, Major in Revolutionary War, died without issue.

III. Charles West, Ensign in Army, died.

IV. William West, married Hannah Sharp, daughter of James Sharp and Mary Newton, and had:

I. Mary Sharp West, married John Stewart, and moved to Alabama.

II. Hannah West, married James Robarts, and died without issue.

III. Charles West, married Sarah Evelyn Nephew, and lived and practiced medicine in Darien; removed later to Houstoun County, where he died. Their issue were ten children.

*Note.—By reference to Dunwody family it will be seen that Simon Munro had also Sevmour Munro, who married James Smith, of Darien, Ga., and had Elizabeth West Smith, who married Col. James Dunwody, and had, among others, Jane Adelaide Dunwody, who married Rev. John Jones. William West, a brother of Charles West, married Hannah Sharpe, a sister of Mary Sharpe, who married Major John Jones, both daughters of James Sharpe and Mary Newton, of Charleston, S. C.; and thus is seen the connection between the Wests, Munros, Dunwodys, Andersons, Nephews and many others.

1. Charles Wm. West, M. D., married (see Berrien) Eliza Whitehead; practiced in Savannah, Ga.; had issue:
   A. Evelyn Nephew West, died without issue.
   B. Wm. Whitehead West, married Sarah Byrd Shippen, of Philadelphia, Penn., and had seven children.
   C. May West, died without issue.
   D. Charles Nephew West, married Mary, granddaughter of Hon. Langdon Cheves, and had four children.
   E. Clifford Catharine West, married Col. Clifford Anderson, and had Clifford Anderson (see Anderson).
   F. John Randolph West, married Lillie Soullard, and had four children.
   G. James Gignilliat West, married Belle Davant.
   H. Laura Maxwell West, unmarried.
   I. Thomas Berrien West, married Ellen Walker (four children).
   J. Henry Cumming West, married Sarah Whitehead.

Charles West and Sarah Evelyn Nephew had also:
2. Hannah Sharp West, married David Anderson, died.
3. Mary West, married Henry H. Tucker.
4. Susan West, died.
5. Elizabeth Munro West, died.
6. James Nephew West, married Isabella Atkinson.
7. Clifford Stiles West, married John Powers.
8. Sarah Evelyn West, died.
9. Joseph Jones West, M. D., married Anna Munro Rogers.
10. Maria Louisa West, married Dr. Julius Cæsar Gilbert.

James Nephew West and Isabella Atkinson had:
   A. Mary Evelyn West.
   B. Hamilton West, M. D., Galveston, Texas.
   C. Charles West.
   D. Sarah West.
   E. James West.
   F. Isabelle West.
   G. Barrington West.
   H. Georgia West.
   I. Joseph West.
   J. Clifford West.

Clifford Stiles West and John Powers had:

I. John Powers, married Corinne Smith.

II. Evelyn Powers, married Talmadge Walker.

Joseph Jones West died 1869; married Anna Munro Rogers, and had:

A. Annie Munro West.

B. Catharine Nephew West, died.

C. Elizabeth Wade West, died.

D. Joseph Woodford West, died.

E. Francis Bartow West, married Ruth Tinsley, and lives in Macon; issue:

a. Addison Tinsley West.

b. Francis Bartow West, Jr.

c. Anna Munro West.

Maria Louisa West and Dr. Gilbert had:

I. Evelyn Gilbert, married Holtzclaw.

II. Charles Gilbert, married Corinne Mann.

III. Kate Gilbert, married Henry Holtzclaw.

IV. Clifford Gilbert, married Henry Holtzclaw.

V. Fannie Gilbert, married Virgil Hurd.

VI. James Gilbert, unmarried.

DE GIGNILLIAT

In writing an account of this family, it is not by any means intended to give all the lines, but simply to show descent of a few of line and one of them from McIntosh of "Mala," mentioned in my work on "Baillie of Dunain," and to show descent of the Kings, Wests, &c., from Nephews and the Holmes. Abraham Gignilliat came to America, July 30, 1685, before Revocation of Edict of Nantes, October 22, 1688. He married Mary DeVille, and had Jean Francis de Gignilliat, who had a grant of 3,000 acres granted to him as first of Swiss nation to settle in Carolina; he married Susanne Le Serrurier, daughter of Count Jacques Le Serrurier and Elizabeth Leger, and had:

*I. Henry Gignilliat, married Hester Marion, aunt of Gen. Marion, and had Gabriel Gignilliat, member of S. C. Provincial Congress, 1775, from St. Johns, Berkeley.

II. Abraham Gignilliat, married, and had:

1. John Gignilliat, died May 25, 1750; married Mary Magdalen DuPre, daughter of Cornelius DuPre, who married, 1708, Jean Brabant, and had issue:

*Other children were Pierre, Mary and Elizabeth Gignilliat.

A. James Gignilliat, born July 30, 1746; married Charlotte, daughter of Dr. Pepper and Sarah Evelyn, and had:
  a. Mary Magdalen Gignilliat, married James Nephew.
  b. Gilbert Gignilliat, married Mary McDonald.
  c. Henry Gignilliat, married Jane McIntosh, of Mala, or Mallow, and had:
I. Wm. McIntosh Gignilliat, married Mary Manley, and had Jane, Mary, Henry, Margaret and Wm. Gignilliat, of Wayne Co., Ga. Gilbert Gignilliat and Mary McDonald had Norman Gignilliat; married Charlotte Trezevant, and had Margaret Helen Gignilliat, who married James Edward Holmes, son of Dr. James Holmes, of Darien, Ga.

PRATT

This family trace their descent from the 10th and 11th century, and Charles Pratt, Earl of Camden, Lord Chief Justice of England in the time of George III., was of this ancient line. Lieut. Wm. Pratt and his brother, John Pratt, went from England to New England in 1633, and settled in Connecticut. Of this family, Rev. Nathaniel Alpheus Pratt, born 1796, and his brother, Rev. Horace Southworth Pratt, born 1794, went to Georgia about 1820. Rev. Horace Pratt settled in St. Marys, Ga., and married, first, Jane Wood, and had:

I. Isabella Pratt, married Rev. Abner Porter.
II. Laleah Pratt, married Rev. Jas. B. Dunwody.
III. Pratt, married Rev. John Wood.

Rev. Horace Pratt, married, second, Isabella Drysdale, and had:

I. Horace Pratt, died young.
II. Sarah Pratt, married Judge James Lapsley.
III. Mary Pratt, married Robt. Lapsley.

Rev. Nathaniel A. Pratt, married 1830, Catharine Barrington King, daughter of Roswell King and Catharine Barrington, and had:

1. Horace A. Pratt, born 1830; married Lillias Logan, of Virginia.
2. Rev. Henry Barrington Pratt, born 1832; married Janie Gildersleeve, of Virginia.
3. Nathaniel Alpheus Pratt, born 1834; married Julia E. Stubbs.

4. Francis Lorinda Pratt, born 1835; married Rev. Jno. W. Baker.
5. Bayard Hand Pratt, born 1838; married Miss Wood, of Alabama.
6. Catharine Barrington Pratt, born 1840; died young.
7. Charles Pratt, born 1842; married Emma C. Stubbs.
8. Sarah Anna Pratt, born 1844.
9. Isabel Julia Pratt, born 1846; married Rev. Walker, of Ohio.
10. William Nephew Pratt, born 1848.
11. Kate Quintard Pratt, born 1850; married A. T. Heath.

Nathaniel A. Pratt, M. D., a noted chemist connected with the phosphate industry at Charleston at one time, and I believe instrumental in its development. He married, and had two sons:

1. Nathaniel Palmer Pratt, chemical mineralogist and chemical engineer, has been very successful and is proprietor of the N. K. Pratt Laboratory, the largest of the kind in the South. He married Frances, daughter of Rev. W. E. Baker and Evelyn, daughter of Barrington King.
2. Henry Jemison Pratt, married Frances, daughter of James Roswell King and Frances, daughter of Oliver Prince, formerly U. S. Senator from Georgia. James Roswell King was son of *Barrington King and Catharine M. Nephew.

Horace A. Pratt and Lillias Logan had issue:

A. Kate Lee Pratt, died in childhood.
B. Daughter, died in childhood.
C. John Henry Pratt, analytical chemist, Bartow, Fla.; married Lucy Breedlove, and had:
  a. Lillias Pratt.
  b. John Henry Pratt.
D. Horace A. Pratt, died in Texas, 1884.

Rev. Henry Barrington Pratt and Miss Gildersleeve had:

*It is said the Barringtons came from Virginia. There was Josiah Barrington, the father, who came to Georgia before the Revolution, and was a tax collector under Royal Government. He had a family, we suppose, as there were several Barrington ladies.

A. Benj. Gildersleeve Pratt, married Emma Dunn, of Chester, S. C.
B. Kate Pratt, married Jno. N. Webb, of North Carolina.
C. Louisa Pratt, married Richard Evans Wylie, of Lancaster, S. C.
D. Paul Pratt, married Belle Newell, Baltimore, Md.
E. Maria Pratt, died Richmond, Va.
F. Henry Basil Pratt, unmarried, in New York.
G. Juanita Pratt, died young.

Benj. G. Pratt and Emma Dunn had:
a. William Pratt.
b. Benj. Gildersleeve Pratt.
c. Julia Pratt.
d. Pratt.

Dr. Nathaniel Alpheus Pratt, an eminent chemist, closely at one time connected with the phosphate interests of South Carolina, son of Rev. Nathaniel A. Pratt and Catharine Barrington King, married Julia E. Stubbs (see King), and had the following children:
A. Robert Small Pratt, died infancy.
B. Nathaniel Palmer Pratt, President N. P. Pratt Laboratory, Atlanta, Ga., married Frances Baker, of Roswell, Ga., daughter of Rev. W. E. Baker and Evelyn King, daughter of Barrington King and Catharine M. Nephew, and had:
  a. Palmer Pratt.
  b. Evelyn Pratt.
  c. Julia Pratt.
  d. Nathaniel Alpheus Pratt.
C. Henry Jemison Pratt, died 1891, Rome, Ga., married Fanny Prince King.
D. Frances Lorinda Pratt, married Rev. John W. Baker, and had Francis Lorinda Baker, died in infancy.
E. Arthur William Pratt, died Atlanta, 1899.
F. Geo. Lewis Pratt, engineering director N. P. Pratt Laboratory.
G. Julia E. Pratt, of Decatur, Ga., married Sherrod Kennedy, of Atlanta, Ga., and had, Fanny Pratt Kennedy.

Henry Jemison Pratt married Frances Prince King, daughter of James Roswell King* (son of Barrington King and Catharine M. Nephew) and Fanny Prince, daughter †Oliver Prince (at one time U. S. Senator from Ga.), and had:

a. Richard Pratt.
b. Norman Pratt.
c. Henry Jemison Pratt.
F. Geo. Lewis Pratt, married Meta ——, of New Orleans, and had Margaret Pratt.

Bayard Hand Pratt, son of Rev. N. H. Pratt, married Mattie ——, of Alabama, and had:

A. Joanna Pratt.
B. Margaret Pratt.
C. John Pratt.
D. Oliver Pratt.
E. Kate Pratt.
F. Lloyd Pratt.

Capt. Charles Pratt, C. E., son Rev. N. A. Pratt and Catharine B. King, had:

A. John Pryor Pratt, died in Savannah.
B. Eliza Richard Pratt.
C. William Stubbs Pratt.
D. Emma Pratt.
E. Ellen Palmer Pratt.
F. Eugene Charles Pratt.

Kate Quintard Pratt married A. T. Heath, of Roswell, Ga., and had:

I. Wm. Pratt Heath, chief chemist N. P. Pratt Laboratory, married Susan Taylor.
II. Natalie Heath.
III. Elise Ansley Heath.
IV. Alfred Taylor Heath, Jr.

Louisa Pratt and Richard Evans Wylie had:

I. Louisa Wylie.
II. Juanita Wylie.
III. Eliza Wylie, died in infancy.
IV. John D. Wylie, died.
V. Louise Wylie.
VI. Kate Wylie.

*James Roswell King married, second, Meta Lewis, daughter of R. Adams Lewis.

†The Princes came from the North. Oliver, son of Hon. Oliver Prince, married a Jackson, of Georgia, descended also from the Rootes, Cobbes, Reades, &c., of Virginia, and sister of Gen. H. R. Jackson.

Paul Pratt and Belle Newell had:
- a. Algio Pratt.
- b. Janet Pratt.
- c. Marie Pratt.

Kate Pratt and Jno. N. Webb had:
- I. Kate Webb.
- II. Henry Webb.
- III. Katharine Webb.
- IV. Margaret Webb.

DE TREVILLE

This ancient French family is of undoubted noble origin, and bears the same name, though perhaps different coats-of-arms, from the Counts De Treville, and the stock from which it springs truly bears within its bosom the motto *"Noblesse oblige;"* for in peace and in war, and in all walks of life, it has exemplified itself as a family to be trusted and depended upon; and this assertion is borne out not by tradition only, but by consultation with historical evidences so clear that South Carolina should be proud to have within her borders the family of De Treville.

Cadet John La Bouladrie de Treville was born in France, emigrated to America and settled in St. Helena Parish, S. C., and, at the breaking out of hostilities between the Colonies and Great Britain, was appointed Lieutenant, and soon after became Captain in the 4th Regiment of Artillery of the South Carolina contingent of the Continental line. He proved a very efficient officer and served with distinction, and, had his life been prolonged, might have attained much higher rank; but an unfortunate difficulty which resulted in two duels with the same man, caused his untimely death; for though he fought first with swords and in the second encounter with pistols, at last killing his antagonist, he received a sword cut from which he ultimately died, and thus the State was deprived of this gallant soldier and member of the eminent Society of the Cincinnati.*

Capt. De Treville married Julia Wilkinson, an heiress of English extraction, and by her had two children:

I. Robert L. de Treville, married Sarah Ellis, born Beaufort, S. C., 17—; died in Charleston, 1862.

II. Harriet de Treville, married, first, Robert Guerard, son of Godin Guerard and Ann Mathews, sister of Hon. John Mathews, son of Hon. John Guerard, member of His Majesty's Council.

Harriet de Treville and Robert Guerard had a number of children, all of whom died young. She married, secondly, March 2, 1814, Samuel Lawrence, of Beaufort, S. C., and had:

I. Samuel Lawrence, born Beaufort, S. C., December 24, 1815; and after practicing law some time with his kinsman, Col. Richard de Treville, removed to Marietta, Ga., where, after practicing with marked success, he became Judge, and held the position for many years, dying October 2, 1890. Judge Samuel Lawrence married, first, Amanda Malvina Bolan (sister of Mrs. John Heyward Glover), who was born in South Carolina, January 3, 1818, and died in Marietta, Ga., June 25, 1871. He married, second, December, 1873, Clara E. Green, of Atlanta, Ga. His children by his first wife are:

1. James Bolan Lawrence, born Beaufort, S. C., March 2, 1838; died Atlanta, Ga., July 3, 1884.
2. Robert de Treville Lawrence, born South Carolina, February 9, 1841; a soldier in the late war, member of the Washington Light Infantry, Hampton's Legion, with which he for some time served, and then was transferred to the Signal Corps, with which he remained until the close of the war. He returned to his home, and married, September 14,

*Moultrie's Memoirs; McCrady's History of South Carolina, Vol. III., etc.

1887, Anna E. Atkinson, of Marietta, and had:

A. Alexander Atkinson Lawrence, born in Marietta, Ga., April, 1869; married, November 27, 1900, Isabel A. Paine, of Charleston, S. C. He is now practicing law in Savannah, Ga.

B. Amanda Bolan Lawrence, born in Marietta, Ga., 1871.

C. Robt. de T. Lawrence, born in Marietta, Ga., 1872; died there October 12, 1895.

D. Samuel Lawrence, born in Marietta, Ga., July, 1874.

E. James Bolan Lawrence, born January 2, 1878.

F. M—— McDonald Lawrence, born in Marietta, Ga., September 4, 1881.

3. Samuel Lawrence was born in South Carolina, January 3, 1843; died in Marietta, Ga., September, 1872.

4. Proctor Bolan Lawrence was born in South Carolina, November 2, 1844. He served throughout the Confederate war; he married, November 1, 1867, Alice Smith, of Talbotton, Ga., who died in Alabama, 1870; married, second, Caroline Pooler, 1872, who died in Marietta, Ga., September, 1874. His children are:

A. Letitia Mary Lawrence, born March, 1873.

B. Chas. Colding Lawrence, born May, 1874.

5. Annie Edith Lawrence, born in South Carolina, June 15, 1846; died in Atlanta, Ga., April 9, 1867.

6. Amanda Lawrence, born August 4, 1849, in Marietta, Ga.; died there, April 16, 1866.

7. Jane Glover Lawrence, born in Marietta, Ga., January, 1852; died in Atlanta, Ga., September 10, 1889.

8. Stephen Lawrence, born January 5, 1854, in Marietta, Ga.; died there, July 28, 1855.

9. John de T. Lawrence, born in Marietta, Ga., June 10, 1856; married, 1885, Ella Belle Beale, of Baton Rouge, La. Their children are:

A. Mary Beale Lawrence, born New Orleans.

B. Ella Belle Beale Lawrence, born New Orleans.

C. Ella Beale Lawrence, born Atlanta, Ga.

Robert L. de Treville, only son of Capt. John La Bouladrie de Treville and Julia Wilkinson, married Sarah Ellis, daughter of

Richard Ellis and Sarah Hogg. (Richard Ellis married Elizabeth Green, April 28, 1784. Last Thursday, Mr. Richard Ellis to Miss Elizabeth Greene.—*S. C. Gazette.*) He married, also, Sarah Hogg.* Robert L. de Treville and Sarah Ellis (daughter of Richard Ellis, brother of Mrs. Nathaniel Adams, children of Edmund Ellis), had the following children:

1. Richard de Treville.
2. Caroline de Treville, born, Beaufort, S. C., died Charleston, 18—.
3. Harriet de Treville, born Beaufort, S. C.; died Summerville, 18—.
4. Elizabeth de Treville, born Beaufort, S. C.; died Charleston, August 4, 1893.
5. Ellis de Treville, born Beaufort, S. C., about 1816; died May 7, 1870, Charleston.

Richard de Treville, eldest son of Robert L. de Treville and Sarah Ellis, was born in Beaufort, S. C., November 29, 1801; attended the school of Hon. James L. Petigru, and entered West Point Military Academy; graduating from that institution in 1823, and received the appointment of brevet Colonel of Artillery in the U. S. Army, and served until 1825, when he resigned. He afterward studied law and practiced in his native State to the time of his death, which occurred in Summerville, S. C., November 25, 1874. He filled many offices of honor and among them that of Lieutenant Governor of South Carolina in her palmy days, and when South Carolina seceded, he was called to the command of the 17th Regiment, S. C. M., and as its leader took part in the defense of the sea islands. And thus do we see this honorable scion of an honored family giving to his country his services in all times of need.

Lt. Gov. de Treville married, first, February 23, 1826, Esther Hutson, daughter of Alexander Frazier Gregorie and Esther Hutson, both of Prince William's Parish, S. C. She died, November 21, 1826. He married, second, at Gillisonville, S. C., 4th August, 1829, Cornelia Matilda, daughter of Capt. William Joyner,† of the Continental Artillery, who married the

*NOTE.—The following shows the military services of the Hogg family: "William Hogg, under Capt. Cowan, 1780; James Hogg, Col. Waters' Regiment, 1780; John Hogg, 1779-80-81-82; Lewis Hogg, 1780-81-83. Major Hogg also did good service." Jane H. Hogg married, in 1840, Alexander Moultrie.

†NOTE.—She was also a niece of Capt. John Joyner, of the Continental Navy during the Revolution, and half-sister of Hon. Wm. John Gray-

widow of Capt. William Grayson, of the Revolution, her maiden name being Susan Greene; born Beaufort, S. C., about 1777; died in Charleston, March 30, 1854. By his second marriage, Lt. Gov. de Treville had:

A. Wm. Joyner de Treville, born Beaufort, S. C., May 23, 1830.
B. Sarah de Treville, born Beaufort, December 12, 1831; died July 1, 1833.
C. Robert de Treville, born Beaufort, S. C., August 24, 1833.
D. Richard de Treville, born Beaufort, S. C., December 3, 1834.
E. Cornelia Ellen de Treville, born Beaufort, S. C., July 10, 1836; died New York, January 11, 1892.
F. Florence Matilda de Treville, born Beaufort, S. C., July 30, 1838; married, February 1, 1883, Wm. N. Symington, of Washington, D. C.
G. Emma Elizabeth de Treville, born Beaufort, S. C., April 30, 1840; died New York, August 25, 1880.
H. Edward White de Treville, born Beaufort, S. C., September 8, 1842.
I. John La Bouladrie de Treville, born Beaufort, S. C., January 8, 1846.
J. Louis de Treville, born Beaufort, S. C., November 23, 1849.

Cornelia Matilda Joyner, second wife of Hon. R. de Treville, was born in Beaufort, S. C., December 23, 1810; died in Charleston, S. C., April 6, 1854.

William Joyner de Treville received his early education and preparation for college at the old Beaufort Academy under such teachers as the Rev. Stiles Mellichamp and the Rev. John Fielding. He entered Princeton College in 1850, and was distinguished as a student in that famous institution. He graduated well up in a distinguished class, and returning home, read law, and was admitted to the Bar in May, 1857. During

son, the poet, biographer, and member of Congress. Susan Greene claimed to be closely related to Gen. Nathaniel Greene, and was probably a daughter of Daniel John Greene, one of His Majesty's Justices of the Peace. Hon. Wm. John Grayson married Sarah Matilda Somarsall, grand-daughter of Daniel Stevens (marriage settlement in office of Secretary of State, 1814), and among their issue were the late Mrs. T. L. Ogier, of Charleston, S. C., and Henry Grayson, who married his cousin, Cornelia, second daughter of the Rev. Dr. Brantley.

the early years of his practice in Beaufort he taught school. His practice prospered, and he acquired a handsome residence in the old town, and lived the happy, elegant home life of the gentlemen of those palmy days, in the courtly and literary society of Beaufort. But this scene and chapter of his life was briefly closed by "the purple testament of bleeding war." Exposed to the first rude impression of the gathering storm, his native town was soon deserted as a place of residence, and converted into a citadel. The interruption of war broke up his practice and scattered his clientele. He held several legal positions under the government of the Confederate States, and endured the privation, and groped amid the disruptions of the times. The disastrous end of the conflict found him stranded amid the wrecks of his life, even his beautiful home lost by the confiscation of an unprecedented and impossible tax, sold without process of law or possibility of redemption, and now owned and occupied—climax of reversal—by a former slave! Driven by adverse fate, he sought other shores, removed to Barnwell, where he practiced his profession for a brief period, and then went to Orangeburg, where for about twenty-five years he lived and practiced, founding and rearing another happy home, whose hearth-stones and mahogany shone with culture and hospitality, and that in the days of the homes of Judge Glover, Gen. Jamison, the Hutsons, the Legares, of Dr. Alex. S. Salley and of Murray Robinson. Here he reached the zenith of his life, and had for years a remunerative practice whose income he enjoyed with the zest and relish of a perfect *savoir vivre*. But his pockets, like Dr. Johnson's, "had holes in them," the strings of his purse were loose to every applicant. "He was so kind, that he paid interest for it." Troubles came, domestic afflictions, loss of fortune, decadence of practice, ills incident to human life. But both in vicissitudes and contrasts of fortune, he bore himself with a cheerfulness that was his great characteristic. He hurled sarcastic jests at misfortune, he forgot privation when he met a friend. This genial sunniness astonished, and attracted to him. His wit was keen. He had the perception and sensibility of the artist. He felt the pathetic and descried the ludicrous in literature, nature and in men; with catholic penetration he could detect deceit and unmask the Tartuffe and the Pecksniff in the Court and in the world. And he could express his perception by word and pencil, and frequently tossed off a couplet or a sketch that amused the Court, and affected the verdict. Some of his portraits and drawings are preserved as reliques by admiring friends, and his portraitures and caricatures of the drowsy and patient judge, the perplexed advocate and the confounded witness, sketched at his desk, have been carried home as souvenirs and favors of the Court. As a lawyer he had advantages; of heredity, his father, Col. Richard de Treville, of the old 17th Regiment, of Charleston, and Lieutenant Governor of the State in her chivalrous days, was one of that group of courtly men and brilliant lawyers who graced the Bar at its best period; of training, for he sat at the feet of those Gamaliels; of education, for he graduated at Princeton, and of natural gifts developed in the genial atmosphere of such association and antecedents. Among his legal experiences he acted for a time as solicitor in the Second Circuit, and exhibited rare talent as a prosecuting officer. In the journals and dockets and judgment books of Orangeburg, the evidence of his legal business will delight the eye of the lawyer. Some of his written and printed arguments on Circuit and in the Supreme Court, are models of learning and industry. In his prime he was a wary and skilful adversary and a persuasive advocate before a judge and jury. He was strikingly handsome, and in appearance seemed possessed of Pierian youth. He removed to Brevard, N. C., and was admitted to the Bar of that State; but waning strength showed all too plainly that his days were numbered, and after several months sojourn there he returned to his native State and located in Columbia; and soon after was for a second time appointed U. S. Commissioner, and this office he held up to the time of his death, which occurred September 11, 1897. He married, first, August 17, 1852, Agnes Givens, daughter of Philip Givens and *Mary Eliza Firth, both of St. Helena Parish, and had:

a. Mary Cornelia de Treville, born Beaufort, S. C., 23 July, 1853.
b. Franklin Sams de Treville, born Charleston, S. C., May 2, 1855; died near White Hall, S. C.
c. Wm. Joyner de Treville, Jr., now of Austin, Texas, born Beaufort, S. C., September 19, 1857.
d. Minnie de Treville, died in infancy.
e. Ada de Treville, born Beaufort, S. C., October, 1860;

*Mary Eliza Firth was the daughter of Samuel Firth, of Philadelphia, Penn., a descendant of Samuel Carpenter, who came over with Penn and founded the city of Philadelphia.

married Rev. James Henry Fowles LaRoche;* died February 10, 1881.

f. Sarah Isabelle de Treville, born Barnwell C. H., September, 1863; lives now in New York City.

Mary Cornelia de Treville, married, November 3, 1875, Julius, youngest son of Judge Thomas Worth Glover, of St. James Goose Creek Parish, and afterward of Orangeburg, S. C., and his wife, Caroline Elizabeth Jamison, sister of Gen. Jamison, of St. Matthew's Parish, S. C., died September 19, 1881, leaving one son:

I. Wm. Lloyd Glover, born Orangeburg, S. C., June 13, 1878; married January 16, 1901, Julia Evelina, third daughter of Joel Townsend Salley, of Orangeburg, S. C., and Lydia Matthews Walpole, of John's Island, S. C.

Wm. Joyner de Treville, Jr., son of Wm. Joyner de Treville and Agnes Givens, married Rose, daughter of Warren Ransom Davis and Ruth H——, and had:

1. James LaRoche de Treville.
2. Ransom (?) Davis de Treville.
3. William de Treville.

Wm. Joyner de Treville, Sr., married, second, December 20, 1877, Mary Eugenia Ann, eldest daughter of Derrill Hart Darby, of St. Matthews Parish, S. C., and Charlotte Olympia Garnett, of Virginia, sister of the distinguished Gen. Richard Brooke Garnett, whose lineage is from some of the finest of old Virginia. Through the Darbys she descends from Col. Wm. Thomson, so celebrated in the History of South Carolina, also from the ancient family of Elliott, who came with the Screvens from the North, and from the Screvens and Cutts families. Col. Thomson is ancestor of a branch of families of Haskells and others equally noted. She is also a grand-

NOTE.—"About 1730, Moses Thomson and his connections moved from Pennsylvania to Amelia Township. A member of this family, Wm. Thomson, married Eugenia, daughter of Capt. Charles Russell, and her sister, Sophabanista Russell, married John McCord. From these marriages spring many of the early Orangeburg families, among whom are branches of Cheves, McCord, Taber, Rhett, Goodwyn, Darbye, Hane, Stuart, Sinkler, &c." (Salley's History of Orangeburg County).

*Rev. Wm. La Roche, now of Oakley, Md., says Ada, second daughter of Wm. de Treville and Agnes Givens, married Rev. James Henry Fowles La Roche, son of Richard La Roche and Miss Mackay. His father always lived on Toogoodoo River, twenty miles south of Charleston. His mother's early home was at Pocotaligo, S. C.

daughter of Col. Wm. Mercer Garnett and Anna Maria, daughter of Richard Brooke, of Essex Co., Va.

Wm. Joyner de Treville and Mary Eugenia Ann Darby have one son: Derrill de Treville.

Robert de Treville, second son of Hon. Richard de Treville and C. M. Joyner, attended the schools of the Revs. Mellichamp and Fielding; entered the South Carolina College and graduated in 1853; studied law and was admitted to the Bar in 1855, and practiced with his father until the beginning of the war, at which time he was a member of the Washington Light Infantry. After a short term of service with that command, he was commissioned First Lieutenant in the (Confederate States) Provisional Army, in the regiment that became the 1st South Carolina Infantry (Regulars), and rose to be its Lieutenant Colonel. He was killed in the hard-fought battle of Averysboro, N. C., March 16, 1865, while in command of that regiment.* Ever conspicuous for gallantry, he participated in most of the engagements in Charleston harbor, and it was while under his command that Fort Moultrie underwent the severest ordeal in its whole history, September 8, 1863.† He married, December 4, 1860, Eliza, eldest daughter of John Heyward Glover, of Marietta, Ga., formerly of Colleton Co., S. C., and Jane Porter Bolan, and left two children:

a. Robert Glover de Treville, born November 17, 1861.
b. Ruth de Treville, born August 2, 1863.

Robert Glover de Treville married, February 20, 1881, Annie Emera, daughter of William Augustus Thrasher, of Elmore Co., Ala., and Mary Eliza Watson, of Georgia, and had:

1. Helen Lieze de Treville, born April 19, 1882.
2. Annie Ruth de Treville, born December 5, 1891.

Ruth de Treville married, December 31, 1881, Luther Love, son of Calvin Wellborn Hunnicut, of Mecklenburg Co., and Letitia Ann Payne, of Newton Co., Ga., and died May 12, 1883, leaving one son:

I. Luther Love Hunnicut.

Richard de Treville, third son of Hon. Richard de Treville

*NOTE.—In this action, Rhett's brigade of regulars, composed of the 1st S. C. Infantry, the 1st S. C. Artillery and Lucas' Battalion, and commanded by Col. William Butler, was engaged from 7 a. m. to about 4 p. m., handsomely repulsing the continued assaults of Kilpatrick's division and Slocum's corps, and held the field against this vastly superior force of veterans.

†See Johnson's "Defense of Charleston Harbor."

and Cornelia M. Joyner, was born in Beaufort, S. C., December 3, 1834; was prepared for college in the schools of Revs. Mellichamp and Fielding; entered the S. C. College and graduated in 1855; after which he studied law at Cambridge University, Mass. At the breaking out of the war between the States, he joined the Washington Light Infantry (Hampton Legion), and served with same until discharged on account of ill health; and was appointed clerk in the Treasury Department in Richmond, Va., with which he remained until the end of the war. He married, February 17, 1863, Ella, daughter of William Mitchell and Julia Burnham, of Virginia, and had:

1. Eva de Treville, born August 19, 1864; married, June 12, 1900, Rodman Paul Snelling, of Boston, Mass., and has a daughter, born April 15, 1901.

Edward White de Treville, fourth son of Hon. R. de Treville and C. M. Joyner, was born in Beaufort, S. C., June 23, 1841; was prepared for college in the best schools of Charleston; entered the S. C. Military Academy, but his health proving unequal to barrack life, left before graduating. Soon after was appointed Sergeant Major of the 17th Regiment S. C. M., and served in that capacity until the command was disbanded, when he joined the Washington Light Infantry (Hampton Legion), and served with this company until discharged on account of ill health. He then accepted an appointment in the Confederate Treasury Department, and remained with same until the close of the war. While in the Treasury Department he studied medicine, and after the close of the war returned to his native State, where he began the practice of his profession; but by this time his health was utterly ruined, and he died while on a visit, in Orangeburg, S. C., May 28, 1867.

John La Bouladrie de Treville, fifth son of Hon. Richard de Treville and C. M. Joyner, was born in Beaufort, S. C., January 8, 1846; and when quite a youth joined the Beaufort Volunteer Artillery, and served gallantly and faithfully with that command until the close of the war, when he returned to South Carolina, and soon after engaged in business at the North, and died in Richmond, Va., January 3, 1902. He married, October, 1875, Ida, daughter of John Vandeventer and Mary Greenlease, of Richmond, Va. (Mrs. De Treville died April 21, 1896), and had one son:

a. John La Bouladrie de Treville, born Richmond, Va., July 10, 1876.

Louis de Treville, sixth son of Hon. R. de Treville and C. M. Joyner, married, August 31, 1871, Eleanora Norval, eldest daughter of Dr. Robert Witsell, of Walterboro, S. C., and Thomasina Susan Davis, daughter of John Norval Davis and Julia Mary Lehre, daughter of Thomas Lehre and Mrs. James Stanyarne, *nee* Susannah Scott, daughter of Col. Wm. Scott, of the Revolution, and Mary, daughter of Richard and Florence Waring. John Norval Davis was son of Capt. Wm. Ransom Davis and Eleanora de Norvelle. Dr. Witsell was full surgeon in Sloan's Regiment during the war between the States, 1861-65, and he was a first cousin of ex-Gov. Johnson Hagood. The Scotts, of South Carolina, married in the Stobo-Stanyarne families and also into that of Adam Daniel, who married a daughter of Landgrave Blake.

Louis de Treville and Eleanora Norval Witsell had the following children:

a. Thomasina Davis de Treville, born Beaufort, S. C., July 11, 1872.
b. Wm. Ransom de Treville, born Summerville, S. C., October 22, 1873; died November 19, 1876.
c. John La Bouladrie de Treville, born Summerville, S. C., February 10, 1875.
d. Eleanora Norval de Treville, born Summerville, S. C., June 25, 1878.
e. Marie Louise de Treville, born Summerville, S. C., August 21, 1879.
f. Robert de Treville (1), born Summerville, S. C., July 19, 1880; died there June 10, 1881.
g. Richard de Treville, born Summerville, S. C., November 14, 1882.
h. Cornelia Ellen de Treville, born Summerville, S. C., February, 27, 1884; died there April 1, 1884.
i. Robert de Treville (2), born Summerville, S. C., April 16, 1885; died there April 22, 1885.
j. Thomas Lehre de Treville, born Summerville, S. C., July 10, 1886; died there August 10, 1886.

NOTE.—Mrs. De Treville, through her mother, is related to the Richardsons, of Clarendon County, the Fludds, the Spanns, the Calhouns, of Abbeville, S. C., and to many descendants of Thomas Smith, first Landgrave, and among her cousins was that able officer, Col. Wm. Ransom Calhoun, of the 1st S. C. Artillery (regulars), who was killed in a duel with Lieut. Col. Alfred Rhett, September 5, 1862, of the same command.

k. Daniel Flud de Treville, born Orangeburg, S. C., May 19, 1888.

John La Bouladrie de Treville married, November 5, 1894, Ella Marguerite, eldest daughter of William Eugene McNulty, of ——, and Mary L. Durham, of Fairfield, S. C.

Eleanora N. de Treville married, October 3, 1900, Christopher, eldest son of Rev. William Robert Atkinson, D. D., of Georgetown, S. C., and Lucy Morton Hannah, of Gravel Hill, Charlotte Co., Va. Dr. William Robert Atkinson was a member of a family that belongs to Georgetown District. He removed to Alabama, and from Mobile entered the Sophomore Class of the South Carolina College in 1859. Here he was soon distinguished for his ability and earnest disposition. Upon the opening of hostilities between the States, the students of the college went to Charleston. Later on, upon the fall of Beaufort, the Governor ordered the college company to the defense of the coast, and senior examinations were not held in December, 1861. But, at the suggestion of the Trustees, the Faculty recommended the granting of diplomas to those members of the Senior Class who were then in service. Dr. Atkinson was one of the three or four best men in the class. He served for a while in the Richmond Rifles, and then was made a member of the Signal Service Corps, which did most excellent and responsible work in Charleston and Savannah. At the close of the war he went to Virginia University, and then taught school in Abbeville County. During a portion of the year he assisted Mr. Edward R. Miles, in the town of Abbeville. He was a very thorough and cultivated teacher, and his familiarity with Latin grammar especially was the envy of his class. At the end of this year, a protracted religious meeting having been organized among all the churches, Dr. Atkinson was much impressed and began to study for the Episcopal ministry. But he shortly arrived at the conclusion that Presbyterian tenets were more in accordance with his ideas, and entered the Presbyterian Seminary in Columbia. Here he graduated. Some time after this he was appointed Chaplain of the Virginia University. But he had so great a fondness, and so great an aptitude for teaching that he again entered the work in Raleigh. After this he took charge of the Charlotte Female College and achieved great success. Believing, however, that Columbia was an admirable educational centre, he founded, in 1890, the South Carolina College for Women. His determination was to have a first-class College in every respect, and under his administration the College soon attained a high reputation for scholarship and high standards. This was a trying financial and political period, and in his work Dr. Atkinson taxed a constitution never very robust. At the end of six years, failing health rendered it necessary for him to abandon his chosen work and to sell his magnificent property. After this, Dr. Atkinson visited Florida, and then resided a while at Lake Saranac. For some time before his death he lived in Williamsport, Penn. Dr. Atkinson received his honorary degree from the South Carolina College while President of the College for Women in Columbia. An exceedingly positive, earnest, aggressive man, Dr. Atkinson sometimes gave offense. But he was always manly, and ever ready to make reparation when convinced that it was right. He always commanded respect from others for himself. By his first marriage, with Miss Hannah, Dr. Atkinson had several children. Mr. Cristopher Atkinson is now in Columbia. The Rev. George Atkinson is engaged in devoted pastoral work in the mining regions of Pennsylvania. His daughter, Miss Annie Atkinson, a musical artiste of great merit, married the pianist and composer, Burmeister, and resides in New York. A few years ago Dr. Atkinson married a second time, Miss Thompson, of Williamsport, Pa. She survives him.

Marie Louise de Treville married, April 18, 1900, Alexander Washington Ellerbe, seventh son of Madison Farr Ellerbe, of Cheraw, S. C., and Eleanor Adele La Coste (now the wife of T. Stobo Farrow), and had:

I. Harry La Coste Ellerbe, born Columbia, S. C., January 13. 1901.

Hon. Richard de Treville married, third, Angelina Ketchum, of Charleston, S. C., daughter of Joel Ketchum and Elizabeth Burns, and had:

1. Lena de Treville, born Charleston, S. C.; died there.
2. Elizabeth de Treville, born Charleston, now of New Jersey.
3. Richard de Treville, born Greenville, S. C., artist, who illustrates a paper in Stockton, California.

Elizabeth de Treville, third daughter of Robert L. de Treville and Sarah Ellis, was born in Beaufort, S. C.; died in Charleston, S. C., August 4, 1893. She married John Blake Washnigton, son of William Washington and Martha Ferguson

Blake, daughter of Capt. John Blake, of the Revolution, and Margaret Mercier, daughter of Lieut. St. Pierre Mercier, who married the widow of Capt. George Haig, born Margaret Watson. William Washington was son of Col. Wm. Washington, the famous Revolutionary officer. Elizabeth de Treville and John Blake Washington had:

I. Wm. Washington, born Charleston, S. C., 1853; died.

II. Harriet de Treville Washington, born Charleston, October, 1856.

III. John Blake Washington, born Charleston, S. C., December 29, 1858; married June 20, 1888, Margaret Thomson, second daughter of the late Albert Rhett Taber and his second wife, Louisa Burnham Darby, of St. Matthew's Parish, S. C.—descended from the Elliotts, Screvens, Col. Wm. Thomson, Cutts, &c., and had:

1. Margaret Thomson Washington, born April 17, 1889.
2. John Blake Washington, born April 9, 1890.
3. Charlotte Garnett Washington, born June 20, 1893.
4. William Washington, born January 15, 1897.

Harriet de Treville Washington, married Charles Palmer Sanders, eldest son of Thomas Lining Sanders, of Charleston, S. C., and Rebecca Witsell, of Walterboro, S. C., and had:

I. Lilly Blake Sanders, born Charleston, S. C., March 25, 1879.

II. Marie de Treville Sanders, born Charleston, S. C., April 15, 1881.

The Blakes are connected by marriage to the Merciers, Haigs, Wilsons, Bowens, Washingtons, Goodwyns, Perrys, Lesesnes, DeVeauxs, Barnwells, Palmers, Bellingers, Lewis, Legares, Mazycks, Habershams, Middletons, &c., and, though not of the Landgrave family of Blake, are of noted Revolutionary stock.

John and Lawrence Washington, brothers, came to America. Lawrence Washington married Jane Fleming, and had: John Washington, married Mary Townsend, and had, probably, besides others:

I. Anne Washington, married Wm. Strother (issue twenty-one children).

II. —. Washington, married, and had: Col. Bailey Washington, who married Miss Strother, sister of Anne Strother, who maried John James.

William Strother and Anne Washington had:

I. Anne Strother, married John James.

II. —. Strother, married Col. Bailey (Baillie?) Washington, and had:

1. Col. Wm. Washington, married, 1782, Jane Riley Elliott, daughter of Charles Elliott,* of St. Paul's Parish, S. C., and Jane Stanyarne, daughter of Joseph Stanyarne and Elizabeth Stobo,† and had:

A. Jane Washington, married Jas. Hasel Ancrum; left issue.

B. William Washington, married Martha Ferguson Blake, and had:

1. William Washington, born 1810; died 1849; married Theodosia Narcissa McPherson.
2. Margaret Mercier Washington, married Thomas Pinckney Lowndes; left issue.
3. Jane Washington, died in infancy.
4. Elizabeth Emily Washington, died unmarried, 1855.
5. Cornelia Washington, married James Skirving McPherson; left issue.
6. John Blake Washington, married Elizabeth, third daughter of Robt. L. and Sarah de Treville; left issue.
7. Septima Martha Washington, married Jas. Albert Strobhart; no issue.
8. Harriet Mary Washington, unmarried.
9. Martha Blake Washington, married Wm. Henry Peronneau; left issue.

Lieut. James Elliott McPherson Washington, C. S. A., aide to Gen. R. S. Garnett, was the son of William and Narcissa Washington; born October 15, 1836; died at Monteray, Highland Co., Va., August 25, 1861.

John James and Annie Strother had:

I. Benjamin James, married Jane Stobo, from whom descend the Garlingtons, Simpsons, Farrows, etc.

Ellis de Treville, second son of Robert L. de Treville and

*Note.—Charles Elliott married, second, Anne, only daughter of Thomas Ferguson, by the second of five wives, "the widow North, of the Perry family." She (Anne) subsequently married Richard Beresford. She had no children. (Johnson's Traditions of the Revolution.)

†Note.—Elizabeth Stanyarne, sister of Mrs. Jean Bulloch, daughter of Rev. Archibald Stobo.

Sarah Ellis, was born in Beaufort about 1816; graduated from Cambridge University; studied law and was admitted to the Bar in 1838; practiced for many years prior to the War between the States, and afterwards to the time of his death, in Charleston, S. C., May 7, 1870. He married, October 11, 1849, Julia Emma, daughter of Capt. James Copes, of Charleston, and Harriet Eliza Chambers, and had:

A. James Copes de Treville, born Charleston, S. C., August 10, 1850.
B. Richard Henry de Treville, born Charleston, S. C., March 10, 1854.

James Copes de Treville married, April 4, 1880, Julia Mary, daughter of Caleb Sauls, of Colleton Co., S. C., and Georgiana Austin, of Lexington, S. C., and had:

a. Cornelia de Treville, born January 25, 1881.
b. Richard de Treville, born January 9, 1883.
c. George de Treville, born June 6, 1884.
d. Nell Pressley de Treville, born October 29, 1885.
e. Benjamin Ellis de Treville, born November 30, 1886.
f. Sallie de Treville, born September 14, 1888; died —.
g. Julian de Treville, born March 2, 1890.
h. James de Treville, born January 3, 1892.
i. Jesse Campbell de Treville, born August 11, 1893.
j. Katharine de Treville, born May 20, 1895.
k. Morgan de Treville, born July 15, 1897.
l. An infant, unnamed, born August 9, 1899.

Richard Henry de Treville was born in Charleston, S. C., March 10, 1854; removed to Hopkinsville, Ky. (where he now resides), September, 1876; married, November 11, 1880, Sudie C., daughter of James A. Wallace and Cornelia Gant, of Kentucky, and had:

a. Cornelia Wallace de Treville, born April 27, 1885.
b. Julia Copes de Treville, born July 31, 1887.
c. Wm. Wallace de Treville, born April 24, 1890.
d. Richard Ellis de Treville, born December 3, 1894.

c

JOYNER, OF BEAUFORT, S. C.

This family furnished two men of note to the service of the Province of South Carolina—Capt. William Joyner, of the army, and Capt. John Joyner, of the navy, and the author has seen the "Arms of Joyner," which would indicate a gentle origin of the family, who were of English extraction. Capt. Wm. Joyner married Susan Grayson, widow, born Susan Greene, and had:

I. Margaret Joyner, married Rev. Dr. Brantley, one of the first pastors of the First Baptist Church of Charleston.

II. Ann Joyner, married, first, Jas. Agnew, of St. Helena Island, S. C.; he died, leaving no issue.

III. Elizabeth Joyner, married Edward Fripp, and had:

(a.) Annie Perry Fripp, born 1836; married Col. Chas. Cochran Lee, of North Carolina, who was killed in the battle of Gaines' Mill.

(b.) Elizabeth Fripp, married Elvira Fripp, her first cousin.

II. Mrs. Jas. Agnew (*nee* Ann Joyner) married, second, Edward Fripp (widower of Elizabeth J.), and had:

1. Edward James (or St. James) Fripp, born July 12, 1845; died June 12, 1891; married, first, May 7, 1874, Margaret, only daughter of Chas. Lining, of Charleston, S. C.; she left no issue. He married, second, October 9, 1881, Ellen, widow of Theodore Kimball, of Baltimore, Md., and daughter of Geo. M. Le Vigal, of Macon, Ga., and Lucy Pritchard, of Newbern, N. C., and left one child, Ellen St. James Fripp, of Savannah, Ga., born November 12, 1891.

IV. Cornelia Matilda Joyner married, August 4, 1829, Hon. R. de Treville.

V. James Joyner; removed to Georgia; married, and had Cornelia Joyner.

VI. John Joyner, died unmarried.

VII. Frank Joyner, died unmarried.

Rev. Dr. Brantley came from the North; married Margaret Joyner, and had:

I. —. Brantley, married Mr. Cress; issue two daughters. Removed to Europe.
II. Cornelia Brantley, married her cousin, Henry Grayson, and had:
I. Margaret Grayson, married . Martin; died.
II. Henry Grayson.
III. Matilda Grayson, died unmarried.
III. Rev. John Brantley, eminent Baptist minister, who went from Atlanta, Ga., to Baltimore, Md.; had issue, John Brantley, and a daughter, who married Morehead, of Charlotte, N. C.
IV. Hemans Brantley.
V. Beverly Brantley, a gallant young soldier of the Washington Light Infantry; killed first battle of Manassas.
a. Anne Perry Fripp, married, first, July, 1856, Col. Chas. Cochran Lee, C. S. A., and second, Matthew Moyle, of Cornwall, England; had by first marriage:
1. Annie Cornelia Lee, born July 1, 1857; married Geo. Matthew Moyle, of North Carolina, son of Matthew Moyle, of Cornwall, England.
2. Eula Elizabeth Lee, died in infancy.
3. Charles Florence Lee, married Jas. Harris, of Spartanburg, S. C., who died, leaving four children.
1. Mrs. Matthew Moyle had:
a. William Wallace Moyle, married Dora Cuthberson, of North Carolina.
b. John Moyle.
c. Susan Elizabeth Moyle.
d. Chas. Cochran Moyle.

Charles Florence Lee, born August 10, 1862; married, April 11, 1883, James Gilliam Harris, of Spartanburg, S. C., who died leaving the following children:
I. Jas. Gilliam Harris.
II. Laurence Benjamin Harris.
III. Eula Lee Harris.
IV. Bessie Lee Harris.
b. Elizabeth and Elvira Fripp had:
1. Harriet Fripp, married J. L. McWhirter, of Jonesville, S. C.
2. Annie Fripp, married G. H. Williams, who died

leaving one son.

3. Julia Fripp, married Geo. G. Boozer, now of Mississippi.
4. Norah Fripp, married Bailey.
5. Pinckney Fripp, married.

Capt. John Joyner, of the navy, married, and had Margaret Joyner, married Archibald Smith, son of John Smith and Elizabeth Williamson, son of Rev. Archibald Smith, of Dalkeith, Scotland, and Jane Wallace. Archibald Smith, married, second, Helen Zubly, daughter of David Zubly, son of Rev. John Joachim Zubly (a branch of Barnwell descend from last marriage). The late John Joyner Smith is a descendant of first marriage. His estate lay between Beaufort and Battery Point, in South Carolina.

John Smith and Elizabeth Williamson had:

I. Mary Smith.
II. Elizabeth Smith.
III. John Smith.
IV. Anne Smith, married Capt. Jno. McQueen.
V. Jane Smith, married Thomas Bourke.
VI. Sarah Smith, married Sir James Wright, Bart., son of Gov. Wright, of Georgia.
VII. Archibald Smith, married, first, Margaret Joyner; second, Helen Zubly.

STANYARNE

This ancient family, connected to so many of the best people in South Carolina, appears to be extinct in the male line.

Joseph Stanyarne, of St. Paul's Parish, S. C., born 1700, died April 7, 1772, married *Elizabeth, daughter of Rev. Archibald Stobo, and had:

*NOTE.—James Bulloch, Esq., married her sister, Jane Stobo, and had:
I. Archibald Bulloch, President of Georgia, 1776; married Mary DeVeaux.
II. Jane Bulloch, married Josiah Perry.
III. Christiana Bulloch, married Hon. Henry Yonge.

Rev. Archibald Stobo had, also, James and William Stobo.

There was a Mary Stanyarne, who married, October 29, 1753, Morton Brailsford, also a James Stanyarne, who married Mrs. Henrietta, relict of William Raven.

William Scott, Jr., married, on Tuesday, February 14, 1771, Elizabeth Legare. Also, a William Scott, married, October 9, 1765, Sarah, daughter of Joseph Brailsford. These are the dates in *Gazette*, they may nave married a few days prior.

I. James Stanyarne, married, June 25, 1772, Susannah, only daughter of Col. William Scott, of Revolutionary fame, and Mary, daughter of Richard and Florence Waring, of Pine Hill, St. George's Parish (James Stanyarne died 1784).

II. Archibald Stanyarne, married, May 19, 1759, Sarah, daughter of Thomas Elliott, of Stono; she died 1772.

III. Jane Stanyarne, married Charles Elliott, of "Sandy Hill," St. Paul's Parish.

IV. William Stanyarne.

V. Elizabeth Stanyarne, married Isaac Holmes.

VI. Joseph Stanyarne, married, December 13, 1773, Mary, widow of Thomas Hartley.

VII. Anne Stanyarne, died unmarried.

Jane Stanyarne, married Charles Elliott, and had:

I. Jane Riley Elliott, who married, 1782, Col. William Washington.

Elizabeth Stanyarne and Isaac Holmes had:

I. Isaac Holmes.

II. Elizabeth Holmes, married John R. Mathews.

James Stanyarne and Susannah Scott had:

I. Jane Stanyarne, died unmarried.

II. Mary Stanyarne.

III. James Stanyarne.

Mary Stanyarne married Daniel Flud (died December, 1849), and had:

(A.) Augustus Fludd.

(B.) Edward Flud., M. D., died unmarried.

(C.) Julia Caroline Flud.

(D.) Daniel Flud, M. D.

(E.) W. Ransom Davis Flud, married Martha Jane Boone, and had Thomas Boone Flud.

(F.) Milton Flud, died in childhood.

(G.) Julius Flud, died in childhood.

(A.) Augustus Fludd, married Matilda, daughter of Gov. James Burchill Richardson and Anna Sinkler, and had:

(a.) Augustsus Fludd, served with distinction throughout the War of Secession as 1st Lieut. in Schulz's Light Battery; died unmarried.

(b.) Jane Stanyarne Fludd, died unmarried.

(c.) William R. Fludd, who served most creditably as 2d Lieut. in Schulz's Light Artillery during the Confederate War, married Sarah, daughter of Dr. Matthew Moore and Martha Murray, and had:

1. Martha Fludd.
2. Augustus Fludd.
3. Matilda Fludd.
4. Sarah Fludd.

(d.) Mary Matilda Fludd, died unmarried.

(e.) Augusta Julia Fludd, died unmarried.

(C.) Julia Caroline Flud, who married William Burrows, had:

(a.) Elizabeth Screven Burrows, married Capt. Colclough.

(b.) Edward Flud Burrows, married Sallie Kennedy.

(c.) Mary Stanyarne Burrows, married Samuel Gaillard.

(D.) Daniel Flud: This eminent and well-beloved physician, after a useful and well-spent life, died in Summerville, S. C., March 24, 1896, in the 78th year of his age, transmitting as spotless as he had received it, the good name he had inherited. He was a firm believer in the precepts of the Great Physician, and by never-ending deeds of charity, known to the recipients and himself alone, and graced with tender manifestations of his sympathetic nature, beautifully exemplified the faith he professed; he was a true Carolinian and by his devotion to his State illustrated an exalted type of citizenship. He was a signer of the Ordinance of Secession, and upon the declaration of war following its adoption, promptly volunteered for the defense of his State, and, with the courage of his race, served faithfully throughout the struggle for Southern Independence, first in the Rutledge Mounted Rifles, and subsequently in the Charleston Light Dragoons. He married Harriet Hampton, daughter of John Christopher Schulz and Susan Flud Cantey, and had:

(a.) Susan Cantey Flud, died in childhood.

(b.) Edward Augustus Flud.

(c.) Daniel Flud.

(d.) William Ransom Flud, died in childhood.
(e.) William Ransom Flud, died in childhood.
(f.) Harriet Hampton Schulz Flud, died quite young.
(g.) Henry Cantey Flud.
(h.) Julia Caroline Flud.
(i.) Mary Stanyarne Flud.

III. James Stanyarne, married Elizabeth Wilson, and had:

(A.) Sarah Stanyarne, married Thomas Boone.
(B.) Joseph R. Stanyarne, married Mazyck.
(C.) William Stanyarne, married Mazyck.

DAVIS

Davis, Esq., came from England and settled on James River, Va. He married Miss Ransom, and had:

I. Capt. Wm. Ransom Davis,* born in Virginia; removed to South Carolina and settled on the Santee River, his estate lying in what are now known as Berkeley, Clarendon (or perhaps Sumter) and Orangeburg Counties, and taking in Vance's and Nelson's Ferries. He died on his estate, December, 1799. He served as Captain in the 5th Regiment of regular Continental Army, Marion's Brigade. Capt. Davis married, first, Eleanora de Nor-

*NOTE.—Besides Capt. William Ransom Davis, there were his sisters: Ann Davis, who died March 4, 1847, aged 90, married William Bay; and Letitia Davis, married Col. Henderson, from whom descend a family of Hunter, in the West.

Ann Davis and William Bay had:

I. Anna Isabella, married Rev. P. H. Falker.
II. Margaret Ransom Bay, died October 25, 1831; married Joseph Maybank.
III. Martha Davis Bay, born January 27, 1798; died at Columbia, S. C., December 18, 1877; married Alexander Herbemont.
IV. Sarah Davis Bay, married William Mayrant.
V. William Bay, went West.

Alexander Herbemont and Martha Davis Bay had one son, Alexander Herbemont, Jr., who died abroad; married Clara Isabel Fraser, daughter of John Fraser, of Charleston, S. C.; she died in Columbia, S. C., April 15, 1898. Alexander Herbemont, Sr., died November 24, 1865, in 73d year of his age. He was Clerk of Court of Appeals in Columbia, S. C., for more than twenty years, and United States Consul to Genoa, Italy.

Thomas Lehre and Mrs. Stanyarne had:

1. Col. Thomas Lehre.
2. Julia Mary Lehre, married John N. Davis.

velle, of Davis Hill, Statesburg, S. C., and had the following issue:

I. John Norval Davis.

II. Leonora Davis, married Col. James G. Spann.

III. William Ransom Davis, died in service during Seminole War, aged about 21 years.

John Norval Davis graduated from the South Carolina College in 1808; afterward took a course at Yale College, Conn., and returned to South Carolina, where he was elected to the State Senate. He married Julia Mary (or Martha) Lehre, daughter of Thomas Lehre and Mrs. James Stanyarne (*nee* Susannah Scott), only daughter of Col. Wm. Scott,* of the Revolutionary War, who married Mary, daughter of Richard and Florence Waring, of Pine Hill, St. George's Parish, S. C. (for issue by James Stanyarne, see Stanyarne).

John Norval Davis and Julia Mary (or Martha) Lehre, had:

1. Martha Mary Davis, married Thomas Priestly Cooper.
2. Julia Ransom Davis, married William Boone Richardson Mitchell.
3. Eleanora Norvelle Davis, married Charles Ryan Boyle, of St. Paul's Parish, Colleton Co., S. C.
4. William Ransom Davis, planter on Santee, entered Confederate States Army in Charleston Light Dragoons, was killed near Petersburg, Va., 1864, while skirmishing.
5. Thomasina Susan Davis, married Dr. Robert Witsell.

Martha Mary Davis and Thomas Priestly Cooper (son of Thomas Cooper, one of the Presidents of the South Carolina College,) had issue:

I. Thomas Cooper, died.

II. Julia Lehre Cooper, married, first, William Ingraham; second, Waddell; no issue.

III. Caroline Lehre Cooper, died in infancy.

Julia Ransom Davis and William Boone Richardson Mitchell had one surviving child, Wm. Rufus Mitchell, who married Mary Dangerfield, of Berkeley, and had Wm. Rufus Mitchell. W. B. Richardson Mitchell married, second, Mary, eldest daughter of Rev. Phillip Gadsden and Susan Hamilton, of Beaufort, S. C., and had:

*There were Scotts in South Carolina connected to Stanyarnes.

I. William Mitchell, died unmarried.

II. John Mitchell, married Ellen Harleston, of Charleston, and had issue.

Eleanora Norvelle Davis and Charles Ryan Boyle had:

I. Julia Lehre Boyle.

II. Charles Boyle, married Calista, daughter of Dr. Brownfield and Pauline Brazilia Sumter.*

III. John Davis Boyle.

Thomasina Susan Davis, married Dr. Robert Witsell, of Walterboro, S. C., and had:

1. Eleanora Norval Witsell, married Louis de Treville.
2. Thomasina Ann Witsell, married Jno. Charles Bulow.
3. Caroline Lehre Witsell, died when a child.

Eleanora Norval Witsell, born Walterboro, S. C., August 31, 1852; married Summerville, S. C., August 31, 1871, Louis, sixth son of Hon. Richard de Treville and Cornelia Matilda Joyner, daughter Capt. William Joyner, of the Continental Artillery, and had:

I. Thomasina Davis de Treville.

II. Wm. Ransom de Treville.

III. Jno. La Bouladrie de Treville.

IV. Eleanora Norval de Treville.

V. Marie Louise de Treville.

VI. Robert de Treville.

VII. Richard de Treville (see De Treville).

VIII. Cornelia Ellen de Treville.

IX. Robert de Treville.

*NOTE.—Mrs. Brownfield was born in Rio Janeiro, in 1812. She was the daughter of Col. Thomas Sumter, who was the son of Gen. Thomas Sumter, of Revolutionary fame. Her mother was Natalie de Lage, who was the daughter of the Countess d'Amblement de Lage. Natalie de Lage was a child at the Court when the storm of the French Revolution was about to burst. Her mother, with others of the nobility, were obliged to emigrate. The assured death of Marie Antoinette and Louis XVI. offered no hope to the nobility, and the Countess de Lage determined to seek an asylum in America. In this design she was aided by Madame Tallien. When the edict of Napoleon permitted the return of the nobility to France, on the same ship on which Natalie took passage was Col. Thomas Sumter, then Secretary of the American Legation at Paris. Col. Sumter and Natalie became acquainted on the passage, and before reaching France were engaged. Their marriage took place in Paris, in probably the year 1808. In 1809, Col. Sumter was made Minister to the Court of Brazil; and in Rio Janeiro, Mrs. Brownfield (Pauline Brazilica Sumter) was born; and when about thirteen years of age came to this State with her parents, and spent some years on the family estate near Statesburg. In 1866, she removed to Summerville, where she died in 1889, leaving a large family.

X. Thomas Lehre de Treville.

XI. Daniel Flud de Treville.

Thomasina Ann Witsell, married *John Charles, second son of Thomas Lehre Bulow and Martha Caroline, daughter of Alwyn Ball and Esther McClellan, and had: Julia Carlita Bulow.

Leonora Davis and Col. James G. Spann had issue:

I. Eleanora Norval Spann, married Richard Charles, son of ex-Gov. James Burchill Richardson.

II. Ransom Davis Spann, died recently.

III. Mary Spann, married John Athol Murray.

IV. James G. Spann, married Elizabeth Richardson.

Capt. Wm. Ransom Davis, married, second, Martha Cantey, of Kershaw, S. C., sister of a wife of the first Wade Hampton, and had:

I. Warren Ransom Davis, member of Congress, poet, Solicitor, etc. (see O'Neal's Bench and Bar).

II. Martha Maria Davis, married John Ewing Calhoun, first cousin and brother-in-law of John C. Calhoun, the Vice-President.

III. Henry Davis, died young.

Martha Maria Davis and Jno. Ewing Calhoun had:

I. Jno. Ewing Calhoun, died.

II. Martha Maria Calhoun, died.

III. Wm. Ransom Calhoun, unmarried (Capt. and Col.).

IV. Susan Calhoun.

V. Jno. Ewing Calhoun.

VI. Florence Calhoun, died young.

VII. Warren Davis Calhoun, died young.

VIII. Henry Davis Calhoun, born September 22, 1838; died March, 1866; was First Lieut. Ferguson's Light Battery, C. S. A.

IX. Edward Boiseau Calhoun, born April 28, 1841; married Sarah Calhoun Norwood, of Abbeville, S. C.

Wm. Ransom Calhoun, born July 22, 1827; graduated from West Point; appointed Aid to Gov. Richard I. Manning; was Secretary of Legation and acting Minister to France; soon after Secession was commissioned Captain in First S. C. Artil-

*Killed a few months after, in an altercation in Summerville, S. C., in 1876.

lery (Regulars)—became Colonel, commanded at Fort Sumter for a while, and on September 5th, 1862, was killed in duel with his Lieutenant Colonel.

Edward Boiseau Calhoun served through the war in Lucas' Battalion of Artillery and attained rank of Captain. He and Sarah C. Norwood had issue:

1. Martha Maria Calhoun.
2. Sarah Louise Calhoun, married Allen McLee Schoen, of Richmond, Va., and had Edward Calhoun Schoen.
3. Floride Bonneau Calhoun.
4. Willie N. Calhoun.

✓ ELLIS, OF SOUTH CAROLINA

It is said that the first of this Ellis family was a landed proprietor in County of Durham, England; and tradition says that he was accosted by a fortune-teller, who asked to be allowed to tell his fortune, which was permitted, when it was foretold he would meet adverse circumstances and emigrate to America. In a few years he did so, and on board ship found a Bible with the name of Mary Wilkinson* in it; he made her acquaintance and they became man and wife, and had a son, Edmund Ellis, who married, and had the following children:

I. Richard Ellis,† married, first, Sarah Hogg; second, Elizabeth Greene.
II. Edmund Ellis, (?) married Elizabeth Capers, daughter of Thomas Capers; moved North.
III. Margaret Ellis, married Nathaniel Adams, Sr., of South Carolina, and had, besides others, Nathaniel Adams, who moved to Georgia, and married Annie Bolton.

NOTE.—Richard Ellis was a resident and owner of two tracts of land during and at the close of the Revolutionary War, known as the "Old Quarter House Tract" and "New Quarter House Tract." When he left Charleston to join the American army, he delivered to the care of James Rugge his papers, &c. (see *Rugge* vs. *Ellis*). In Ellis *vs.* Ellis it appears that Richard Ellis made his will 17th June, 1802, and that his four sons, Charles, Richard, Edmund, William, and two daughters, Elizabeth and

*Murdered by Indians.

†Richard Ellis joined the Colonists, but had a brother who remained loyal to the Crown; he was banished, suffered under confiscation act, and moved North.

Sarah, and his wife, Sarah, but after making his will, before his death another son was born, Wilkinson Ellis, who died before coming to maturity. Richard Ellis, testator, died October 20, 1804; and it further appears that Sarah Ellis or De Treville, was only a sister of the half-blood. Now, as Richard Ellis married twice, he probably married Sarah Hogg first; as in the *South Carolina Gazette*, April 28, 1784, we find that on "Thursday last, Miss Elizabeth Green was married to Richard Ellis." So that it is likely that Sarah and Elizabeth Ellis were issue of the Greene marriage, and that Richard, Charles, Edmund, William and Wilkinson Ellis were children of marriage to Miss Hogg—unless it be that Sarah and Wilkinson were by last marriage. At any rate, it is shown in the De Treville *vs.* Ellis case that Sarah de Treville was daughter of Richard Ellis and half-sister of Richard W. Ellis; and in same case that William Ellis, brother of above, died unmarried, in 1825. It also shows marriage of Sarah to De Treville, and that she was sister of half blood (see Reynolds *vs.* Executors of Calder).

Richard Ellis,* eldest son of Edmund Ellis and brother of Margaret Adams, married Sarah Hogg,† and had:

I. Charles Ellis, married Martha Dahlgren.
II. Richard W. Ellis, married, 1841, Sarah Witter, daughter Jonathan Witter.
III. William Ellis, died, unmarried, 1825.
IV. Edmund Ellis.
V. Elizabeth Ellis, married David Adams (?).
VI. Sarah Ellis, half-sister of above, married Robert L. de Treville.
VII. Wilkinson Ellis.

Richard W. Ellis and Sarah Witter had:

1. Stephen G. Ellis, married Juliana S. Baynard.
2. Robert de Treville Ellis.
3. Edmund Ellis, M. D., in 1841, married Sarah Ellen Perreyclear.
4. Thomas B. Ellis, married, first, Ella Rhodes; second, Julia Hall.
5. Caroline de Treville Ellis, married Thomas S. Baynard.

Charles Ellis and Martha Dahlgren, sister of the inventor, Dahlgren, Jr., had:

1. Henry Ellis, attorney at law, Orangeburg, S. C.
2. Elizabeth Ellis.

Stephen G. Ellis, son of Richard W. Ellis and Sarah Witter,*

*Went into Revolutionary War. "He (Richard Ellis) married, second, Thursday last, Miss Elizabeth Green."—*S. C. Gazette*, April 28, 1784.

†"Died, September 20, 1783, Mrs. Sarah Ellis."—*S. C. Gazette*.

*The Witters of James Island descend from Judith Manigault.

married Juliana S. Baynard, daughter of Archibald Calder Baynard, and widow of Rev. Wilson Edward Hall, who died about 1844; son of Dr. Wm. Hall, of Charleston; son of that Capt. Wm. Hall who commanded the Brig Notre Dame, which with two other brigs captured two and destroyed one of seven British war vessels, the rest escaping. Stephen G. Ellis and Juliana S. Baynard had:

1. Richard A. Ellis, of Barnwell, attorney at law, who already is a man of some note.
2. Sarah G. Ellis, married E. A. Furse.
3. Martha E. Ellis, married C. C. Baggs, of Liberty Co., Ga., and had, beside others:
   I. Lavinia Baggs, married Wm. H. Harper.
   II. Daisy Baggs.
4. Caroline de Treville Ellis.
5. J. L. Ellis, married Anna Wilson, and had:
   A. J. L. Ellis.
6. Thomas B. Ellis, Jr., married Lizzie Harper.
7. Calder B. Ellis, married Fannie Vincent.
8. Dr. E. W. Ellis, married Miss Heathe, of Heatheville, Barnwell Co., S. C.
9. Cecelia F. Ellis, married Charles B. Dunbar, and had:
   I. Stephen Dunbar.
   II. Charles Dunbar and others.
10. Lavinia Ellis.

Dr. Edmund Ellis, died 1878 or '9; married Ellen Perreyclear, and had:

1. Richard W. Ellis, married Miss Rhodes, and had
   A. Cecil Ellis.
2. Thomas B. Ellis, of James Island, S. C., married daughter of Dr. Lebby, of James Island.
3. Rosa Ellis, married Benton.
4. Sarah Ellis, married Andrew Hasell.

Thomas B. Ellis, brother of Dr. Edmund Ellis, married, first, Ella Rhodes, and had:

1. George Ellis, married.
2. Margaret Ellis, married Etheridge, of Alabama, son of Hon.——. Etheridge.

Thomas B. Ellis, married, second, Julia Hall, half-sister of R. A. Ellis, Esq., and daughter of Rev. W. E. Hall, Jr., son of Capt. William Hall, of the Navy during Revolutionary War. He served through the whole of the late war and lost his foot at Averysboro, N. C.

Rev. Wilson Edward Hall and Juliana S. Baynard had:

I. Wilson Edward Hall, a brave soldier of C. S. Navy, at battle of Port Royal; married Laura D. Roberts, and had Tillie Hall, married W. L. Lagerquist.

II. Julia A. Hall, married P. B. Ellis; no issue.

BAYNARD

This family, of Edisto Island, were planters and well known people. Thomas Baynard married Sarah Calder, daughter of Archibald Calder, who apparently by the records was a son of Miss Bailey and a Mr. Calder, of Edisto, sister of Henry Bailey, who died 1774. Sarah Calder was half-sister of Archibald John Calder, who left a son, A. G. Calder, who died, April 15, 1804, and of Mrs. E. Mikell, mother of Ephraim Mikell, Jr., and of Ann Seabrook, wife of Gabriel Seabrook, Elizabeth, wife of Mingo Mackie, previously wife of Wm. Baynard, and Mary Ann, wife of Wm. Seabrook. The Guerard family of Georgia intermarried twice into that of Baynard. We can imagine the wealth and great style of these planters of St. Helena Parish, Port Royal and Edisto Island, and we see by records how patriotic they were during the Revolution. Thomas Baynard and Sarah Calder had:

I. Archibald Calder Baynard, a graduate of South Carolina College with second honor, about 1816, and then elected to the South Carolina Legislature; died 1862.

II. Wm. M. Baynard.

III. Ephraim Mikell Baynard, died after the war, aged 80 years, one of the wealthiest men of his section, owning 600 slaves and many plantations. Left by deed of trust to Charleston College $160,000 in city of Charleston scrip, which has been the chief support of the college.*

IV. Jno. Baynard.

Archibald Calder Baynard, son of Thomas Baynard and Sarah Calder, married Martha Chaplain, grand-daughter of John Chaplain, and left issue:

1. Juhana S. Baynard, married, first, Rev. Wilson Edward Hall; second, Stephen G. Ellis (see Ellis).†

* Will of John Chaplain, 1765.

†Robert G. Willingham, D. D., of Richmond, is a nephew of Mrs. Ellis.

2. Thomas S. Baynard, married Caroline de Treville Ellis, and had Julia M. Baynard, who married Geo. A. Rhodes.
3. Rev. Calder A. Baynard.
4. Cecilia M. Baynard, married Thomas H. Willingham.
5. Sarah Calder Baynard, married Dr. James Stoney Lawton, first cousin of Gen. Lawton, of Savannah
6. Elizabeth Baynard, married Benj. L. Willingham.
7. Florence Baynard, married W. G. Willingham.

Wm. M. Baynard, brother of Archibald C. and Ephraim Mikell Baynard, had:

1. Ephraim M. Baynard, Jr.
2. Joseph S. Baynard.
3. Wm. Baynard; in Heyward's company, killed in skirmish in Georgia, 1863, near Ogeechee River.

Hon. Jno. Guerard married Sarah C. Baynard, second daughter of Wm. E. Baynard, of South Carolina. Wm. Percy Guerard married Adelaide Scott Baynard, fourth daughter of Wm. Edings Baynard, Esq., of South Carolina, and sister of Hon. Joseph S. Baynard, of Guyton, Ga., and had:

I. Wm. Edings Guerard.
II. Geo. Cuthbert Guerard, married Inez B. Guyton.
III. Sophia Percy Guerard.
IV. Anna Baynard Guerard.
V. Lucile Guerard.
VI. Ethel Guerard.
VII. Adelaide Guerard.
VIII. Nathalie Guerard.
IX. Ruth Guerard.
X. John M. Guerard.

YONGE, OF SOUTH CAROLINA

Hon. Robert Yonge, Associate Justice of South Carolina 1733-1744. His Majesty grants, 6th April, 1733, to Robert Yonge 500 acres in Colleton Co., S. C. His residence was at Torgordo, where he died, September 9, 1758. He married Elizabeth , and had:

I. Lydia Yonge, married Fuller.
II. Francis Yonge, Sr., of Torgordo, died November 4,

1780; married, first, Sarah Clifford, 6th December, 1752, and had:

1. Eliza Yonge, married, first, Wilkinson; second, Peter Porcher.
2. Francis Yonge, of St. Paul's, died 1788; married Sarah Legare.
3. Yonge.

Francis Yonge, Sr., married, second, Susanna, and had:

1. Sarah Hope Yonge.
2. Harriet P. Yonge.

Eliza Yonge and Peter Porcher had Francis George Porcher, M. D., who married, first, Sarah Julia Pelot; second, Susan Postell, by whom he had: Francis James Porcher, married Abbey Louisa Gilman, and had:

I. Louisa Porcher.
II. Francis Yonge Porcher.
III. Wilmot DeSaussure Porcher.

Francis Yonge, of St. Paul's, and Sarah Legare had: Sarah M., Elizabeth, Mary and Susanna Yonge. By Lydia, his second wife, had:

I. Margaret Yonge, christened September 18, 1729.
II. Francis Yonge, christened July 21, 1730; died October 26, 1730.
III. Charles Yonge, christened October 6, 1732.

Hon. Francis Yonge, Surveyor General of South Carolina, 1717-1719; Member of King's Council, 1717-1719; Agent of South Carolina in England, 1722-26; Chief Justice South Carolina, 1721; died 1733 or 1734. "In 1732, Francis Yonge speaks of his wife Lydia and cozen Robert Yonge." In 1734, Lydia and Robert Yonge, attorneys for Francis.

Hon. Francis Yonge married, first, the widow of Geo. Fletcher, of Barbadoes, who died December 7, 1721. His second wife was Lydia. By Mrs. Fletcher, he had:

I. Hon. Henry Yonge, Surveyor General of Georgia, 1760; Member of His Hajesty's Council. He married twice: first, 1758, Eliza Bellinger, one of the sisters of Wm. Bellinger, who was nephew of Landgrave Edmund Bellinger (died April 9, 1774), and had:

1. Henry Yonge, married.
2. Ann Agnes Yonge, married Abraham Jackson, brother of Gov. James Jackson, and had:

I. Anna Jackson, married Gov. Schley, and had:
1. Henry Schley.
3. Elizabeth Yonge.
4. Dr. William John Yonge, married Hon. Frances Pitt, of Shropshire, England.

Hon. Henry Yonge married, second, Christiana Bulloch (September 14, 1744), daughter of James Bulloch, Esq., had no issue. He had grant of land, 1734-35-40. Resided at Williston, S. C. 1758, in Georgia, advertised for sale 500 acres on Skidaway Island.

II. Jane Yonge.

BREWTON

Col. Miles Brewton, Powder Receiver of the Province of South Carolina and distinguished in other ways, married, first, Susannah (born Pinckney), widow of Capt. Matthew Porter; she was born in 1671; died 1741. Married, second, Mary Legare, widow of James Payne. By his first marriage Col. Brewton's issue was as follows:

I. Robert Brewton, born 1697; died 1759; married, first, Millicent, daughter of John Bulloch and Mary——; married, second, Mary Loughton. Issue by first marriage:
(A.) Robert Brewton, who married Elleanor ——.
(B.) Mary Brewton, born 1720; married, 1742, Joseph Jones, of St. John's, Colleton, S. C.
(C.) Elizabeth Brewton, born 1724; married, 1741, Mumford Milner.

Issue by second marriage:
(A.) Miles Brewton, born 1731; married Mary Izard.
(B.) Frances Anne Brewton, born 1733; married Charles Pinckney; died 1750.
(C.) Rebecca Brewton, born 1737; married Jacob Motte.
(D.) Susannah Brewton, died 1755.

Mary Brewton, who married Joseph Jones, of St. John's, Colleton, had:
(a.) Joseph Jones, died.
(b.) John Jones.
(c.) Millicent Jones, married John Colcock, 1768.

II. Jane Brewton, married —— Bruce.

III. Elizabeth Brewton, married Edward Croft.
IV. Ruth Brewton, married Maj. William Pinckney.
V. Mary Brewton, married Thomas Dale.
VI. Rebecca Brewton, married, 1734, Jordan Roche.

The Brewton family is allied to the following families: Pinckneys, Jones, Izards, Mottes, and others, and has as descendants a branch of Middleton, Pinckney, Alston, etc. To a branch of Pinckney was connected by marriage the eminent families of Laurens and Ramsay of South Carolina. (See *S. C. Genealogical Magazine*, April, 1901.)

JONES, of Liberty and McIntosh Counties, Ga.

This line springs from Joseph Jones, of St. John's, Colleton, S. C., whose son, Maj. John Jones, was killed at the siege of Savannah, while bravely storming the ramparts of the enemy. Among his descendants are: the eminent historian, Col. Charles Colcock Jones, the well known writer and professor, Dr. Joseph Jones, of Tulane University, La., Rev. John Jones, Rev. Charles Colcock Jones, Capt. Joseph Jones, Charles Edgeworth Jones, writer and historian, and others. This family is connected to the Brewtons, Pinckneys, Mottes, Alstons, Middletons, Sharpes, Dunwodys, Wests, Munroes and many others of South Carolina and Georgia, as the following descent will show:

Descent of the Captain Joseph Jones Family, of Liberty County, Ga.

Col. Miles Brewton married, first, Susannah, widow of Capt. Mathew Porter, and had:

I. Robert Brewton, born 1697; married, first, Millicent, daughter of John and Mary Bulloch; second, Mary Loughton.
II. Jane Brewton, married —— Bruce.
III. Elizabeth Brewton, married Edward Croft.
IV. Ruth Brewton, married Maj. William Pinckney.
V. Mary Brewton, married Thomas Dale.
VI. Rebecca Brewton, married, 1734, Jordan Roche.

Robert and Millicent Brewton had Mary, who married, 1720, Joseph Jones (who died 1751), had John Jones, born 1720.

John Jones married Miss Pinckney, daughter of Wm. Pinckney, of South Carolina, 1742, and had:

I. Millicent Jones, born 1745; died April 23, 1829; married John Colcock, of Charleston, S. C., 1768 (who died August 21, 1783).

II. Maj. John Jones, born January 20, 1749; married Mary Sharpe, December 28, 1769, and had:

1. Mary, born 1770.
2. John, born 1772; died March 28, 1805, at Liberty Hall plantation.
3. Millicent, born 1774.
4. Hannah, born 1778.
5. Joseph, born November 6, 1779.

Mary Sharpe, wife of Maj. John Jones, born November 2, 1753, was the daughter of James Sharpe and Mary Newton; they had two daughters, Mary and Hannah Sharpe.

NOTE.—On the 28th past, Mr. John Jones was married to Mrs. Mary Sharp, daughter of James Sharp Esq., of Pon Pon.—*South Carolina Gazette*, January 11, 1770. Says Mr. C. J. Colcock:

I have now before me two copies of the *South Carolina Gazette*, of dates November 1, 1768, and January 13, 1775. From the first I copy, "Married, John Colcock, Esq., to Miss Millicent Jones, daughter of Mr. John Jones, deceased." The second paper contains a mention of the election of John Colcock to the South Carolina Assembly, from the district between the Broad and Saluda.

From page 761 of the second volume of McCrady's History of South Carolina, I quote: "But under all the circumstances of the time, we cannot but look upon the appearance of such prominent lower country men as Edward Rutledge, returned from 96, and John Colcock and Rowland Rugeby from the district between the Broad and Saluda," etc. Mr. Salley, Secretary of the South Carolina branch of the Historical Society, has convinced me by a personal interview, and references offered by him, that instead of John Jones, the paper should have published Millicent Jones, daughter of Joseph Jones, and sister of John Jones, killed at the siege of Savannah.

The Jones family is not descended from the Pinckney family, unless one of the three wives of Col. Miles Brewton was a Miss Pinckney. By the marriage of Mary Brewton to Joseph Jones, and of her aunt, Ruth Brewton, to William Pinckney, a connection was established between the families of Jones, Pinckney and Colcock.

I believe what Mr. A. S. Salley published in his account of the genealogy of the Brewton family and their descendants, is reliable, and would advise you to procure a copy of the *South Carolina Genealogical and Historical Magazine*, published April, 1901.

Hannah Sharpe married William West, and had:

I. Mary, married James Robarts. No issue.

II. A daughter, married John Stewart.

III. Dr. Charles West, Sr.

Mary Jones, daughter Maj. John Jones, married, first, Joel Walker, no issue; married, second, Nathaniel Law, and had one daughter, Harriet Law, who married Mr. Handley, son of Gov. Handley, of Georgia, and had:

I. William Handley, no issue.

II. George Handley, no issue.

III. Mary Handley, married Henry Law, of Savannah, Ga., and had a large family.

John Jones (eldest son of Maj. John Jones), married, first, Elizabeth Stewart, and had:

1. Elizabeth Jones, born 1794; married Col. Wm. Maxwell.
2. Mary Newton Jones, born 1796, no issue.
3. John Jones, born 1798, no issue.

Col. William Maxwell's mother was a sister of Senator John Elliott, of Liberty Co., Ga. Capt. Maxwell commanded a United States gunboat in the war of 1812-15.

John Jones, eldest son of Maj. John Jones, married, second, August 4, 1801, Susannah Hyrne Girardeau (she died July 1, 1810, was the daughter of John Girardeau and Hannah Splatt), and had:

1. Peter Girardeau Jones, born 1802, no issue.
2. Susannah H. Jones, born 1803.
3. Rev. Charles Colcock Jones, born December 20, 1804; died March 16, 1863.

Ann Le Sade married Peter Girardeau and came to America after the revocation of the Edict of Nantes, 1621, and settled in Carolina; they were the grand-parents of Susannah Hyrne Girardeau.

Susannah Hyrne Jones married, first, Jas Audley Maxwell; second, Mr. Cummings, no issue. By Maxwell marriage had:

I. Charles Edward Maxwell, died in early manhood.

II. Laura E. Maxwell, married Rev. D. L. Buttolph, and had:

I. *Charles Edward Maxwell Buttolph.

II. James D. Buttolph.

III. William Smythe Buttolph.

IV. Susan Mary Buttolph.

V. Wallace Stuart Buttolph, died August 26, 1899.

Rev. Charles Colcock Jones married his cousin, Mary Jones, daughter of Capt. Joseph Jones, of Liberty Co., Ga., and had:

1. Col. Charles Colcock Jones, born October 28, 1831.

*Note.—Margaret Bellinger, daughter of Edmund Bellinger, first Landgrave, married Nicholas Bohun, and had Margaret Bohun, who married John Girardeau.

*Residence Summerville, Augusta, Ga.

2. Dr. Joseph Jones, born 1833; died, 1896, New Orleans, La.
3. Mary Sharpe Jones, born 1835; died, 1889; buried New Orleans, La.

Col. Charles Colcock Jones married, first, November 9, 1858, Ruth Whitehead, of Burke Co., Ga. (born May 31, 1837; died July 7, 1861), and had:

1. Julia Berrien Jones, born November 18, 1859; died July 2, 1861.
2. Ruth Jones, born June 25, 1861; married Rev. S. B. Carpenter, February 13, 1890, and had:
   I. Eva Berrien Carpenter, born 1891.
   II. Josephine Clarence Carpenter, born 1895.

Col. Charles Colcock Jones married, second, Eva Berrien Eve, of Augusta, Ga. (born November 9, 1841; died October 25, 1890), and had:

1. Charles Edgeworth Jones, born July 27, 1867.

Col. Jones died, July 19, 1893, at his home, Summerville, near Augusta, Ga. He was in command of all of the siege artillery of the Georgia and Florida coast during the war of 1861-65; an eminent lawyer, historian and author, standing at the top of every department of life.

Dr. Joseph Jones, M. D., late of New Orleans, married, first, Miss Davis,* of Augusta, Ga., and had:

1. Dr. Stanhope Jones, of New Orleans, La.
2. Susan Caroline Jones.
3. Charles Colcock Jones.
4. Mary Cuthbert Jones.

Dr. Joseph Jones married, second, Susan Polk, daughter of Gen. Leonidas Polk, "the fighting Bishop" of the Civil War, 1861-65, and had:

1. Francis D. Jones.
2. Dr. Hamilton Jones.
3. Laura Jones.

Dr. Jones was most eminent in his profession as practitioner, teacher, chemist, anatomist, microscopist, writer and author; at the head of the State Board of Health, and an authority in medical affairs not only in America but also in Europe. He died at New Orleans, aged sixty-odd years.

Mary Sharpe Jones married Rev. Robert Quarterman Mallard, D. D., and had:

*Descended from the Habershams, Clays and Cuthberts (see Cuthbert).

I. Mary Jones Mallard.

II. Georgia Maxwell Mallard, married Mr. Seago, had issue.

III. Charles Colcock Mallard.

Capt. Joseph Jones (youngest son of Maj. John Jones and Mary Sharpe), married, first, Mary Maybank, and had Joseph Maybank Jones, no issue.

Capt. Joseph Jones married, second, 1806, Sarah Anderson (daughter of David Anderson and Mary Cooper, who was born June 30, 1783, Sumter District, S. C.), and had eight children, six dying in infancy; the two who lived were:

I. Mary, married Rev. Charles Colcock Jones, D. D.

II. Rev. John Jones, married Jane Adaline Dunwody (daughter of Col. James Dunwody and Elizabeth West Smith), and had:

1. James Dunwody Jones, born May 1, 1842.
2. Mary Elizabeth Jones, born 1849; died 1852.
3. John Carolyn Jones, born 1852.
4. Joseph Henry Jones, born 1854.

Rev. John Jones was an eminent Presbyterian divine, and served as Chaplain of the 8th Regiment of Georgia Volunteers in 1861; also Chaplain of the Legislature and Senate of Georgia for twenty-three years, and was buried with senatorial honors. Born November 15, 1815, Liberty Co., Ga.; died November 26, 1893, Atlanta, Ga.

James Dunwody Jones married, November 2, 1870, Mary Cornelia Ashley (daughter of Col. Wm. Percy Morford Ashley and Fanny Baisden Dunham), and had:

1. John Ashley Jones, born August 27, 1871.
2. Fanny Adaline Jones, born October 21, 1872.
3. James Logan Jones, born April 12, 1874.
4. Rosabell Margaret Jones, born January 12, 1876.
5. Ruby Cornelia Jones, born December 18, 1877.
6. Elizabeth Munro Jones, born February 17, 1881; died April 29, 1885.
7. Mary Dunwody Jones, born January 25, 1883.
8. Jane Dunham Jones, born February 17, 1885.
9. William Percy Jones, born August 4, 1888.

John Ashley Jones married Maude Allgood, 1898. Fanny Adaline Jones married Malcolm Cunningham, 1900. Rosabell Margaret Jones married Capt. Wm. Calhoun Massey, 1899.

Maj. John Jones (son of John Jones and Miss Pinckney),

daughter of Maj. William Pinckney, of Charleston, S. C.), was born Charleston, January 20, 1749, and was killed in the "forlorn-hope" charge on the Spring Hill battery, siege of Savannah, Ga., October 9, 1779. He was an Aide-de-camp on the staff of Gen. McIntosh. Maj. Jones came to Georgia in 1774, and did a large importing mercantile business in the then flourishing town of Sunbury, Liberty Co., Ga., and was also a large planter of rice—his plantation is still known as Rice Hope. There will be found in White's Historical Collections of Georgia and also in Col. C. C. Jones' History of Georgia, a full account of the services of Maj. John Jones in the War of the Revolution. I here append a letter from Maj. John Jones to his wife while he was in camp at Savannah, Ga.:

CAMP BEFORE SAVANNAH, GA., 5th October, 1779.

My dear Polly: The enemy still being obstinate, and not knowing how long they may continue so, I must beg the favor of you to send off Ishmael immediately, on Black Sloven, with a pair of thick breeches, my blue coat, and three ruffled shirts, without stocks, and one pair of black silk breeches. Ishmael is to go no farther than Mrs. McPherson's at Indian Land, where Jacob will meet him. I have sent home my English horse; he has been very sick. The time I have been absent from you appears almost an age. As soon as this important affair is over, I shall immediately return home.

Your ever affectionate husband, JOHN JONES.

There is a street in Savannah, Ga., named in honor of Maj. Jones.

The widow of Maj. John Jones married Maj. Phillip Lowe (a cousin of Gen. Nathaniel Greene), also of the American Revolution, and had Eliza Greene Lowe, born 1785, in Liberty Co., Ga.; married, first, Charles Walker, no issue. Married, second, James Robarts, and had Mary Green Robarts, born 1805; died December 2, 1878. Married, third, David Robarts, and had:

I. Joseph Robarts, born 1811; died 1858.

II. Louisa J. Robarts, born 1813; died 1896.

Joseph Robarts married Sophia L. Gibson, of St. Mary's, Ga. (daughter Wm. Gibson and Mary Fatio), and had:

I. Mary Sophia Robarts, born 1838.

II. Lilla Walton Robarts, born 1840; unmarried.

III. Ellen Douglas Robarts, born 1842.

IV. Joseph Jones Robarts, born 1843; died from wound in battle, 1864.

Mary Sophia Robarts married T. D. Adams, and had:

I. Lill Ellen Adams.
II. Zadie Douglas Adams.
III. T. D. Adams, Jr.

Ellen Douglas Robarts married Dr. A. B. Brumby, and had:

I. Mary Brevard Brumby.
II. Louis Joseph Brumby.
III. Richard Brumby, died.
IV. Lilla Livingston Brumby.
V. Sophia Adams Brumby.
VI. Hattie Davison Brumby, born 1876.
VII. Ernestine Alberta Brumby.

Descent of Sarah Anderson.

She was the second wife of Capt. Joseph Jones and mother of Mary (Mrs. C. C. Jones) and Rev. John Jones, D. D. Her mother was Mary Cooper, daughter of John Cooper and Miss Merian or Meriam; she was full sister of Col. John Cooper, who commanded a squadron of cavalry at the siege of Savannah, Ga., October 9, 1779, and was severely wounded in the battle of October 9th. Col. John Cooper was the grand-father of Col. Charles P. Cooper, of Jacksonville, Fla. This family hold that they are a collateral branch of the same root from which came Sir Anthony Ashley Cooper (son of Sir John Cooper), and afterward created by Charles II. of England Earl of Shaftsbury (see English history). Sir John Cooper married Miss Ashley, daughter of Lord Ashley, of England. The Ashleys of Georgia hold that they are a collateral branch of the root of the Ashley line. Mary Cornelia Ashley married James Dunwody Jones. Her great-grand-father was Wm. Ludovic Ashley; her grand-father, Wm. Anthony Ashley; her father, Col. Wm. Percy Morford Ashley; and the Coopers of the old line claimed relationship with the old Ashleys. Hence two old families are reunited in the children of James Dunwody Jones and Mary Cornelia Ashley.

Col. John Cooper married Miss Merriam, who was probably a daughter of John Merriam, who went from England to Georgia with the celebrated Rev. Geo. Whitfield, in 1739, and who became a teacher at Bethesda Orphans Home. These

Merriams were probably rich, but such was the enthusiasm of John Merriam that he determined to go with Whitfield to Georgia.

Capt. Joseph Jones married, third, Elizabeth Screven Hart,* of Sunbury, Liberty Co., Ga., and had:

1. Charles Berrien, born November 11, 1820; died May, 1856.
2. Evelyn Elouisa, born June 16, 1822; died November 21, 1849.
3. Henry Hart, born December 2, 1823; died February 13, 1892.
4. James Newton, born September 25, 1825; died October 6, 1854.
5. Emma Adelaide, born August 23, 1827.
6. Hetty Augusta, born February 15, 1829; died October, 1856.
7. Edward Joseph, born April 10, 1830; died October, 1832.
8. Andrew Maybank, born October 16, 1831; died September 13, 1895.
9. Edwin West, born September 11, 1833; killed in battle, October 12, 1862.
10. Thomas Screven, born August 28, 1835; died September 16, 1837.
11. Elliott Maxwell, born January 6, 1837; died July 6, 1838.
12. Josephine Elizabeth Caroline, born May 13, 1839; died October, 1856.
13. Helen Louisa, born September 23, 1841.
14. Laura Matilda, born May 16, 1843; died April, 1853.

Charles Berrien Jones married Marion Anderson, of Liberty Co., Ga., January 26, 1843, and had:

1. Charles Marion, Jr., born 1844; married.
2. Mary Genevieve, born 1845; married Finn Moore, and had issue.
3. William Anderson, born 1846; married Kate B. King, and have issue.

*Elizabeth Screven Hart was daughter of John Hart and Mary Screven, daughter of James Screven and Mary Hyrne Smith, a daughter of Thomas Smith, son of second Landgrave (see Screven and book of James B. Heyward).

4. Sarah Anderson, born 1847; married Tilman White, and have issue.
5. Joseph Maxwell, born 1848.

Evelyn Elouisa Jones married, first, Joseph Anderson, January 24, 1843, and had:

I. Elizabeth Mary Anderson, born 1844; married Dr. Raymond Harris, Sr.; no issue.
II. Evelyn Josephine Anderson, born 1846; married James Ross, and had two children.

Mrs. E. E. Anderson married, second, her cousin, John Hart, and had a large family.

Col. Henry Hart Jones married, May 6, 1846, Abby Dowse, of Burke Co., Ga. (both dead), and had:

1. Joseph Henry, Ella, James, died in infancy.
2. Eliza, married Cooper Winn, and had issue.
3. Stewart, married Miss Rogers, of Macon, Ga.
4. John Sturgis, married Miss Rogers, of Macon, Ga., and has issue.
5. Augusta, married, first, Mr. Mitchel, and had issue; married, second, Cooper Winn.
6. Henry Jones, married, and has issue.
7. Minnie Jones, died in infancy.

James Newton Jones married, 1851, Sarah Jane Norman, of Liberty Co., Ga., and had Ellen Elizabeth, who married G. B. Dettre, of Norristown, Pa., and had two daughters.

Emma Adelaide Jones married, June 16, 1846, Dr. Stephen N. Harris, of Liberty Co., Ga., and had:

I. Mary Louisa Harris, unmarried.
II. Emma Adelaide Harris, married Harry Ghalager, and had issue.
III. Stephen Raymond Harris, married, and has issue.
IV. Evelyn Elizabeth Harris, married Wm. Barnard, and left issue.
V. R. B. Harris, married.

Emma Adelaide Jones married, second, November 10, 1858, Columbus Harris, brother of first husband, and had:

I. Susan Josephine, married twice, and has issue.
II. Wm. Joseph Harris.
III. James Newton Harris.
IV. Walter Starnes Harris.

Hetty Augusta Jones married, 1849, Dr. Troup Maxwell (died yellow fever, Key West, Fla., October, 1856), and had:

I. George Troup Maxwell.
II. Elliott Maxwell.
III. Augusta Maxwell, married a Mr. Maxwell (her cousin), has issue.

Col. Andrew Maybank Jones married, first, May, 1855, Evelyn Harrison, of Florida, and had:

1. Robert Harrison Jones, married Susan Baker, daughter Judge Baker, of Jacksonville, Fla., and have issue.
2. Mary Lee Jones, married E. Hamilton; has issue.
3. Evelyn Sanderson Jones, married, and has issue.

Col. A. M. Jones married, second, 1870, Miss Electra Dodge, and had:

1. Annie Welford Jones, married Ed. Fuller; has issue.
2. Electra Jones.
3. Josephine Jones.
4. Andrew Maybank Jones, Jr.

Edwin West Jones married, 1857, Elizabeth Howitt Le Hardy; no issue.

Josephine Elizabeth Caroline Jones married, August, 1856, Dr. Jackson Maxwell; died of yellow fever, Key West, Fla., October, 1856.

Helen Louisa Jones, married, July, 1861, Dr. Axon Keith Quarterman, and had: Ellen Elizabeth, James Newton, William Henry, Keith Axon, Helen Adelaide, Arthur Matherson, Matilda Louisa, and Alexander Sanford Quarterman.

The Jones and Nephew Relationship.

Mr. Peter Nephew, an English gentleman of whose origin we know nothing, married the widow of John Cooper—she was a Miss Merian, and was the mother of Mary Cooper, who was the mother of Sarah Anderson, who was the mother of Mrs. C. C. Jones and Rev. John Jones, D. D., who was the father of James Dunwody Jones. Peter Nephew had: James Nephew, who married Mary Magdalene Gignilliatt, and had Evelyn, Clifford and others. Evelyn married Dr. Charles West, Sr., and had: Dr. Charles West, Jr., Dr. Joseph West, and eight others. Mr. James Nephew began life with small means, but his energy commended him to an Englishman named Leavett, the first planter of sea island cotton in Georgia. He settled Julianton plantation, Harris Neck, McIntosh Co., Ga., and James Nephew managed the business, and also planted a small crop for himself, that was shipped to England with Leavett's. His daughter Evelyn was born there. Nephew later settled his own plantation near Baisden's Bluff, and called it Manchester, and it remains so called to this day; and in time he settled a fine rice plantation on Cathead Creek, near Darien, Ga., known as Ceylon, even to the present time, and was afterwards owned by Dr. Charles West. Mr. James Nephew died 1827, and left $2,000 to the Darien Presbyterian Church, and also endowed a scholarship in the Columbia, S. C., Presbyterian Seminary. David Anderson (a cousin of Mary and John Jones) married Hannah West, who was a grand-daughter of James Nephew. She died in 1837—buried in Nephew Cemetery, McIntosh Co., Ga. On her tomb are these words: "God must have needed thee in Heaven, or He would not have taken thee from one who almost adored thee."

The Jones and West Relationship.

*The emigrant West came from Dorchester, England, to America—Dorchester, Mass., 1621. The family came to Dorchester, S. C., 1695, and to Liberty Co., Ga., then St. John's Parish, 1752.

James Sharpe and Mary Newton, his wife, had:

1. Mary Sharpe, married Maj. John Jones.
2. Hannah Sharpe, married William West.

William was a son of Charles, who came, 1752, to St. John's Parish, and obtained a grant of rice land on Bine Swamp, and called his place Westfield. His only daughter, Elizabeth, married Col. Simon Munro, 1767—which makes the West family also related to the Dunwodys. Charles West also had a son, Samuel, a bold soldier of the Revolution. He once, single-handed, pursued the infamous tory, McGirt. West was mounted upon a powerful English horse, McGirt on his famous American mare, "The Fair America." Finding West was gaining on him, he turned from the high lands to the swamp, and rice fields, where his lighter horse would have the advantage. Reaching a wide canal, McGirt's mare cleared it. West came thundering close behind, sabre in hand, but the heavier horse failed to reach the further bank. McGirt heard the splash, and looking back saw the mishap of his pursuer, and without stopping, raised his hat, and sung out to West,

*Miss Anne M. West says the ancestor came directly from England (see West history), which is probably quite correct.

"Hurrah for the Fair America!" Even the redoubtable McGirt had no taste for the powerful sabre of the red-headed Samuel West. He died suddenly, while walking in the garden of his sister, Mrs. Simon Munro. Charles, Jr., died in youth.

William West and his wife, Hannah Sharpe, had:

1. Mary West, married James Robarts, who afterwards married Eliza G. Lowe.
2. Daughter, married John Stewart and moved to Alabama; no trace.
3. Dr. Charles West, Sr., married Evelyn Nephew, and had ten children, among whom were Dr. Charles, Jr., and Dr. Joseph Jones West.

Dr. Chas. West, Sr., was a ward of his cousin, Capt. Joseph Jones.

Dr. Charles West, Jr., married Eliza Whitehead, and had:

1. Charles Nephew West, married Mary Cheves; have issue.
2. William Whitehead West, married Sadie Shippen; have issue.
3. Eva Nephew West.
4. Clifford West, married Col. Clifford A. Anderson; issue.
5. John West, married Miss Soullard; have issue.
6. James West, married Belle Davant.
7. Thomas West, married Miss Tinsley.
8. Henry Cumming West, married Miss Whitehead.

Dr. Joseph Jones West married Annie Munro Rogers, and had:

I. Annie Munro West.
II. Catharine, Elizabeth and Joseph died in infancy.
III. Francis Bartow West, married Miss Tinsley.

Rev. Charles Rogers (son of Dr. Chas. Rogers and Annie Munroe, daughter of Col. Simon Munro and Elizabeth West), married Caroline Woodford, and had:

I. Annie Munro Rogers, married Dr. Joseph Jones West.
II. Caroline Matilda Rogers, married Samuel Vernon Stiles; have issue.
III. Georgia Woodford Rogers, married, first, Peyton Wade; second, H. Fraser Grant, and have issue:
   I. Rogers Grant, married.
   II. Annie Grant.

III. Rosa Grant.
IV. —— Grant.
IV. Charles Woodford Rogers.

Samuel V. Stiles and Caroline Matilda Rogers had Samuel V. Stiles, married Georgia Jacobs; issue.

Jones and Pinckney Relationship.

The maternal grand-father of Maj. John Jones was Maj. William Pinckney, Master in Chancery, born Charleston, 1702, son of Thomas Pinckney and his wife, Miss Cotesworth, and came to America from Lincolnshire, Eng., 1687, and settled in Carolina. They were people of gentle birth and ample fortune, and in religious belief Protestant Episcopalians. They had three sons, who were educated in England:

1. Charles Cotesworth, who had Col. Charles Cotesworth, Jr., who commanded a regiment at the siege of Savannah, Ga., 1779, and mentions in a letter written home the fact: "My cousin, Jack Jones, is among the killed."
2. Thomas, Jr., died in youth.
3. Maj. William Pinckney, born 1702.*

History gives an account of the family.

*Thomas Pinckney and Mary Cotesworth had:
I. Thomas Pinckney.
II. Charles Pinckney, married Elizabeth Lucas.
III. William Pinckney (Major), married Ruth Brewton.

DUNWODY

The ancestor of the Dunwody family, of Liberty and McIntosh Counties, was John Dunwody, who went to Chester Co., Penn., about 1730, from the "Old Country," a man of education and a school teacher, and married, 1740, Susanna Creswell, daughter of William Creswell, of Faggs Manor, Chester Co., Penn. Of this family, Georgia has just cause to be proud, for in the first Executive Council of the Independent Colony she had James and John Dunwody; and later, Col. James Dunwody, a Senator of the State; John Dunwody, Esq., of Roswell; and in the late war between the States, Col. John Dunwody, of Mexican and Confederate States War; Rev. James Bulloch Dunwody, Chaplain in C. S. Army; Col. Henry Dunwody, who died on field of Gettysburg, thirty paces in front of his regiment; Capt. Charles A. Dunwody, at first battle of Manassas; Dr. Wm. Elliott Dunwody, a well known physician of Marietta and Macon, Ga.; the eminent Revs. James and Samuel Dunwody; Mayor Harry Dunwody, of Brunswick; Dr. Jno. Dunwody, surgeon U. S. A., and other well known members of the family. This family is connected to the Bullochs, Elliotts, Jones, McDonalds, McIntoshs and others.

John Dunwody and Susannah Creswell had:

I. Dr. James Dunwody, married Esther Splatt, *nee* Dean.

II. Robert Dunwody, married Mary, daughter James and Mary Phillips Creswell, of Chester Co., Penn.

III. John Dunwody, married Jane Hamilton, of Chester Co., Penn., and had:

1. Agnes Dunwody, married Freeland, of Tennessee.

IV. Margaret Dunwody, married Mr. McMahon.

V. Mary Dunwody, married Mr. Euart.

VI. Rebecca Dunwody, married, first, McKahn; second, Lieut. Hugh McWilliams; third, Jas. Cousart.

VII. Sarah Dunwody, married James Freeland, of North Carolina.

VIII. Susanna Dunwody, married, first, Wm. Hamill; second, Col. Daniel McKaraher.

Robert Dunwody and his wife, Mary Creswell, his cousin, moved to Georgia, settled in Screven County, and had:

1. Samuel Dunwody.
2. John Dunwody, married Lelia Pearce.
3. Susanna Dunwody, born Chester Co., Penn.
4. Rev. James Dunwody, born May 4, 1790, in Screven Co., Ga.
5. Mary Dunwody, married B. A. Saxon.
6. Robert Dunwody.
7. Esther Dunwody, born Dr. Dunwody's plantation, Arcadia, Liberty Co., Ga. Some of this line in Louisiana.

The Dunwody Family of Liberty and McIntosh Counties, Georgia.

The original emigrant, John Dunwody, came to America, about 1730; was an educated man, and commenced teaching school in Chester Co., Penn. Married, 1740, Susanna Creswell, daughter of Wm. Creswell, of Faggo Manor, Chester Co., Penn., and had:

1st. Dr. James Dunwody. 2d. Robert. 3d. John. 4th. Margaret. 5th. Mary. 6th. Rebecca. 7th. Sarah. 8th. Susanna. All born Chester Co., Pa.

Margaret married Mr. McMahon.

Mary married Mr. Euart.

Rebecca married, first, Mr. McKann; second, Lieut. Hugh McWilliams; and third, James Cousart.

Sarah Married James Freeland, Esq., of North Carolina.

Susanna married, first, William Hamill; second, Col. Daniel McKaraher, and had Elizabeth, who married Louis Bomeisler, and had Edwin Louis, married Helen Pomeroy Ives, of Hamilton, Ontario, and had Louis Edwin Bomeister, of New York.

John married Jane Hamilton, of Chester Co., Pa., and had Agnes, who married Mr. Freeland, of Tennessee.

Robert married his cousin, Mary Creswell (daughter of James Creswell and Mary Phillips, of Chester Co., Pa.). They moved to Georgia and settled in Screven Co., and had: 1. Samuel. 2. John. 3. Susanna, born Chester Co., Pa. 4. Rev. James Dunwody. 5. Mary. 6. Robert, born Screven Co., Ga. 7. Esther, born at Dr. James Dunwody's plantation, Arcadia, Liberty Co., Ga.

Rev. James Dunwody, born May 4, 1790, was a minister of the South Georgia Conference M. E. Church. He mentions in his reminiscences that "My uncle John and several of my mother's brothers fought at the battle of Brandywine of the American Revolution."

John Dunwody married Delia Pearce, of Georgia.

Mary Dunwody married B. A. Saxon, of Georgia.

Dunwodys of Liberty and McIntosh Counties, Ga.

Dr. James Dunwody came to Georgia about 1770, and was a member of the Executive Council of Georgia, 1776. He settled in St. John's Parish, now Liberty Co., Ga., and practiced medicine; married Mrs. Esther Splatt, widow of Edward Splatt, and lived at his plantation, known as Arcadia to the present time. Esther, his wife, was a Miss Dean; she had a sister Mary, who married Mr. Ladson. The father of Esther and Mary was Abraham Dean, born 1704, and married Ann Dupont,* who was born 1707, and were related to the family of

*Gideon Dupont was one of the church wardens at St. James Goose Creek, S. C., 1746. Esther Elliott died 1815.

Gen. Francis Marion, of the American Revolution. Dr. Dunwody died 1807.

Dr. James Dunwody and his wife Esther had:

I. Col. James Dunwody, born December 1, 1789; died February 15, 1833; married Elizabeth West Smith.

II. John Dunwody, married, Sunbury, Ga., June 7, 1808, Jane Bulloch.

III. Esther Dunwody, married, October 1, 1795, John Elliott, U. S. Senator, and had:

I. Hester A. Elliott, born December 12, 1797; married Maj. James Stephens Bulloch, December 31, 1817, and had:

1. Capt. James D. Bulloch.

Col. James Dunwody married, 1815, Elizabeth West Smith, daughter of James Smith† and Seymour Munro, daughter of Col. Simon Munro, of Inverness, Scotland, late of Liberty Co., Ga., and had:

1. Caroline Seymour Dunwody, born 1816; died Philadelphia, Pa.
2. Mary Elizabeth Dunwody, born August 14, 1818; died March 13, 1884.
3. Jane Adaline Dunwody, born October 10, 1820; died March 20, 1884.
4. William James Dunwody, born 1823; died June 6, 1873.
5. Dean Munro Dunwody, born March 19, 1825; died February 5, 1879.
6. Sarah Ann Dunwody, born 1827; died August 3, 1849.
7. John Franklin Dunwody, born 1829.

Col. James Dunwody, born December 1, 1789; died February 15, 1833; interred Medway.

Mrs. Elizabeth West Dunwody, born April 25, 1794; died June 30, 1879. Born at Sunbury, Liberty Co., Ga.; died Atlanta, Ga.; buried Marietta, Ga.

Caroline Seymour Dunwody married Francis Shackelford, of South Carolina, 1835, and had:

I. Caroline Shackelford, married C. B. Howard, July 18, 1860, and had:

†James Smith married, second, Jane Farquharson, daughter of Dr. John Irvine (no issue).

I. Chessley Bostick Howard, born June 9, 1867; married Miss O'Hear; has issue.
II. Caroline Virginia Howard, born February 26, 1863; married Frank R. Logan, of Atlanta.
III. George Troup Howard, born April 13, 1869; married.
IV. Caroline Shackelford Howard, born May 5, 1837, Hopestill plantation, McIntosh Co., Ga.

Jane Adaline Dunwody married Rev. John Jones, D. D., February 18, 1841, and had:
I. James Dunwody Jones, born May 1, 1842, at Hopestill plantation, McIntosh Co., Ga.
II. Mary Elizabeth Jones, born 1849; died 1852, Marietta, Ga.
III. John Carolyn Jones, born 1852, Marietta, Ga.
IV. Joseph Henry Jones, born 1854, Hopestill plantation, McIntosh Co., Ga.

James Dunwody Jones married Mary Cornelia Ashley, November 2, 1870, and had:
1. John Ashley Jones, born August 27, 1871; married Maude Allgood, October 12, 1898.
2. Fanny Adaline Jones, born October 2, 1872; married Malcolm Cunningham, September 25, 1900.
3. James Logan Jones, born April 12, 1874.
4. Rosabell Margaret Jones, born January 12, 1876; married Capt. Wm. Calhoun Massey, June 15, 1890.
5. Ruby Cornelia Jones, born December 18, 1877.
6. Elizabeth Munro Jones, born February 17, 1881; died April 29, 1885.
7. Mary Dunwody Jones, born January 25, 1883.
8. Jane Dunham Jones, born February 17, 1885.
9. William Percy Jones, born August 4, 1888.

Mary Cornelia (Ashley) Jones, born October 30, 1848, daughter of Col. Wm. Percy Morford Ashley, of Camden Co., Ga. He, his father and grand-father, were large rice planters on the Satilla River, Ga. The Ashleys descend from the English family of that name.

Jane Adaline Dunwody married Rev. John Jones, D. D., son of Capt. Joseph Jones, February 18, 1841, at Hopestill plantation, the winter home of her father and mother, McIntosh Co., Ga. It was one of those old time weddings. The family and its connections, and friends present, that night, in the parlors of the old plantation house, represented over $2,000,000 worth of property.

Dean Munro Dunwody married Catharine E. McDonald, daughter of Gov. Charles McDonald (Governor of Georgia 1839-42) and his wife, Annie Franklin, and had:

1. James Smith Dunwody, born January 12, 1851; married, first, Lettie Hall, January 12, 1878; son, died; married, second, Sallie McIntosh, November 19, 1890, daughter Rev. William McIntosh, and had William McIntosh Dunwody, born March 12, 1894.
2. Annie Elizabeth Dunwody, born November 2, 1853; married, February 16, 1873, Richard L. Morris, of McIntosh Co., Ga., and had Charlotte M. Morris, born July 10, 1874; married Welby Jordan, and had:
   I. Louis Jordan, born 1900.
   II. Catharine McDonald Jordan, born October 17, 1878.
   III. Richard L. Jordan, Jr., born March 30, 1876.

Richard L. Morris, Sr., died October 15, 1885.

3. Ella McDonald Dunwody, born September 11, 1855; married Capt. Campbell Wylly, of McIntosh Co., Ga., April 11, 1882, and had: Elizabeth Spalding Wylly, born May 24, 1887.
4. McDonald Dunwody, born June 29, 1857; married Charlotte Morall, November 16, 1881, and had:
   A. Carrie Gignilliat Dunwody, born October 18, 1882.
   B. Annie Phoebe Dunwody, born March 23, 1885.
   C. Catharine McDonald Dunwody, born July 19, 1886.
   D. Charlotte Morall Dunwody, born July 30, 1887.
   E. Edith Dunwody, born June 28, 1888.
   F. Dean Munro Dunwody, born November 5, 1893.

Residence, Darien, McIntosh Co., Ga.

5. Dean Munro Dunwody, Jr., born September 29, 1859.
6. Mary Jane Dunwody, born June 11, 1862; married October 26, 1888, Samuel Barnett, died; no issue.
7. Harry Franklin Dunwody, born October 1, 1863; died May 15, 1890; married, first, Eula Brown, January, 2, 1890; second, Scotia Tyson Waller, January 21, 1897, and had: Harry F. Dunwody, born 1898.

8. Dr. John Atkinson Dunwody, born December 17, 1864.
9. Richard Gailliard Dunwody, born May 18, 1867; married, February 5, 1895, Mrs. Smythe (*nee* Brown), and had:
   A. Harry Franklin Dunwody, born December 22, 1895.
   B. Gailliard Dunwody.

John Franklin Dunwody, youngest son of Col. James Dunwody, born 1829; married Miss Annie Bryan, of North Carolina, March, 1854, and had:

1. Mary Elison (Minnie) Dunwody, born June 10, 1855; married September, 1871, Henry Baars, and had:
   I. J. Ernest Baars, born 1874; married Olive Blackshear.
   II. Theo. Dunwody, born 1876.
   III. Annie Elison, born 1879.
   IV. Henry Baars, born 1888.
2. Sarah Ann Dunwody, born October, 1856.
3. John Franklin, Jr., born 1857.
4. Bryan, born 1858; married Sallie Hyer, of Pensacola, Fla.
5. Adrian Van Bokelen, born 1865; resides Paris, France.

Descent of Elizabeth West Smith, wife of Col. James Dunwody, from Munros of Scotland, and grand-daughter of Sir Simon Munro, known as Col. Simon Munro, of Liberty Co., Ga., whose daughter, Seymour, married James Smith, whose daughter married Col. James Dunwody (see Simon Munros coats of arms, also arms of House of Munro). Simon Munro, born 1741; died December 29, 1790. His plantation was called Novare, the name of the home of the Munros, Barons of Foulis, Inverness, Scotland.

Dunwody and West relationship: Col. Simon Munro, 1767, married Elizabeth West, daughter of Charles West, Sr., and sister of Wm. West, who married Hannah Sharpe, sister of Mary Sharpe, who married Maj. John Jones.

NOTE.—Col. Simon Munro held a commission in Colonial Troops as Lieutenant in Capt. William Young's company, 1st Regiment of Foot, 1765, Savannah Division, and after war was Colonel of militia in Georgia.

Col. Simon Munro and Elizabeth West, his wife, had:

I. Elizabeth Munro, married, first, Alexander McIvor, and had Alexander Munro McIvor, who left issue; second, John Bettis, no issue.

II. Amarinthia Munro, married Maj. John Stevens, and had: Henry, William, Joseph, Harriet Louisa, married Col. Quarterman.

III. Annie, married Dr. Charles Rogers, of Bryan Co., Ga., and had: Charles, William, David and Seymour Rogers.

IV. Seymour, who married Mr. James Smith, and had Elizabeth West Smith, who married Col. James Dunwody, Sr., died December 9, 1828; buried at Sunbury, Ga.

V. Harry Munro, died young.

Descent of James Smith, born 1767; Robert Yeamans, died Bristol, Eng., 1643, and had Sir John Yeamans, Baronet, commissioned January 11, 1664, Governor and Lieut. General of the Province of Carolina, and had Ann, who married James Moore, Governor of Carolina 1700-2, and had:

I. Betsey Moore, died, no issue.

II. Mary Moore, married Mr. Porcher, of South Carolina, and have issue.

III. Matsey Moore, married Mr. Postell, of South Carolina, have descendants.

IV. James Moore, Governor of South Carolina 1719.

V. Maurice Moore.

VI. Roger Moore.

VII. Margaret Moore, married Wm. Sanders, and had Margaret Sanders, who married Thomas Smith, and had James Smith (and others), who married Seymour Munro, and had Elizabeth West, who married Col. James Dunwody, and had Jane Adaline (and others), who married Rev. John Jones, D. D., and had James Dunwody, who married Mary Cornelia Ashley, and had John Ashley (and others), who married Maude Allgood.

Mr. James Smith's descent from Sir John Smith, of Exeter, England, 1565, had Sir George Smith, Sheriff of Devon, Eng.,

NOTE.—Col. Simon Munro, a younger son of Munro, Barons of Foulis, went to Georgia and settled in St. John Parish, afterward Liberty County, Ga.

1615, and had Sir George Smith, whose son was Gov. Thomas Smith, of the Colony of Carolina, 1693, and his son was Thomas Smith, whose son, Thomas Smith, married Margaret Sanders, and had James Smith, who married Seymour Munro, and had Elizabeth West Smith, who married Col. Jas. Dunwody, etc. Mr. James Smith died 1854; buried Midway, Liberty Co., Ga.

The John Dunwody family, of Liberty and Cobb Counties, Ga.: Son of Dr. James Dunwody and his wife, Esther (Dean Splatt) Dunwody, John Dunwody, born January 14, 1786, Liberty Co., Ga.; died Roswell, Ga., 1858; married June 7, 1808, Jane Bulloch, born April 8, 1788, Savannah, Ga. She was the daughter of James Bulloch and Anne Irvine, daughter of Dr. Irvine and Anne E. Baillie, daughter of Col. Kenneth Baillie, son of John Baillie, of Torbreck and Balrobert and Catharine Dunbar (of Dunain family).

John and Jane Bulloch Dunwody had:

I. Rev. James Bulloch, born September 24, 1816.
II. Major John, born November 6, 1818.
III. Jane Marion, born June 22, 1820.
IV. Dr. William Elliott, born November 6, 1823; died June 15, 1891.
V. Col. Henry Macon, born March 13, 1826; died July 3, 1863.
VI. Major Charles A., born June 6, 1828.

I. Rev. James Bulloch Dunwody married, first, Laleah Pratt, and had:

1. Laleah Georgiana, born 1843; married December 5, 1890, Joseph Addison Waddell, and has issue.
2. John Henry Dunwody.

Rev. James B. Dunwody married, second, Ellen Martin; third, Caroline Haygood, and had issue.

II. Major John Dunwody married Elizabeth Clark Wing, June 11, 1849, and had:

1. Alice Augusta, born March 16, 1854.
2. Clara Jane, born May 3, 1856.
3. John Elliott, born November 10, 1858.
4. Jefferson Davis, born Februry 12, 1861.
5. Henry Macon, born July 27, 1863.
6. Dora Elizabeth, born June 10, 1866.
7. Marion Franklin, born December 24, 1871.

Mrs. E. C. Dunwody, born October 9, 1825; died 1898, Atlanta, Ga.

John Elliott married Ella Wing, and had issue.

Clara Jane married Wm. Ira Smith, and had issue.

Jefferson Davis married Cornelia Robson, and had issue.

Henry Macon married Helen D. Keese, and had issue.

Dora Elizabeth married E. P. Chalfant, and had issue.

III. Jane Marion married, first, Stanhope Irwin; second, Dr. W. E. Glen; third, Adam Alexander, of Washington, Ga.

IV. Dr. William Elliott married, March 12, 1846, Ruth Ann Atwood, born March 13, 1826, and had:

1. Henry Atwood, born December 23, 1846; died December 6, 1890.
2. William Elliott, Jr., born July 15, 1848.
3. Jane Esther, born July 7, 1850; died August 27, 1855.
4. John Alford, born May 25, 1854.
5. James Marion, born August 28, 1857.

Henry Atwood* married, April 7, 1869, Hattie W. Morris, of Marietta, Ga., and had:

1. Ruth Atwood, born March 28, 1870; married Mr. Cole.
2. James Morris, born January 29, 1872.
3. Hattie Weyland, born October 22, 1876.
4. Henry Atwood, Jr., born July 29, 1874.
5. John Alford, Jr., born December 31, 1878.
6. William Elliott, Jr., born September 20, 1882.

William Elliott, Jr., married January, 1870, Annie Taylor La Roche, of Savannah, Ga., and had:

1. William Elliott, Jr., born December 17, 1870; married.
2. Isaac La Roche, born October 4, 1872; married.
3. Felix Lessing, born December 5, 1874.
4. Ralph, born October 10, 1876.
5. Annie or Amy La Roche, born March 27, 1878; married J. W. Glover.
6. James Marion, born December 28, 1880.

W. E. Dunwody, died Macon, Ga., June 5, 1890.

John Alford married, November 20, 1884, Dora Hargrove, of Macon, Ga., and had:

1. John Alford, Jr., born October 8, 1890.

*Said to have had also Frederick, Marion and Bishop.

2. Dora Elizabeth, born March 7, 1892.
3. James Marion, Jr., born July 21, 1893; married October 4, 1892, Georgia E. Marsh.

V. Col. Henry Macon married Matilda Maxwell, of Georgia, and had Leilia or Laleah, Edward, Corinne, all dead. Col. H. M. Dunwody was killed at the battle of Gettysburg, while leading his regiment, the 51st Georgia Volunteers, July 3, 1863.

VI. Maj. Charles A. Dunwody married, May 6, 1852, Ellen J. Rice, of Charleston, S. C., born July 22, 1827; died June 19, 1895, and had:

1. William Glen Dunwody, born February 16, 1854.
2. Caroline R. Dunwody.
3. Ellen G. Dunwody, born 1856.
4. Charles A. Dunwody, born May 22, 1863.
5. George H. Dunwody, born November, 1864.
6. Rosaline M. Dunwody, dead.

Esther Dunwody, only daughter of Dr. James and his wife, Esther Splatt, married U. S. Senator John Elliott, of Liberty Co., Ga. (who died 1827), and had:

I. Esther or Hettie Elliott.
II. Caroline, died unmarried.
III. Jane Elliott.
IV. And V. Charles and John died in boyhood.
VI. Corinne Elliott, married Robert Hutchinson, an English gentleman, who resided in Savannah, Ga. His wife and two children were lost in the disaster to the steamer Pulaski.

Esther (or Hettie) Elliott married Maj. James Stephens Bulloch (brother of Mrs. Jane Bulloch Dunwody), and had Capt. James Dunwody Bulloch, who married Harriet Cross, daughter of Brig. Gen. Osborne Cross, U. S. A., and had:

I. James Bulloch, died.
II. Dunwody Bulloch, died.
III. Stewart Bulloch, in Australia.
IV. Jessie Bulloch, married M. Hyslop-Maxwell.
V. Louisa Bulloch.

Senator John Elliott married, second, Martha Stewart, daughter of Gen. Daniel Stewart, and had:

I. Susan Elliott, married Dr. Hilborne West.
II. Georgia Elliott.

III. Daniel Stuart Elliott, married Lucy Sorrel, and had:

1. John S. Elliott, married Helena Ellis, and had issue.
2. Maude Elliott.

Maj. James Stephens Bulloch married, second, Mrs. Martha (Stewart) Elliott, widow of John Elliott, and had:

1. Anna Bulloch, married James K. Gracie.
2. Mitty (or Martha), married Theodore Roosevelt.
3. Irvine Stephens Bulloch, married Ella Sears.
4. Charles Irvine Bulloch, died young.

Martha Bulloch married Theodore Roosevelt, Sr., and had:

I. Theodore Roosevelt, Jr., born October 27, 1858, married, first, Alice Lee; second, Edith Kermit Carow.

II. Anna L. Roosevelt, born January 18, 1858; married Commander W. S. Cowles, of U. S. Navy.

III. Elliott Roosevelt, born February 26, 1860; married Anna Hall.

IV. Corinne Roosevelt, born September 27, 1861; married Douglas Robinson.

NOTE.—As the issue of the Roosevelts have been given in my work on Baillie of Dunain, will not repeat it here, except to say that Commander Cowles has a son, William Sheffield Cowles.

Capt. James Bulloch, eldest son of Governor Archibald Bulloch and Mary De Veaux, married, April 13, 1786, Ann Irvine, daughter of Dr. John Irvine and Ann Elizabeth Baillie, and had:

I. John Irvine Bulloch, married Charlotte Glen, issue.

II. James Stephens Bulloch, married, first, Esther Elliott; second, Martha Stewart.

III. Jane Bulloch, married John Dunwody.

IV. Ann Bulloch, dead.

NOTE.—Munro: Col. Sir Simon Munro, grand-father of Elizabeth West Smith, who married James Dunwody, was from Inverness, Scotland. He held a commission in the Colonial Army in Georgia as a Lieutenant in Captain William Young's Company, 1st Regiment of Foot, 1765, Savannah Division, and after the war was Colonel of militia in Georgia. He was a younger son of the family of Munro, of Foulis; went to America and settled in St. John's Parish. He was born 1741; married Elizabeth, daughter of Charles West, who settled in St. John's Parish, 1748.

Hugh Munro was the first of family designated of Foulis; died 1126, and succeeded by Robert Munro, 16th Baron of Foulis, and so on down to Sir Robert Munro, 23d Baron of Foulis, who was appointed High Sheriff of Ross by George I., June 9, 1725. He married Jean, daughter of Sir John Forbes, of Culloden, by whom he had three sons and one daughter, Anne, who married Alexander Gordon, Esq. Sir Robert died 1729; was succeeded by his eldest son, Sir Robert, 24th Baron of Foulis, who fell at the battle of Falkirk, January 17, 1746. He married Mary, daughter of Henry Seymour, Esq., of Woodland County, Dorset, and was succeeded by his eldest son, Sir Harry Munro; Sir Simon being a younger son, came to America as narrated above; from him descend the branch of Dunwody and Jones.

BULLOCH

IRVINE OF CULTS

DENNIS

*John Dennis, of Brunswide, New Jersey, a distinguished patriot of the Revolutionary War, member of Provincial Congress and one who held many offices of trust, is the progenitor of branches of the following families: Guerard, Anderson, Arnold, Millen, Gordon and others. The great-grand-father of John Dennis was †Capt. William Sanford, of New Jersey, was member of the Lords Proprietors Council under the following: Lord Proprietor Philip Carteret, 1675; Governor Laurie, 1683-1686, and one of the other Governors, 1682; and when we remember that in those days to be a member of the Council under the Lords Proprietors was almost equivalent to a title of nobility, and carried with the position great influence, we can appreciate the great honor, for New Jersey at one time was a part of the County Palatine of New Albion, and the Lord Proprietor was entitled Earl Palatine. In the days of the Proprietary and Royal Governors, to be a Judge, Justice of the Peace, member of the Council, Speaker of Colonial Assembly and member thereof, or County Clerk and other positions, were then truly honors held by gentlemen or by men of influence; and so, too, to have taken part in freeing the Colonies was a deed commensurate with the earlier honors of the Colonies, and gave to the

*See Force's American Archives.

†See Whitehead's History of East Jersey under the Proprietors.

patriot position and honor. John Dennis, Esq., had a son, Richard Dennis, who served in the war of 1812 with the rank of Colonel. He married, first, July 11, 1797, in Savannah, Ga., Eliza Jane Williams, and had:

I. Eliza Jane Dennis, married Dr. Milne, and had:
I. McPherson Milne.
II. Mary Milne.

Col. Richard Dennis married, second, by Bishop White, November 25, 1812, Harriet Eliza Duffield, of Philadelphia, Penn., and had:

I. Madeline Dennis, married John Posey Williamson, of Savannah.

II. Harriet Dennis, married Peter Guerard, of Savannah.

II. *Sarah C. Dennis, daughter of John Dennis, married, first, Major Richard Stites, of New Jersey, who was killed in battle during the Revolutionary War, and had:

I. Richard M. Stites, who moved from New Jersey to Savannah; married, June 10, 1801, Mary Wayne, daughter of Richard Wayne and Elizabeth Clifford, and had:

1. Richard Stites.
2. Eliza Stites, married George Anderson.
3. Sarah Anderson Stites, married, 1821, William Washington Gordon.

*Mrs. Stites married, second, Dr. Noel.

III. Elizabeth Dennis, daughter of John Dennis, married Arnold, of Savannah, and had Richard Dennis Arnold, a well known physician of Savannah, Professor Savannah Medical College, and several times Mayor of Savannah, whose daughter, Ellen, married Geo. Cosens, and had:

I. Richard D. Cosens.
II. Geo. Cosens, married Miss Henderson, daughter of Rev. M. H. Henderson and Miss Screven.
III. Margaret Cosens.

IV. Margaret Dennis, daughter of John Dennis, married Millen, of Savannah, and had:

I. Col. John Millen, a distinguished lawyer of Savannah.
II. Cornelia Millen.

III. Millen, who married, and left:

1. McPherson Berrien Millen, killed in battle during Confederate war.
2. Geo. Millen, who married, and left issue.

Hon. John Guerard, member of His Majesty's Council in South Carolina, 1761 (son of John Guerard, of Normandy, France), married, first, Miss Hill, daughter of Charles Hill, Chief Justice of South Carolina, issue; he married, second, Marianne Godin, daughter of Benj. Godin, a Huguenot of noble extraction, who married a daughter of Isaac Mazyck, one of the largest land owners in the Province of South Carolina, at whose wife's death most of the chief merchants and public officers attended her funeral.

The eldest son of Hon. John Guerard and Marianne Godin was Godin Guerard, who married Ann Mathews, a sister of Gov. John Mathews and daughter of Mathews and Sarah Gibbes, grand-daughter of Gov. Robert Gibbes. Godin Guerard and Ann Mathews had:

I. Marianne Guerard, married Isaac Wright.

II. Robert Guerard, married Miss De Treville. She married, second, Samuel Lawrence.

III. Peter Guerard, member of Union Society, died at Philadelphia, Pa., December 24, 1842, aged 56. He married, first, Harriet Dennis, grand-daughter of John Dennis, of Brunswick, N. J., a distinguished patriot of the Revolution, grand-son of Hon. Capt. William Sandford, member of the Proprietary and King's Council of New Jersey, 1675, 1682, 1683-1686. Married, second, Elizabeth Haist, and by both had issue.

IV. Sarah Guerard.

V. Louis Guerard, married, first, February 2, 1798, Richard McAllister; second, Dr. Wm. Parker.

VI. Amelia Guerard, married Timothy Barnard, from whom descends Judge Chisholm, who married Georgia Anderson.

NOTE.—Stephen Millen had a daughter, Catharine, who married, first, a Waldburg; second, John Henry Morel, and had issue.

The alliances of Guerard are too numerous to mention, but of the best in Carolina.

Through the Le Serruriers, the families of Le Noble, Gignilliat, Mazyck, Ravenel, Taylor, Du Bose, De Veaux, McDuffie, Chastagnier, Izard, Guerard and others are related and descended.

VII. Anna Guerard, married Steel White.

VIII. Catharine Guerard, married James Barnard.

Peter Guerard and Harriet Dennis had:

1. Harriette Eliza Guerard, married Thos. Alfred Haywood, died.
2. John Mathews Guerard (Hon). married Sarah Baynard, died.
3. Richard Dennis Guerard (Hon.), died.
4. Edgar Lennox Guerard, married Charlotte Strother, of Edgefield, S. C., died.
5. Anna Lois Guerard, married, first, John Naff McGuffin; married, second, Col. Robert Brice McComb.
6. Marian Sophia Guerard.
7. Wm. Elliott Guerard, married Leona Ross, of Macon, Ga., issue.
8. Joseph Nancrede Guerard, fatally wounded at Sailor's Creek, in Virginia, last battle of Confederacy.

Anna Lois Guerard had issue by John Naff McGuffin, of New Castle, Penn. Johnanna Guerard McGuffin, who married William White Rogers, of Savannah, no issue. Anna Lois Guerard married, second, Col. Robert Brice McComb, of New Castle, Penn., and had Harriet Guerard McComb, who married Lewis Birely Hamilton, of Waterbury, Conn., and had:

I. Edgar Guerard Hamilton.

II. Charles Hamilton.

III. William Rogers Hamilton.

William Elliott Guerard, son of Peter Guerard and Harriet Dennis, married, November 14, 1871, Leona H. Ross, of Macon, Ga., and had:

1. Leona Ross Guerard, born March 8, 1873; married, July 8, 1896, John Sullivan Schley, had Marianne Sullivan Schley, born January 15, 1898.
2. Joseph Nancrede Guerard, M. D., born January 13, 1875; married, April 19, 1899, Elizabeth Allen; had Elizabeth Allen Guerard, born January 28, 1900.
3. Kate L. Guerard, born July 12, 1877; married, November 29, 1899, Eldred Simkins.
4. Anna Guerard, born April 1, 1879.
5. William Elliott Guerard, born January 6, 1881; married May 2, 1898, May Lucille Silva, had William Elliott Guerard, born July 21, 1900.

6. Harriott Guerard, born April 26, 1883.
7. Francis Ross Guerard, born July 22, 1886.

NOTE.—The Guerards are allied by marriage to many of the best people of Carolina, and descended and connected to such families as Middleton, Hill, Godin, Mazyck, Izard, St. Julien, Ravenel, Barnwell, De Veaux, Mathews, Bull, De Treville, Barnard, Parker, Morel, Dennis, Anderson, Gordon, Waring, Howard, Gadsden, Carter, Schley, Colcock, Cuthbert, Heyward, Bee, Moultrie, Rose, Prioleau, Lawton, Screven, Baynard, White, Chisolm and many others, and have from time to time furnished to the State in war and peace men of eminent worth.

ELLIOTT OF THE NORTH

Two families, the Screvens and a branch of the Elliotts, came to South Carolina in 168—. John Cutts, first President of New Hampshire, had Robert and Richard Cutts, his brothers. Robert Cutts married Mary Hoel (she married, second, Capt. Francis Champernowne), and had:

I. Robert Cutts.
II. Bridget Cutts, married Rev. Wm. Screven, of Kittery, Me.
III. Sarah Cutts.
IV. Elizabeth Cutts, married Humphrey Elliott.
V. Mary Cutts.

Rev. Wm. Screven, progenitor of Screvens of South Carolina and Georgia, founded Georgetown, S. C., and was pioneer of the Baptist faith in South Carolina. One of his children, Elizabeth Screven, married Robert Elliott, one of Tax Commissioners of South Carolina, son of Humphrey Elliott and Elizabeth Cutts, and had the following children:

I. Artemas Elliott, married, June 24, 1744, a daughter of Charles and Mary Burnham, and had:
1. Mary Elliott.
2. Eleanor Elliott.
3. Elizabeth Elliott, married Lewis Lestargette.
4. Margaret Elliott, married, May 10, 1773, James Darbye.
5. Charlotte Elliott, married, September 10, 1765, Capt. Henry Reeves.
6. Annie Elliott (mentions her niece, Mrs. Elizabeth Elliott Bremar, wife of Francis Bremar, and his nephew, Artemas Burnham Darbye).
7. Elliott, married Bremar.

II. Humphrey Elliott, married Catharine Booth, daughter of Robert Booth and grand-daughter of Wm. Elliott, of South Carolina, of Bermuda or South Carolina Elliotts, and had issue, at least, two children.

III. Dorothy Elliott.

IV. Eliza Elliott, married Benj. Williamson, and had:

I. Benj. Williamson.

II. Champernowne Williamson, married Charlotte, daughter Benj. Mazyck.

Robert Elliott, of Great Island, N. H., King's Councillor, married Sarah, daughter of Hon. Nathan Fryer, and had:

I. Humphrey Elliott, married Elizabeth Cutts, and removed with the Screvens to South Carolina.

II. Jane Elliott, married, first, Andrew Pepperell; second, Simon Frost.

III. Elizabeth Elliott, married Lt. Gov. Geo. Vaughan.

Humphrey Elliott and Elizabeth Cutts had:

I. Robert Elliott, married Elizabeth Screven; second, Elizabeth Harford, of South Carolina, who married, second, Wm. Emms.

II. Champernowne Elliott (Deputy to Surveyor General). Robert Elliott and Elizabeth Screven had (see as per above).

NOTE.—This family must not be confounded with the Bermuda Elliotts, nor with Hon. Grey Elliott of King's Council in Georgia, though they were all probably related.

SCREVEN

It showed a bold and determined spirit when the Rev. Wm. Screven, of Kittery, Maine, decided to migrate to South Carolina rather than give up his tenets of belief. Allied by marriage to the eminent families of Cutts and Elliott, he with the Elliotts removed to South Carolina and founded Georgetown, and became a well known Baptist leader, and founded the Screven family, who have in South Carolina and Georgia furnished to the professions, to the army and to the State, men of eminent worth. Among the members of this family on the roll of honor are to be found the brave Gen. James Screven, killed at Midway, Liberty Co., Ga. His nephew, Maj. John Screven (and later on Dr. James Proctor Screven), Mayor of Savannah and a planter. His son, Col. John Screven, many times Mayor of Savannah; President of the Atlantic and Gulf Railroad; President of Confederate Veterans; President of Sons of Revolution of Georgia; second General Vice-President National Society Sons of Revolution; President Georgia Historical Society, and a gentleman of refined and dignified demeanor, holding various positions of eminence; graduate of Franklin College, and in all walks a typical gentleman of the South. One of his sons, Major Thomas Screven, of Guards Battalion and volunteer in Spanish-American War. Superintendent of Police, Acting Mayor of Savannah, and last Judge of the Court of Ordinary. Nor are these all, for at different periods we find a John Screven, Dr. Richard Bedon Screven and others. So, then, this family, descended from Landgrave Smith, the Hyrnes, the Bryans of Georgia, and many others, was at once a family of high social distinction and eminent in many ways.

Rev. Wm. Screven, born in England, 1629; died at Georgetown, S. C., 1713; married, July 23, 1764, Bridget Cutts, daughter of Robert Cutts and Mary Hoel. He resided at Kittery, Maine, until he removed to South Carolina, about 1683, and became founder of the Baptist faith in South Carolina. His children were:

I. Samuel Screven, died December 3, 1771, aged over 62 years.

II. Mercy Screven.

III. Sarah Screven.

IV. Bridget Screven.

V. Elizabeth Screven, married Robert Elliott, February 5, 1720-1, who with Rev. Screven went to South Carolina. He was one of the Tax Collectors of South Carolina, and a probable relative of the Thomas and Wm. Elliotts of South Carolina, as they all claimed relationship.

VI. Robert Screven.

VII. Parmenius Screven.

VIII. Joshua Screven.

IX. William Screven (will June 11, 1765); died after 1756.

X. Joseph Screven.

XI. Elisha Screven, born September 1, 1698; died December 3, 1757; married and had issue.

Wm. Screven married Catharine, daughter of Justinius Stoll, and had:

1. John Screven, married Guerin.
2. James Screven, born 1704; married, 1736, Mary Hyrne Smith, born October 9, 1717; died 1758.
3. Samuel Screven.
4. Charles Screven.
5. Benjamin Screven.
6. William Screven.
7. Robert Screven.

James Screven, son of Wm. Screven, and grand-son of Rev. Wm. Screven and Bridget Cutts, married, 1736, Mary Hyrne Smith, born October 9, 1717, died 1758, daughter of Thomas Smith and Mary Hyrne; son of Thomas Smith, third Landgrave; son of Thomas Smith, second Landgrave; son of Hon. Governor Thomas Smith, of South Carolina, and a Landgrave, one of Colonial nobility of South Carolina. (Mary Hyrne was daughter of Edward Hyrne, of County Lincoln, England, and Elizabeth, daughter of Sir Drayner Massingbird.) James Screven and Mary Hyrne Smith had the following children:

A. Gen. James Screven, married, 1764, Mary, daughter of Charles Odingsell, of Edisto, S. C.

B. Thomas Smith Screven, 1743-1804; married, first, February 24, 1761, Eleanor Screven; died July 15, 1762, daughter of Wm. Screven, issue; married, second, March 22, 1764, Catharine Nicholson; married, third, Eleanor Hart; married, fourth, Amanda B. Gibbes, and had:

a. Susannah Screven, 1795.
b. Sarah Esther Screven.

C. Barbara Screven, married Jaudon.

D. John Screven, Lieut. in St. John's Rangers, born November 23, 1750; died, September 2, 1801; married, first, January 30, 1772, Patience Holmes, died 24 December, 1774; married, second, January 18, 1776, Elizabeth Pendarvis, widow of Josiah Bryan.

E. Benjamin Screven, member Provincial Congress in South Carolina, January 11, 1775; Capt. of Cavalry during Revolution.

F. Mary Screven, married James Brisbane.

G. Elizabeth Screven, 1722; married, 1767, Seth Gilbert.

Gen. James Screven, born in South Carolina, resident of St.

John's Parish, Liberty Co., Ga., member of Provincial Congress, July 4, 1775; Capt. St. John's Rangers, March 2, 1776; Colonel, 1777-1778; General of Georgia troops, 1778; died from wounds received November 25, 1778, in battle against the British, near Midway Church, Liberty Co., Ga. Screven County and Fort Screven, Tybee Island, recently built, were named for him. By Mary Odingsell he had the following children:

a. Mary Screven, born September 15, 1767; died December 27, 1845; married John Hart.
b. Esther Screven, born September 15, 1767; died December 24, 1802; married, December 11, 1778, Thomas Smith.
c. Martha Screven, born 1769.
d. James Screven, born 1771.
e. Charles Odingsell Screven, born February, 1773; died July, 1830; married, first, Lucy Wilmington Barnard, widow of Jones; second, Barbara R. Galphin, widow of Holmes, and by latter had (see further on):

Wm. Edward Screven married Cornelia E. Harris, and had:

1. Mary Galphin Screven, born 1846; married Francis Edward Davis.
2. Edward William Screven, born 1848; married Mary Parsons *Carroll, and had:
   a. Edward W. Screven, born 1878.
   b. Elizabeth Berrien Screven, born 1880; died 1888.
3. Louisa C. Screven, born 1850; married Samuel Ware Starnes.
4. Raymond Harris Screven, born 1853; married Nora Slade.
5. Ann Elizabeth Screven, born 1855; married D. A. Dansby.

Thomas Smith Screven, by first marriage to Eleanor Screven, had Mary Screven, 1761-1827. By third marriage to Eleanor Hart, he had:

a. Martha Screven, 1772-1793; married Benj. Bonneau.
b. Thomas Smith Screven, 1774-1833; married, first, Mariana Smith; second, Archor Smith.

*This marriage connects the families of Berrien and Screven, Mary Parsons Carroll being the grand-daughter of Judge John McPherson Berrien, alternately on the Supreme bench of Georgia and Attorney General in President Jackson's Cabinet.

c. Eleanor Hart Screven, 1779-1845; married Jno. Cox.

Charles Odingsell Screven married, first, Lucy Wilmington Barnard, and had James Odingsell Screven; married Eleanor Talbird. He married, second, Barbara Robert Galphin, and had:

1. Ann Elizabeth Screven, born 1820; married Thomas S. Mallard.
2. Wm. Edward Screven, 1822-1860; married Cornelia Harris.
3. Benj. Smith Screven, married, first, Ann Baker; second, Rosa Jones.

Rev. James O. Screven and Eleanor Talbird had:

A. Mary Barnard Screven, married Ramsay.
B. Eva Screven, married Lennard.
C. Dr. James Screven, married.
D. Claudia Screven.

Thomas Smith Screven and Mariana Smith had:

1. Marianna Screven, 1811-1844.
2. Martha Eleanor Screven, 1814-1876.
3. Sarah Norton Screven, 1816-1835.
4. Margaret Jane Screven, 1819-1865.

From family Bible record furnished by Dr. Thomas Screven.*

Col. John Screven, son of James Screven and Mary Hyrne Smith, married, second, Elizabeth Pendarvis, widow of Josiah Bryan, and daughter of Josiah Pendarvis and Mary Bedon, daughter of Col. Richard Bedon, son of Major Richard Bedon, son of George Bedon, who came over with Gov. Sayle, March 17, 1670, and who was member of South Carolina Colonial Assembly and a land owner. Josiah Pendarvis was son of John Pendarvis and Hannah Keyes, son of Joseph Pendarvis, who came over with Sayle, 1670; was a land owner and member of South Carolina Colonial Assembly, 1693; receiver of funds for St. Augustine expedition, and a man of importance. Col. John Screven and *Elizabeth Pendarvis had:

1. John Screven, 1777-1830; married, first, Hannah Proctor; second, Sarah Proctor.

*Elisha, son of Rev. William Screven, married, 1724, Hannah Johnson; born 1709; died December 3, 1771, and had:
1. Elisha, born July 18, 1732; married Rebecca .
2. Elizabeth, born December 13, 1738; married James Fowler.
3. Benjamin, born April 26, 1750; died April 10, 1785; married, November 4, 1771, Margaret Brockington.

2. Dr. Richard Bedon Screven, 1778-1856; married, first, Alice Pendarvis, daughter of Josiah Pendarvis and Elizabeth Louisa Stobo; married, second, Mary Hamilton, widow Rhodes; married, third, Charlotte, widow Moser.
3. Sarah Screven, born 1780; married Col. Wm. Hazzard.
3. Benj. Smith Screven, 1783-1826; married Mary Joyner.
4. Martha Screven, born 1786; married James West.
5. Elizabeth Screven, 1788-1848; married John Brookes Posey.
6. Mary Bedon Screven, 1794-1871; married Stephen R. Proctor.
7. Thomas Edward Screven, M. D., married Cornelia McNish.

From this line descends branches of following families: Bond, Henderson, Daniell, Le Hardy, Cuthbert, Edwards, DuBose, Clarkson, Chisholm, Heyward, Guerard, Gadsden, Fraser, Janvier, Hazzard, Huger and others, and the family became later connected to Bryan of Georgia, Izard, Heyward, DeSaussure and many others.

Col. John Screven and Hannah Proctor had:

1. Emily Sophia Screven, married Samuel Miller Bond.
2. Dr. James Proctor Screven, married Georgia Hannah Bryan.
3. Martha Sophia Screven, married Dr. Wm. C. Daniell, a distinguished physician of Savannah and writer, one of the committee appointed by the Legislature to regulate the finances of the State. He was by descent a Virginian.

Col. John Screven and Sarah Ann Proctor had Elizabeth Mary Screven, who also married Dr. Wm. Coffee Daniell, and had:

I. Charles Daniell, married Elizabeth P. Richardson.
II. Sarah E. Daniell, married Dr. J. C. Le Hardy.

Dr. Wm. C. Daniell and Martha Sophia Screven had:

I. Benj. R. Daniell, married Emily Dockery.
II. Thomas Smith Daniell.
III. Tattnall Fouche Daniell, married Susan Ann Footman, daughter of Edward Footman and Susan

*The name was changed to Bedon in 1802.

Ward, daughter of Benj. Ward and Ann, daughter of Major John Habersham (see Habersham).

IV. Marion Sophia Daniell.

V. Wm. Screven Daniell.

Dr. James Proctor Screven and Hannah Georgia Bryan (daughter of Hon. Joseph Bryan and Delia Forman, son of *Josiah Bryan and Elizabeth Pendarvis), had:

I. Col. John Screven, married, first, Mary White Footman, daughter of Richard S. Footmon and Mary C. Maxwell, daughter of James Benjamin Maxwell and Mary Habersham, and had:

1. Georgia Screven, died.
2. Jas. Proctor Screven, died.
3. Elizabeth Screven, married Thomas Arnold, issue.
4. Maj. Thomas Screven, married Bessie Lawton, daughter of Dr. Wm. Lawton and Elizabeth Jones, daughter of Seaborn Jones, Esq.

Col. Jno. Screven married, second, Mary Eleanor Nisbett, daughter of Nisbett and Martha, niece of Judge Berrien; issue married to Atkinson and Wylly.

II. Sarah Ada Screven, married Rev. M. H. Henderson, issue:

I. Marion Henderson.

II. Henderson, married Geo. Cosens (see Dennis).

III. Capt. Thomas F. Screven, M. D., married, first, Adelaide V. Moore, issue; second, Sallie Lloyd Buchanan, daughter of Admiral Buchanan.

IV. George Proctor Screven, married Ellen Buchanan, daughter of Admiral Buchanan, issue.

Dr. Thomas P. Screven and Alelaide V. Moore had:

1. Ellen S. Screven, married W. W. Gordon (see Stites).
2. John Screven, married Miss Bond, daughter of Thomas Bond, Esq., and Miss Gallie.

I am indebted to James B. Heyward, Esq., of Cartersville, Ga., for a perusal of his fine work on Bedon-Pendarvis, in which he fully carries out the lines and descent of the Screvens,

*Josiah Bryan, born August 22, 1746, son of Hon. Jonathan Bryan, who married Mary, daughter of John Williamson and Mary, daughter of William Bower and Martha Hext, son of Joseph Bryan and Janet Cochran.

and shows them to be splendidly connected and ancient in all lines. Also for a loan of his stupendous work on Landgrave Smith, embracing an enormous number of descendants, and also the Screven line. A branch of this family descend from Hon. Jonathan Bryan, of Georgia, and from the Stobo family. See, also, Cutts family for descent of Screven. The lines could be carried out, but this work will not admit of further enlargement, as the object has been shown of two lines of descent from Habersham and Maxwell family.

BOND

Dr. Thomas Bond, a celebrated physician of Philadelphia, Penn. His grand-sons were:

I. Samuel Miller Bond, married Emily Screven.

II. Thomas Phineas Bond, married, October 4, 1829, Mary C. Maxwell, widow of Dr. Richard S. or H. Footman and daughter of Jas. B. Maxwell and Mary Habersham, and had: Thomas Phineas Bond, married Julia Floyd Gallie, daughter of Maj. John B. Gallie, and had:

A. Mary Gallie Bond, married April 23, 1890, John Screven, son of Dr. Thomas P. Screven and Adelaide V. Moore.

B. Claudia Bond.

C. Augusta Bond.

D. Thomas Bond.

E. Edward Bond.

John Screven and Mary Gallie Bond had:

I. Julia Adelaide Screven, born September 10, 1891.

II. Thomas Forman Screven, born August 12, 1893.

III. Mary Bond Screven, born December 9, 1897.

KOLLOCK

Dr. Lemuel Kollock, who went to Georgia, was born in Wrentham, Mass., October 21, 1766. After studying medicine, he settled in Savannah, Ga., and commenced the practice of his profession. He married Maria Campbell, daughter of Macartan Campbell, a patriot of the Revolution, who married Sarah Fenwick, daughter of Edward Fenwick, of South

Carolina, and Mary Drayton. He was one of the incorporators of the Georgia Medical Society, founded in 1804, and its secretary. Dr. Lemuel Kollock and Maria Campbell had the following children:

I. Phineas Miller Kollock, M. D., married, first, Jane P. Johnston; second, Sarah Hull Campbell.

II. Mary Fenwick Kollock, married Rev. Edward Neufville, his second wife (Rev. Edward Neufville married, first, Mary, daughter of Hon. Wm. Bellinger Bulloch).

III. George J. Kollock, married, first, Augusta P. Johnston, and had Augusta Johnston Kollock. Married, second, Susan Marion, youngest daughter of Col. James Johnston and Anne Houstoun, and had issue:

1. George Jones Kollock.
2. John Fenwick Kollock.
3. William Waring Kollock.
4. Susan Marion Kollock.
5. Mary Fenwick Kollock.
6. Annie Houstoun Kollock.
7. Louisa Belle Kollock, married her cousin, Macartan C. Kollock, and had:
   - A. Susan Marion Kollock.
   - B. Edward Campbell Kollock.
   - C. George Jones Kollock.
   - D. Louisa Belle Kollock.
   - E. Macartan Campbell Kollock.
   - F. Percival Miller Kollock.

Dr. P. M. Kollock married, first, Jane P. Johnston, daughter of Col. James Johnston and Anna Houstoun, and had:

1. Louise Caroline Kollock.
2. Maria Kollock.
3. James Johnston Kollock.
4. Jane Johnston Kollock.
5. Edward Campbell Kollock.

Dr. P. M. Kollock, a well known physician of Savannah and professor in the Savannah Medical College, married, second, Sarah Hull, his cousin, daughter of Edward F. Campbell and Sarah Hull, and had:

1. Macartan Campbell Kollock, married Louisa Belle Kollock.

2. Marion Fenwick Kollock, died.
3. Josiah Tattnall Kollock, married Ida Rotureau, and had:
   A. Sarah Campbell Kollock.
   B. Josiah Tattnall Kollock.
3. Sarah Campbell Kollock, married Charles William, son of Rev. Charles B. King and Anna Wylly Habersham, and had Sarah Hull King.

Mary Fenwick Kollock and Rev. Edward Neufville had:
   I. Neufville.
   II. Edward F. Neufville, married Miss Tattnall, daughter of Commodore Josiah Tattnall, and had Mary Neufville, married William James Bulloch Adams, and had:
      I. Edward Neufville Adams.
      II. Richard B. Adams.

James Johnston, of Georgia, one of the old settlers of the Colony of Scotch descent, married Ann Marion, daughter of Sir George Houstoun, Baronet, and Ann Moodie, and from him descend a branch of Kollocks, Johnstons and others; and from the Campbells, who descend from the Bulls, Fenwicks, Draytons and others of Carolina, descend a branch of the Kollocks, Tattnalls, Noble Jones, Harrisons, Kings, Neufvilles and Adams family of Georgia.

JOHNSTON

This old Georgia family is descended from Dr. James Johnston, born 1686, who entered the Royal Navy, and married, in Dumfries, Scotland, in 1722, Jean Nisbet. Who has not heard of the famous Johnstons of the border, so well known in history, and so brave? Well may Georgia be proud of her Johnstons, for James Johnston was the publisher of the *Georgia Gazette*, without which many facts of history would have been forever lost, and his brother, Dr. Lewis Johnston, of Edinburgh, practiced medicine with Dr. John Irvine in Georgia, the latter having married (his second marriage), his daughter, Elizabeth Johnston. Hon. Lewis Johnston was member of His Majesty's Honorable Council, and sided with the Crown during the Revolution. Went to Jamaica, and died there.

Dr. James Johnston, of the Royal Navy, and Jean Nisbet had:

I. Dr. Lewis Johnston, born 1735.
II. Dr. Andrew Johnston.
III. Marion Johnston.
IV. James Johnston.
V. John Johnston.
VI. Rachael Johnston.
VII. Elizabeth Johnston.

Others also died in infancy.

Dr. Andrew Johnston married, in 1761, Bellamy Roche, at Savannah, Ga., and had:

1. Bellamy Johnston.
2. Matthew Johnston.
3. Jean Nisbet Johnston.
4. James Johnston, married Ann Marion Houstoun, daughter of Sir Geo. Houstoun.
5. Marion Anne Johnston.
6. Andrew William Johnston.
7. Rachel Johnston.
8. Louise Laleah Johnston.

Col. James Johnston married, May 31, 1797, at White Bluff, near Savannah, Ga., Ann Marion, daughter of Sir Geo. Houstoun, Bart., and had:

A. Ann Moodie Johnston, married Dr. Wm. R. Waring.
B. Bellamy Roche Johnston.
C. Geo. Houstoun Johnston, married Emily Green Turner.
D. James Robertson Johnston, married Elizabeth Catharine Dowers, of Philadelphia.
E. Jane Priscilla Johnston, married Dr. P. M. Kollock.
F. Louisa Caroline Johnston, married Patrick Houstoun Woodruff.
G. Eliza Heriot Johnston, married Edmund Molyneux.
H. Andrew Johnston, died infant.
I. Priscilla Augusta Johnston, married Geo. J. Kollock.
J. William Patrick Johnston, married Mary Eliza Hool.
K. Mary Helen Johnston, 1814-1872.
L. Susan Marion Johnston, married Geo. J. Kollock.

James Robertson Johnston and Eliza Catharine Dowers had:

a. Susan Woodruff Johnston.
b. James Houstoun Johnston, married Eugenia Cunningham Duncan.
c. Elizabeth Catharine Johnston.

HOUSTOUN

In the reign of Malcolm IV. of Scotland, 1153-65, the grant of a Barony was made to Hugo De Padvinan, and the name of the Baron was changed to Hugh's-town; afterward, when surnames came in vogue, and the name was eventually corrupted to Houstoun. Several descendants of this Hugo received Knighthood, and in 1668 the representative of the family was created a Baronet by King Charles II. of England. When General Oglethorpe went to Georgia, the 5th Baronet, Sir Patrick Houstoun, accompanied him, and founded this ancient and illustrious family of Georgia, who helped lay the foundations of the commonwealth. We find at an early day Dr. Wm. Houstoun a naturalist, being sent by Sir Hans Sloan to gather rare exotics in the West Indies. Sir Patrick Houstoun, member of His Majesty's Council and President of the same, and Registrar General. His sons, Sir Patrick Houstoun and *Sir George Houstoun, member of the Council of Safety, member of Provincial Congress, and a very prominent patriot, 1775. John Houstoun, Delegate to Continental Congress, member of first Executive Council, Governor of Georgia, Mayor of Savannah, Agent of Georgia in boundary disputes, Trustee of State College, Chief Justice of Georgia, &c. William Houstoun, Trustee State College, Agent of Georgia in settlement of boundary disputes, Delegate to Federal Convention for Adoption of Constitution. Dr. James Houstoun, Surgeon in Continental line of Georgia Brigade during the Revolution.

In later days, Edward Houstoun, a man of prominence, and his sons, Dr. J. P. S. Houstoun, a well known physician and oculist, of Savannah, and General Patrick Houstoun, Adjutant General of State of Florida, and really by title a Baronet. Sir Patrick Houstoun, the founder of the family in Georgia, married Lady Priscilla Dunbar, 1736 (Sir Patrick Houstoun came to Georgia in 1735), and had the following children:

I. Patrick Houstoun, 6th Baronet, died, unmarried, in Bath, England.

II. Sir George Houstoun, 7th Baronet, succeeded his brother, married Ann M. Moodie, daughter of Thomas Moodie, Deputy Secretary of Province.

*Sir George did subsequently take the oath of allegiance to the King and was amerced by the Georgia Assembly, but no doubt he thought the day was lost and was a patriot at heart.

III. Wm. Houstoun (Hon.)
IV. Gov. John Houstoun, married Hannah, daughter of Hon. Jonathan Bryan.
V. Dr. James Houston, Surgeon Continental Army.
VI. Ann Houstoun, married George McIntosh, 4th son of John Mohr McIntosh, and from this marriage descend the Clinches, Sadlers, Louds, branch of the Shanklins, Elliotts, of South Carolina, and a branch of Heyward.

Sir George Houstoun, the 7th Baronet, married Ann Moodie, and had:

A. George Houstoun, died.
B. Patrick Houstoun, born 1777; married, 1801, Eliza McQueen.
C. Robert J. M. Houstoun, married Sarah McQueen.
D. Jean Houstoun, married Wednesday, March 30, 1796, George Woodruff.
E. Ann Marion Houstoun, married Col. James Johnston.
F. Priscilla Houstoun, died unmarried.

Patrick Houstoun (son of George Houstoun) and Eliza, daughter of Major Alex. McQueen and Elizabeth Fuller, son of John McQueen and Ann Dallas, son of John McQueen, had:

A. Eliza McQueen Houstoun.
B. Georgia Ann Moodie Houstoun.
C. George Houstoun.
D. Patrick Houstoun.
E. Edward Houstoun, married Claudia Wilhelmina Bond, 1834.
F. James Johnston Houstoun.
G. Robert James Houstoun.
H. Jane Harriet Houstoun.
I. Moodie Houstoun.

Edward Houstoun and Claudia Bond had:

a. Anne Bond Houstoun, married James T. Hopkins.
b. Patrick Houstoun (Gen.), married Martha Bradford.
c. Thomas Bond Houstoun, died early.
d. Edward Houstoun, married Augusta J. Anderson; died 1866.
e. Claudia Wellford Houstoun, died young.
f. Cornelia Elizabeth Houstoun, married George Johnston; died 1882.

g. James Proctor Screven Houstoun, M. D., a well known physician, oculist and officer in Savannah Volunteer Guards, married Sarah G. Cumming, daughter of Wallace Cumming and Harriet Alexander, descended from the Cummings, Clays, Habershams, &c. (See Cumming for issue.)

h. Geo. McQueen Houstoun, died without issue.

i. Eliza McQueen Houstoun, married Raymond Demere, descended from Raymond Demere, an officer in Oglethorpe's regiment, and from the Maxwells and Habershams of Georgia.

j. Claudia Wilhelmina Houstoun, married James Sullivan, son of Dr. Sullivan, of Savannah, Ga., and descended from the noted Sullivan family of Massachusetts.

General Patrick Houstoun, eldest son of Edward Houstoun and Claudia Bond, was a most estimable gentleman and prominent man, Adjutant General of Florida, President of State Senate, and held numerous positions of honor and trust in Florida. He was born in Savannah, and died Monday, May 6, 1901, aged 66 years, in Tallahessee, Fla., his funeral being attended by Confederate Veterans and the State Military. The greatest honor was shown this eminent man and all united in tribute to a worthy son of a distinguished family, who in himself kept up the prestige of the name. He married Martha Bradford, daughter of Col. John Bradford, and had four children:

I. Edward Augustus Houstoun, born 1866, married 1893, Nannie L. King, daughter of Judge Ziba King.

II. Martha Branch Houstoun, born 1869, married 1893, Perry G. Wall.

III. James Proctor Screven Houstoun, born 1875, married 1898, Annie Collins, daughter of State Treasurer C. B. Collins.

IV. Claudia Bond Houstoun, born 1878, married 1896, Geo. P. Rainey, Jr., son of Judge Geo. P. Rainey and Miss Lamar, daughter of Col. Thompson B. Lamar, Colonel of the 5th Florida Regiment, C. S. A., and a brother of Hon. Justice L. Q. C. Lamar, of Mississippi, late of U. S. Supreme Court.

Mrs. Patrick Houstoun was Miss Martha Bradford, great-grand-daughter of Col. John Bradford, of the Revolutionary War, whose mother was a lineal descendant of Oliver Cromwell. Mrs. Houstoun's mother was a daughter of Gov. John Branch, of North Carolina.

Robert James Houstoun, one of the sons of Sir George Houstoun, married Sarah McQueen, sister of Eliza McQueen, who married Patrick Houstoun, brother of Robert, as per above. Robert J. Houstoun and Sarah McQueen had:

I. Sarah Ann Houstoun, who married John W. Anderson, son of Geo. W. Anderson and Eliza Clifford Wayne, son of Capt. Geo. Anderson, of Berwick, Scotland. Eliza Clifford Wayne was daughter of Richard Wayne and Elizabeth Clifford.

Capt. John W. Anderson and Sarah Ann Houstoun had:

I. Robert Houstoun Anderson (Gen. C. S. A.), married Sarah Clitz.

II. George Anderson (Major C. S. A.), married Kate Berrien.

III. John W. Anderson (Capt. C. S. A.), married Jessie C. Wragg.

IV. Clarence Anderson, married Lamar.

V. Clifford W. Anderson (Col. 1st Regiment), married, first, Clifford West; second, Hannah Walker.

VI. Georgia Anderson, married Judge Chisholm, an eminent lawyer and Judge, President of Plant System.

And thus do we see this family united to the Berriens, Wraggs, of South Carolina, Lamars, Wests, Walkers and Houstouns, and descended from the eminent family of Wayne and Anderson, connected to so many of the gentry of Georgia, the Jones, Wallaces, Savages, Owens, &c.

LEWIS

The honorable families of America should keep a faithful record of the noble deeds of ancestors, and emulate them in deeds of valor worthy of the name. When a family rises to importance it should not be forgotten, especially when it has contributed to the country services of value to the community. That the family of Lewis, of Georgia, is an ancient one and that it came to Georgia from Virginia, there can be no doubt, and it would also appear to have been connected by descent to the illustrious family of Washington. Prominent among the members of the Georgia branch may be memtioned such names as Judah Lewis, killed at Midway, in Liberty County, Ga., where the gallant Gen. James Screven met his death wound; Lieut. Joseph Lewis, Liberty County Militia; Capt. Elijah Lewis and others of the name. In earlier times a Samuel Lewis was Sheriff of Liberty County, Ga., and later on we find John Lewis Sergeant of Liberty County Independent Troop and First Corporal and Quartermaster Sergent of the Chatham Troop, 1812, who was a man of sterling integrity, and Elder in Independent Presbyterian Church, Superintendent of Roswell, Cobb County, Sunday School, Chairman of Cherokee Presbytery and Deacons Convention, Cass Co.; Deputy Collector for port of Savannah, Ga., and one of the leading merchants in Savannah; Col. John Nathaniel Lewis, one of the leading citizents of Savannah; Hon. Robert Adams Lewis, his brother, one of the foremost citizens in Savannah, one of Justices of Inferior Court and acting Mayor of Savannah; Lieut. Robert Henry Lewis, a gallant soldier of the war, and his brothers, George Seton and Lt. John Adams Lewis, gallant Confederate soldiers. In fact, all along the line from before the Revolutionary War to the present, we find this family always to the fore, if honor and integrity, patriotism and faith to country, are proof. That they were in Georgia at an early day, we have the proof in records of the name as members of Midway Church; that they held positions as deputy surveyors and other positions, can also be proved, and it is quite certain that they all settled in Liberty County, and that they came first from Virginia and settled in Edgefield District, South Carolina, thence moved to Georgia before 1770. There is a record of Samuel Lewis having land in North Carolina. Samuel Lewis and wife, Mary, came to Georgia, and their children were:

I. Abraham Lewis.

II. *Samuel Lewis, married; killed by Indians in Tennessee.

III. Judah Lewis, killed on Middletons Hill, between Midway Church and Riceboro.

IV. Capt. Elijah Lewis, died February, 1809; married, first, , October 18, 1779; second, †Sarah Hines.

*His widow married, second, Mr. Fulsome, of Natchez, Miss., and had one son, William Fulsome.

†She married, third, Gen. Daniel Stewart.

V. Lt. Joseph Lewis, Liberty Co. Militia, 1777.
VI. Isaac Lewis, died 1809; married Susan Kirkland.‡
VII. Jacob Lewis.
VIII. Demmis Lewis, married Capt. John Webur, of Edgefield District, S. C.
IX. John Lewis, Tutor in Sunbury Academy, in Georgia.

As far as can be learned, this family were in Georgia as early as 1754, and were land owners and patriots of the Revolution. Judah Lewis was killed by the British at Midway, and Elijah Lewis' estate was sequestrated. In 1788, Capt. Elijah Lewis had command of a company for defense against the Indians, and it is related that Joseph Lewis was in his company during the Revolution. In 1774, we find J. Lewis and Elijah Lewis, deputy surveyors, taking oath of allegiance to King George, but subsequently when the Revolution of 1776 came on, they became patriots. Samuel Lewis is mentioned as one of the Tax Collectors of Liberty County, also Sheriff, which in those days were positions of respectability. John Lewis is mentioned as a tutor at Liberty Academy. The name is traced to South Carolina, District of Ninety-Six, where Samuel Lewis had a grant of land, Little Lewis Creek, in 1789; also to State of North Carolina, where Samuel Lewis had located land 29 April, 1786, dated May 18, 1789. One authority traces family to Jamestown, Va.; another tradition is they were related to the Washington family. We see, however, they were an old Georgia family of standing, and that they were an ancient and patriotic race of men. Samuel Lewis married Mary , and had, beside others, Isaac Lewis, married Susan Kirkland, and had Joseph Lewis, married Susannah Baker, and had one son, John Lewis, Sergeant in the Liberty Co. Indepndent Troop, Capt. Williams, under Maj. John McPherson Berrien. John Lewis was Deputy Collector of Port, and Elder in Independent Presbyterian Church, Superintendent Roswell, Cobb Co., Sunday School, Chairman of Cherokee Presbytery Elders and Deacons Convention, November 18, 1858, composed of thirteen counties, and was one of the leading business men of Savannah and a landed proprietor. He died in 1869, at his daughter's residence in Savannah, Ga.

John Lewis, son of Joseph and Susannah Baker Lewis, mar-

‡Probably of the Kirklands, of North Carolina.

ried, first, Susan Adams, on Tuesday, December 12, 1809, daughter of Nathaniel Adams, Esq., planter, of White Bluff, Ga., and his wife, Anne Bolton, born May 2, 1752, died April 27, 1818, daughter of Robert Bolton, Esq., first Postmaster in Georgia, and one who held many positions in Royal Colonial days, but who united with the Colonists, and was Justice of the Peace at White Bluff when he died. Robert Bolton was the son of Robert Bolton, of Philadelphia, a merchant and representative citizen and Church Warden of Christ Church, Philadelphia, who had married Ann Clay, *nee* Curtis, daughter of Winlock Curtis and Ann Bowers, daughter of Benanuel Bowers and Elizabeth, niece of Henry Dunster, first President of Harvard College. Winlock Curtis was son of John Curtis, of Kent on Delaware, and a large landed proprietor. His other son was John Curtis, Chief Justice of Pennsylvania. The Boltons were lineal descendants of the Lords Bolton, descendants of the ancient Saxon Earls of Mercia, descended from one of the Saxon Kings of England. Robert Bolton, of Savannah, married Susannah Mauve, daughter of Mathew and Jane Mauve, French Huguenots, and very rich, who had to leave Switzerland, where they had resided, and fly to America, whither they brought their jewels and an illustrated French Bible, secreted in a chair made for that purpose. Mathew Mauve was born in Vevay, Jane, his wife, in Berne, Switzerland. He died in Savannah, June 28, 1775; she died September 20, 1775. They came to Georgia in 1740. Susannah Mauve was born in Switzerland in 1727, and died in 1762, in Savannah.

Nathaniel Adams was born on St. Helena, in the State of South Carolina, December 20, 1747; died March 7, 1806, in Georgia. He was son of Nathaniel Adams, of South Carolina, who married, September 6, 1744, Margaret Ellis, born October 10, 1727, daughter of Edmund and Anne Ellis, who died March 31, 1738. Edmund Ellis, who died St. Helena, S. C., August 29, 1734, was son of Ellis, a landed proprietor of Durham, England, who came to South Carolina, and who married Mary Wilkinson. The Adams are said to be of same family as that of John Adams, of Massachusetts. John Lewis and Susan Adams had the following children:

I. John Lewis, died.

II. John Nathaniel Lewis, married Frances Simond Henry.

III. Susan Ann Lewis, died.
IV. Robert Adams Lewis, married Catharine Ann Barrington Cook.
V. Margaret Lewis, married Noble Andrew Hardee.
VI. Joseph Lewis, died.

John Lewis married, second, Margaret King, widow of Joseph King, to whom she was married November 8, 1809, by whom she had a child, Susan King. Margaret King was sister to Susan Adams, first wife of John Lewis, and married, second, to John Lewis, by Rev. Henry Kollock, June 13, 1826, and had Mary Eliza Adams Lewis, born January 1, 1828; married by Rev. Nathaniel Pratt, of Roswell, Ga., November 6, 1851, Dr. William Gaston Bulloch.

John Nathaniel Lewis, son of John Lewis and Susan Adams, was born in Savannah, Ga., January 21, 1812; he was educated at Chatham Academy, under the Rev. George White, D. D., and at the age of sixteen entered the counting room of R. & W. King; thence entered counting room of J. Stone & Co.; then went with Geo. B. Cumming, banker, where he remained thirty-three years; after which he entered the Savannah Bank and Trust Co., where he acted as corresponding clerk. He has held numerous positions of honor and trust in several banks. He joined the Odd Fellows and rose to be Noble Grand in the order and also Grand Secretary of Grand Lodge of Georgia. In November, 1829, he joined the Savannah Guards, under Josiah R. Tattnall, and rose to be Lieutenant of the corps under Capt. W. P. Bowen, and at one time was acting commander of the corps. He was also instrumental in organizing the Oglethorpe Light Infantry, and was Captain of the company. In 1843, or about that time, he was Colonel of the First Regiment, and commanded it when it took part in a celebrated sham battle, and his regiment was then composed of the volunteer and militia companies. In 1854, the Savannah Benevolent Association was formed, Mr. Lewis being one of the incorporators, and for years the Secretary of the association, and a noble institution it was—intended to relieve the sick and afflicted in the yellow fever epidemics. Under the separate administrations of Dr. Wayne, John E. Ward and Edward C. Anderson, Esq., Mayors of the city, he was Alderman of Savannah, Chairman of Council and acting Mayor, and he has been Chairman of the Board and one of the Trustees of the Georgia Infirmary. As a member of the Independent Presbyterian Church, he has for years been a Trustee of the church; in home life exemplary as a husband and father. During the late war he entered the Tattnall Home Guards, and was a Lieutenant of the company, which corps built the fortifications around Fort Boggs and the city; and afterward went with the officers of State Bank to Macon, with the assets, and remained there until the close of the war. He married Frances Simond Henry, sister of Judge Charles Seaton Henry, and daughter of Robert Henry, an eminent merchant and gentleman of Albany, New York (son of Robert Henry and Miss Verner), and Isabelle Seaton, daughter of Andrew Seaton, said to be of the Barnes family, and his wife, Margaret Seaton, daughter of John Seaton and his wife, Elizabeth Seaton, of Belssies. These are of the Royal House of Seaton.

John N. Lewis and Margaret Simond Henry had issue:

I. Isabelle Charlotte Lewis, married *Jacob Spivey, banker, and had:

I. Charles Spivey, died.

II. Lewis Spivey.

†II. John Adams Lewis, Lieutenant Conscript Camp, C. S. A., Athens, Ga.

III. Robert Henry Lewis, Lieutenant Co. D, 1st Georgia Regiment, C. S. A.

IV. George Seaton Lewis, private in Co. A, 8th Georgia Cavalry, C. S. A.

V. Margaret Rosina Lewis.

Robert Adams Lewis, second son of John Lewis and Susan Adams, was one of the representative men of Savannah, Ga. He served on the Bench as one of the Justices of the Inferior Court for ten years; also served for many years as member of the City Council, being Chairman of Finance and Chairman of Council; and he could easily have been Mayor—as it was, he was acting Mayor of Savannah, Chairman of Commisisoners

*The Spiveys are an old North Carolina family, whose names are to be found in records of North Carolina. Thomas Spivey, of Chowan, makes his will on December 23, 1729; February 7, 1729-30. Son-in-law, William Hill; daughter, Mary Hill; grand-daughters, Mary and Susannah Hill; sons, Benjamin, Jacob, Thomas and William Spivey. Matthew Spivey, of Norfolk, Va., buys 100 acres of land, December 1, 1714; and other records show them to be an old family of Virginia and North Carolina. In several places in records of North Carolina we find the name as landowners.

†All these served their country faithfully during the late War between the States.

of Pilotage, and was a representative merchant and business man of Savannah, and owner of a fine residence in Roswell, Cobb Co., Ga. He married Catharine Anna Barrington Cook, daughter of Wm. Cook, an English Barrister, and Eliza Barrington. Their children were:

I. Eliza Catharine Lewis, married James Audley Maxwell King, and had:
1. Kate Maxwell King.
2. Julia Rebecca King.
3. Robert Lewis King.
4. Audley Maxwell King.

II. Robert Lewis, married on Staten Island, N. Y., and had issue.

III. Isabella Margaret (Meta) Lewis, married James Roswell King, son of Barrington King and Catharine Nephew, daughter of James Nephew, planter, of an old Georgia family, and Mary Magdalene Gignilliat.

IV. Anne Barrington Lewis, died.

V. Wm. Clarence Lewis, married Augusta E. Pawling, and had:
1. Sophia Lewis.
2. Alice Catharine Lewis.
3. Clarence Lewis.
4. Walter Lewis.

VI. Frances Barrington Lewis, married in Kansas City, Mo., Tuesday, October 9, 1894, Ardena Whitsitt.

The Barrington name is an old one in Georgia, and at an early day we find one Josiah Barrington one of the Tax Collectors in the Colony. One of these Barringtons (probably the above Josiah), who died previously or during the Revolutionary War, married Miss Williams, whose brothers were Thomas Williams, a minister, Richard Williams and Stephen Williams; her other brothers were planters, who lived in Savannah from the earliest times—well known people, respected by all and gentlemen of the "Old School." The issue of the above marriage were two daughters.

I. Eliza Barrington, married Wm. Cook, an English Barrister, an elegant and accomplished gentleman, who had come to Savannah, Ga., on a business trip. Mr. Cook had been a great traveler, and was considered one of the most accomplished and polished gentlemen of the "Old School." His relatives in England had expected him to marry there, but Miss Barrington's beauty captivated him.

II. Katharine Barrington, sister of Eliza, married Roswell King, of Sharon, Conn., a man of sterling integrity and fine mind, and from this marriage the Kings, of Liberty County and Roswell, Ga., descend.

The Maxwells, of Liberty Co., Ga., are an ancient family, and have long been settled in Georgia, and from them and the Kings does James Audley Maxwell King descend. James Maxwell, of Bryan County, and Audley, were brothers, and the family were from Ireland, and undoubtedly of the Maxwells of Nithsdale, Dumfriesshire, Scotland; the "Arms" on will of James Maxwell being three roses, crest; a stag statant. Both of these Liberty and Bryan Co. Maxwells were prominent families, both served their country well, and their connections were both with such ancient families as Bulloch, Dunwody, Mackay, Powell, Habersham, Schley, Screven, Footman, Ways and others. This branch of the Lewis, of Liberty County, descend from the Maxwells, Kings, Barringtons, Cooks, Williams, Adams, Boltons, Mauves, Curtis and others.

Margaret Lewis, daughter of John Lewis and Susan Adams, married Noble Andrew *Hardee, a lawyer and eminent merchant, brother of Gen. Wm. J. Hardee, an eminent Confederate States General, formerly of the U. S. Army and Commandant of the U. S. Military Academy at West Point, sons of Maj. John Hardee and Miss Ellis. The Hardees came originally from North Carolina to South Carolina, thence to Georgia, and can trace back a number of generations. There was a Capt. Hardy, who commanded a galley during the Revolutionary War, in Georgia, and Major Hardee was a Lieutenant in War 1812. Margaret Lewis and Noble Andrew Hardee had the following children:

I. John Lewis Hardee, who married Helen Stoddard of old family, and had:
1. Helen Hardee.
2. Gertrude Hardee, married Frederick Johnston, of old family in Scotland, had issue.
3. Noble A. Hardee.
4. Herbert P. Hardee.

*We have ourselves found the name Hardee in North Carolina History and Genealogical Register; and on May 31, 1738, occurs the name of John Hardee as witness to will of S. Lawson.

5. Marie Hardee, married Chas. Ellis, and had:
   I. Helen Stoddard Ellis.
   II. Margaret Hardee Ellis.

II. Susan Ann Hardee, married, first, Gen. Wm. W. Kirkland, of Hillsboro, N. C. Gen. Kirkland was a gallant General in C. S. Army. They had issue:
1. Margaret Kirkland, married.
2. Noble Hardee Kirkland, married.
4. Elizabeth Lee Kirkland, married, first, Mr. Christman; second, Shepherd, of Shepherdstown, Va.

All of these children evidenced a talent for the stage. Noble H. Kirkland is much more than an ordinary actor and has quite a talent for the stage, and Elizabeth Lee Kirkland (Odette Tyler) is a star actress of some magnitude and an authoress. Mrs. Kirkland married, second, Mr. Mann; third, Capt. Callahan, of U. S. Army; fourth, Dr. Wilkins.

III. Mary Ellis Hardee, married Capt. Clifford A. King, Esq., son of Barrington King, Esq., planter, and President of Roswell Cotton Factory, and Catharine Nephew, daughter of James Nephew, of an old Georgia family, planter.

Away back in annals of Georgia we find a Nephew occupying an official position in Colonial times, and a "Nevie" had a grant of land at an early day in Georgia.

Roswell King was from Sharon, Conn., and was a man of energy and force of character. He married Catharine Barrington, daughter of Josiah (?) Barrington and Miss Williams. The Kings were gallant soldiers during the late war, 1861-65, and among the brothers were Rev. Charles Barrington King, who married Anna W. Habersham; Capt. Thomas King, Lieut. Barrington King, and Capt. James Roswell King, who married, second, Meta Lewis, and Capt. Clifford A. King, who married Mary Ellis Hardee, and had issue (see King). Roswell was a delightful and refined community, composed of settlers from the low country.

Mary Eliza Adams Lewis, only child of John Lewis, by his second marriage to Margaret King, *nee* Adams, sister of Susan Adams, his first wife, married by Rev. Nathaniel Pratt, November 6, 1851.

Dr. Wm. Gaston Bulloch, an eminent surgeon and physician, who served as surgeon, rank of Major, during war between the States, a writer and Professor in Savannah Medical College, graduate of Yale College, 1835, and member of "Skull and Cross Bones Society," of University of Pennsylvania, in medicine. He was the son of John Irvine Bulloch, eldest son of James Bulloch and Ann Irvine, daughter of Dr. John Irvine and Ann Elizabeth Baillie, daughter of Col. Kenneth Baillie. Dr. Irvine was son of Charles Irvine, of Cults, and Euphemia Douglass, of Tilwhilly, John Irvine Bulloch married Charlotte, daughter of Judge John Glen and Sarah, daughter of Dr. N. W. Jones.

GLEN

Dr. Wm. Gaston Bulloch and Mary Eliza Adams Lewis had:

I. Joseph Gaston Baillie Bulloch, M. D., married, April 15, 1880, Eunice H. Bailey, and had issue.

II. Robert H. Bulloch, "M." University of Virginia.

III. Emma Hamilton Bulloch.

Mrs. Bulloch is a poet, and a member of Colonial Dames of America, and was educated at Montpelier, a school founded by late Bishop Elliott. Several children died.

Of the children of Dr. Wm. Gaston Bulloch, all rose to some degree of note. The eldest son, Dr. Joseph Gaston Baillie Bulloch, formerly Recording Secretary of Georgia Medical Society, Vice-President Sons of the Revolution, and President of the Indian Medical Association, A. A. Surgeon M. H. S., author and writer. R. H. Bulloch, a graduate in "M." University of Virginia, architect, and a poet of some parts. Emma Hamilton Bulloch, author of a work on Poetry, a beautiful singer and several times on the Board of Managers of Colonial Dames of Georgia.

Dr. Joseph G. B. Bulloch and Eunice Helena Bailey, descended of the Baileys, of South Carolina and Connecticut, and of the Duttons, of Connecticut, of the Hardens, of Virginia, and Schofields, of North Carolina, daughter of Charles Bailey, Esq., planter and Justice of the Peace, and Ann Cloud, had:

I. Archibald Irvine DeVeaux Bulloch.

II. Wm. Gaston Glen Bulloch.

III. Douglas Eugene St. Cloud Bulloch.

May 12, 1762, we find deed of record of 450 acres of land on Altahama, deeded by Samuel Lewis to his brother, John Lewis, sons of Samuel and Mary, his wife. This second Samuel Lewis went to Nashville, Tenn., thence to Natchez, Miss., where he had a son, Samuel Lewis, the third Samuel Lewis. The second was, it is said, killed by Indians in Tennessee, though it is certain he went to Natchez, Miss., where his son, Samuel, the third, was born, and where his uncle, Capt. Elijah Lewis, went and brought him back to Liberty Co., Ga., where he became a planter. His mother married, second, in Mississippi, Wm. Fulsome, and had a son, Wm. Fulsome. Samuel Lewis, third, married, first, August 22, 1805, Susannah Mann, who died December 25, 1809. He married, second, Drusilla Hines or Way, who married, first, April 2, 1799, Wm. Way, Sr., and had Wm. I. Way.

Samuel Lewis and Drusilla Hines (or Way) had issue:

I. Mary Eliza Lewis, born August 29, 1813, married Frank Parsons.

II. Elijah Lewis, born January 5, 1814.

III. Samuel Newton Lewis, born April 11, 1815.

IV. Sarah Harriet Lewis, married Edward E. Pyncheon.

V. Ann Drusilla Lewis, born June, 1818; married John R. Wilder.

VI. Caroline Rebecca Lewis, born January 14, 1820; married Dr. Wright, of New York, who lived in Georgia, and had issue:

1. James W. Wright, married twice, and had issue.
2. Kingsley Wright.
3. Evelyn Wright, married.
4. Benjamin Wright.

*NOTE.—John Lewis' name occurs on roster of Chatham Hussars as First and Third Corporal, under Capt. Mossman Houstoun, 1812-1813; as Second Quartermaster Sergeant (also under Berrien and Williams); commission to Joseph Lewis in records of Secretary of State at Atlanta as Second Lieutenant of Battalion of Militia, Liberty County, Ga., 9th July, 1777. He was uncle of Joseph Lewis, father of John Lewis.

Ann Drusilla Lewis and John R. Wilder, of an ancient family of New England, and a Consul of one of the foreign powers, had Joseph J. Wilder, merchant, in Savannah, who married Mrs. Smith, daughter of Thomas Butler King, member of Congress, and Ann Page, daughter of Capt. Page; they had Page Wilder, who married Randolph Anderson, attorney at law, son of Col. Edward C. Anderson, Jr., a banker, and Miss Randolph, a descendent of the Randolphs of Virginia and of Thomas Jefferson. Col. Edward C. Anderson was son of George Anderson, Esq., and Miss Stites, daughter of Richard M. Stites, Esq., and Mary Wayne, and George Anderson was son of George Anderson and Eliza Clifford Wayne, daughter of Richard Wayne and Elizabeth Clifford, and the latter George Anderson was a son of Capt. Geo. Anderson, of Berwick, Scotland, and Deborah Grant. This connection embraces branches of the family of Anderson, Owens, Jones, De Renne, Gordon, Stites, Nicol, Mercer, Lamar, Du Bignon, Cunningham and others, such as Williamson, Carmichael, Haskell, Daniel.

Mary Eliza Lewis and Frank Parsons had:

I. Francis Parsons, married Sarah Hervey, at Newberryport, Mass., and had issue:

1. Harriet Parsons, married George W. Owens.
2. Lila Parsons, married Joseph Merrill, of Boston, Mass.

II. Prof. James Parsons, the eminent writer, married Mary Fisher Norris, of Philadelphia, Penn., and had issue:

1. Lewis Parsons.
2. Mary Fisher Parsons.

George W. Owens, attorney at law, was son of Col. George S. Owens, a representative citizen of Savannah, Ga., and Elizabeth Wayne, son of George W. Owens, a former member of Congress, and Sarah Wallace, daughter of Hon. John Wallace, British Consul for Georgia, who married Mary Anderson, daughter of Capt. Geo. Anderson, of Berwick, Scotland, and Deborah Grant. Geo. W. Owens was son of Owen Owens, formerly Alderman in Savannah, and a planter, who came to Georgia at an early day.

Geo. S. Owens and Harriet Parsons had:

I. Mary or May Owens.

II. Clifford Wayne Owens.

Sarah Harriet Lewis and Edward E. Pyncheon had:

I. Lewis Pyncheon, married Miss Hale, of Alabama.
II. Sarah Pyncheon, married.
III. Carrie Pyncheon, married Dr. Braysacher, and had:
1. Harriet Braysacher, married Mr. Eglinston.
2. Maybelle Braysacher.
3. L. Braysacher.

Lewis Pyncheon and Miss Hale had:
1. Edward Hale Pyncheon.
2. Lewis Hale Pyncheon.

Biographical Sketch of John Lewis

John Lewis was born in McIntosh County, Ga., in 1782, and died in 1866, of paralysis, at the residence of his daughter, Mrs. Hardee. He was the son of Joseph Lewis and Susannah Baker, and losing his father at an early age, had to shift for himself. Leaving McIntosh County, and going to Savannah, Ga., when a lad, he early commenced a business career, becoming one of the foremost merchants of his day and time—the firm of Lewis & Stone being a well known and prosperous business house, dealing in every kind of merchandise. Savannah in those days having no railroads, the planters bringing their produce, cotton, rice, etc., to the merchants, who were buyers, cotton factors, and general merchants—the business then being conducted by some of the very best people of the land, and not, as later on, by adventurers and aliens. Afterward, most of the gentlemen retired from business, leaving it to a different sort of people. John Lewis, in his young days, was quite a fashionable man, and at one time owned a large quantity of real estate in Savannah, which was all lost by a large fire, causing his failure; but such was the honor of the man, that he gave up everything, and went to the Suwanee Springs, in Florida, where he made quite a sum of money, though at one time the family had to flee in great haste from the Indians. John Lewis having lost his first wife, ever afterward gave up fashionable life, became a consistent member of the Independent Presbyterian Church, an Elder in it, Superintendent of Roswell, Cobb County, Sunday School, Chairman of Cherokee Deacons and Elders Convention of thirteen counties, was Deputy Collector of Port, was a man pre-eminently noted for the strictest honor, conscientious to a high degree, truthful, moral, and a high-toned gentleman. Nor was he lacking in patriotism. Early, from the age of six, used to the carrying of a gun, when his country called him to arms, we find him Sergeant in Liberty County Independent Troop, 1812, First Corporal and Quartermaster Sergeant in Chatham Troop, Capt. Williams commanding, Major John McPherson Berrien's command, 1812, when they assembled to repel an attack of the British. John Lewis retired from business to his country estate in the beautiful village of Roswell, Cobb County, Ga., and left when he died property in Savannah, Ga., and large bodies of land.

NOTE.—Will of Jacob Lewis and others: Will of Jacob Lewis, wherein he left property to his brothers, Isaac, Judah, Elijah and Joseph Lewis, sister Demmis Lewis, also nephew Joseph Lewis. Will of Abraham Lewis, in which he leaves property to his brothers, Joseph, Judah, Elijah and Isaac, and his sister, Demmis Lewis, dated 17th June, 1774. Will of John Lewis, recorded and dated August 29th, 1763, witnessed by Demmis, Abraham and Joseph Lewis; left property to Samuel Lewis, his father. Will of Evan Lewis on record, seems to be of same line. Samuel Lewis, deed to John, 450 acres on Altamaha River, May 12, 1762. Deed Samuel Lewis to John, of farm stock, June 25, 1762.

BRYAN

As a good many families in this work descend from this old and honorable line of South Carolina and Georgia, and as more reliable records have come to light since the publication of the history of the Bryans in the work on Bellinger and DeVeaux, and as several errors were made, notably in assigning the descent of the Adams, Habershams, Stiles and others from Hugh Bryan and Catharine Barnwell, instead of from Joseph Bryan, grand-son of first Joseph Bryan and Janet Cochran, we here publish the most reliable record of the family taken from the best of references.

NOTE.—One of the Bryans was administrator of James Cochran in 1724.

"In a deed dated October 23, 1735, and recorded in Charleston, Joseph Bryan, the 2d, recites that his father, Joseph Bryan, died intestate, and that his eldest son was the Joseph who makes this deed."

Deeds on record in Charleston from Hugh Bryan mention that his father was Joseph; that his eldest brother was Joseph, and also deeds showing that the brother of Hugh was Jonathan, and the will of William Edwards Cochran, recorded here, leaves as his executrix his wife, Hannah, and her two brothers, Hugh and Jonathan Bryan.

Joseph Bryan (2d), had a son, Joseph (the 3d), for he is mentioned in a conveyance from Hugh Bryan, recorded here, as the son of the brother of Hugh Joseph (2d), who is described as the son and heir of Joseph (the 1st). Elizabeth Bryan is also mentioned in same deed as daughter of Joseph (the wife of Stephen Bull). This Stephen Bull was son of Burnaby Bull, and a cousin of Gen. Stephen Bull, of the Revolutionary War, and was not the Stephen Bull of Sheldon.

In Colonial Park, Savannah, we find an inscription of Mrs. Joseph Bryan, of South Carolina, who died May 26, 1766, aged 64. Near by is buried her son by first marriage with John Williamson, William Bower Williamson, who was father of Mary Bower Williamson, first wife of Edward Barnwell, Sr., and mother of Edward Barnwell, Jr., grand-father on his mother's side of Hon. Joseph W. Barnwell, to whom the author is indebted for these notes. The marriage settlement of Ann Bryan, upon her marriage with James Cuthbert, shows that she was the daughter of Joseph Bryan and the widow Williamson. Now, as John Williamson died in 1732, and Joseph (2d) died in 1735, it is almost certain that Joseph Bryan, 3d, and Elizabeth, Mrs. Bull, must have been by a former wife. . She may have been Mrs. Murray.

Joseph Bryan, 3d, died between the 13th of January, 1750, and February, 1752, for his will is dated and proved on those dates respectively. He married, on January 9, 1741, Mary Storey, and his will mentions his wife, Mary, and daughters, Mary and Agnes.

It would now seem that Hugh Bryan has probably no descendants, though he had a daughter, Mary, mentioned in a deed of William Branford, Jr., dated February 29, 1747. William Branford devised to his daughter, Martha, afterwards Martha Bryan, who died intestate, leaving an only daughter, Mary, now Mary Branford. The St. Andrew's Register shows Hugh Bryan married, first, Martha Branford; the St. Helena Paris Register, a wife, Mary, also Catharine Barnwell, and other records that he married Mary Prioleau. So it seems he married four times and had a daughter, Mrs. Branford, and one styling herself Mrs. E. T., who writes of the death of Catharine, who could not have been her mother, as Mrs. E. T. was grown and married, and Catharine Barnwell's daughter could not have been over five years, if she had one, and the letter was evidently to an older person than a child of five; besides, all testimony now shows that Catharine Barnwell had no children by Hugh Bryan. Both the St. Philips Parish Register and a deed from Mary Bryan, dated April 18, 1758, in which she describes herself as widow of Bryan (shows her to have been Mary Prioleau), and also by her marriage settlement, upon her marriage to Rev. William Hutson, on October 10, 1758, where she describes herself as widow of Hugh Bryan (see Living Christianity).

This honorable family is connected by marriage to the families of Cochran, Barnwell, Prioleau, Bull, Bradford, Storey, Bedon, Pendarvis, Screven, Williamson and others of South Carolina, and to "Cuthbert of Drakies," Houstoun, Screven, Wylly, Adams, Morel, Neyle, King, Stiles, Habersham, Woodbridge, Footman and many others in Georgia, and Randolph, Coulter, &c., of Virginia. Many are its descendants, and the name of Bryan is perpetuated in the names of Bryan County and Bryan street, in Savannah, Ga. The deeds of this eminent family are written on the pages of history, and Georgia owes a debt of gratitude to "The Bryan."

The earliest mention of this family in South Carolina is in a grant to Joseph Bryan, on January 12, 1705, mentioned in a mortgage of June 9, 1737, and recorded in Charleston.

Joseph Bryan and Janet Cochran had the following children:

I. Joseph Bryan, second, died intestate, February 9, 1735; married, first, Mrs. Murray (?); second, Mrs. Williamson.

II. Hugh Bryan, born 1699; died December 31, 1753.

III. Hannah Bryan, will November 5, 1751, and August 20, 1753, married Edward Cockran.

IV. Jonathan Bryan, born September 12, 1708; died March 9, 1788; married October 13, 1737, Mary, daughter of John Williamson and Mary Bower.

Joseph Bryan (son of Joseph Bryan and Janet Cochran), married, first, and had:

1. Joseph Bryan, third, made will January 13, 1750; died February 7, 1752; married January 9, 1741, Mary Story.

2. Elizabeth Bryan, married May 10, 1739, Stephen Bull.

Joseph Bryan married, second, Mrs. Mary Williamson, widow of John Williamson, born Mary Bower, daughter of Wm. Bower and Martha Hext, and had Ann Bryan, married April 12, 1757, Dr. James Cuthbert, Jr., "of Drakies," and had:

I. George Cuthbert.

II. Joseph Cuthbert.

III. Lewis Cuthbert, will August 30, 1803; married Martha Wood, also Miss Bosworth.

IV. Elizabeth Cuthbert, married John Stirk.

V. James Cuthbert, M. D., "of Drakies," will 23 December, 1806.

VI. Jane Cuthbert.

Joseph Bryan (son of Joseph, son of Joseph Bryan and Janet Cochran), married, January 9, 1741, Mary Storey, and had:

1. Mary Bryan, married, September 29, 1774, Col. Richard Wylly.

2. Agnes Bryan (both under 18 years in 1750-52).

Mary Bryan and Col. Richard Wylly had:

I. Alexander Wylly.

II. Mary Wylly, married Nathaniel Adams.

Elizabeth Bryan and Stephen Bull had:

I. John Bull, married Eleanor Purry.

II. Stephen Bull.
III. Josiah T. Bull.
IV. Burnaby Bull.
V. Ann Bryan Bull, married James Garvey.
VI. Lucia Bull, married Jacob Guerard.

Hugh Bryan (brother of Jonathan, son of Joseph Bryan and Janet Cochran), married, first, October 19, 1721, Martha, daughter of Wm. Branford, and had (St. Andrew's Parish Register):

1. Mary Bryan, baptized October 26, 1728; buried May 26, 1750; married April 18, 1746, Wm. Branford, a cousin, died without issue.
2. Elizabeth Bryan, baptized October 26, 1728; married; signs herself E. T.

Hugh Bryan, married, second, Mary ; buried March 20, 1732 (St. Helena Register). He married, third, January 2, 1734, Catharine Barnwell (St. Helena Register), born 1710; died 1740, without issue. He married, fourth, October 25, 1744, Mary, daughter of Samuel Prioleau. She married, second, Rev. Wm. Hutson (St. Philip's Parish Register).

Hannah Bryan and Wm. Edwards Cochran had:

I. Hugh Cochran.
II. William Cochran, will January 17, 1757.
III. Jonathan Cochran, married 1759, Elizabeth Arnold, widow. He also married Mary Tarling and Mrs. Cole.
IV. Elizabeth Cochran, married Elisha Butler.
V. James Cochran, married June 24, 1783, Jane Delegal, widow.
VI. Mary Cochran, married, first, Mr. Tarling; married, second, Samuel Wilkins.

Jonathan Bryan, the patriot, married, October 13, 1737, Mary Williamson, daughter of John Williamson and Mary Bower, and had the following children:

I. Hugh Bryan.
II. Jonathan Bryan.
III. John Bryan.
IV. Joseph Bryan.
V. Mary Bryan, married, first, John Morel, 1766; married, second, Richard Wylly, his second wife.
VI. Josiah Bryan, married, August 14, 1770, Elizabeth Pendarvis.

VII. William Bryan.
VIII. John Bryan.
IX. James Bryan, married March 18, 1790, Elizabeth, daughter of James Langley and Elizabeth Polhill.
X. Elizabeth Bryan.
XI. Hannah Bryan, married Gov. John Houstoun.
XII. Ann Bryan.
XIII. Sarah Janet Cochran Bryan.

Mary Bryan and Hon. John Morel had:

I. Elizabeth Morel, born November 1, 1767; died November 10, 1769.
II. Bryan Morel, born October, 1769; married December 4, 1800, Harriet McQueen.
III. Isaac Morel, born August 27, 1770; died September 12, 1777.
IV. Hester or Esther Morel, born August 1, 1772; married Sampson Neyle about February 20, 1794.
V. Nancy Morel, January 9, 1774.
VI. Hannah Bryan Morel, born August 20, 1776; died April 20, 1790.

Mary Bryan (Morel), widow of Hon. Jno. Morel, married, second, June 3, 1784, Richard Wylly, who first married Mary daughter of Joseph Bryan and Mary Storey, from whom descend a branch of King, Adams, Stiles, Habersham, &c.

Col. Richard Wylly and Mrs. Morel had:

I. Richard Bryan Wylly, born March 2, 1785.
II. Helen Wylly, born August, 1786; married Wm. Woodbridge.
III. Wm. Boyd Wylly, born August 2, 1788.

Josiah Bryan married, August 14, 1770, Elizabeth Pendarvis, daughter of Josiah Pendarvis and Mary, daughter of Col. Richard Bedon, and had Joseph Bryan, born August 17, 1773; died September 8, 1812; married, April 19, 1808, Delia Forman, daughter of Gen. T. M. Forman, of Maryland, issue.

Mrs. Josiah Bryan married, second, John Screven, born 1788; died 16 December, 1825, issue.

James Bryan and Elizabeth Langley had:

1. Ann Bryan, born April 29, 1791, married.
2. Jane Bryan, born February 22, 1802; died June 1, 1881; married.

NOTE.—In concluding this article, I have to present my thanks to Dr. Thomas P. Screven, Hon. Joseph W. Barnwell, Mr. D. E. H. Smith and Langdon Cheves, Esq., for many facts which complete the records of a family in which much confusion has arisen as to the various lines of descent and now is complete and verified by deeds, records, &c.

WILLIAMSON

John Williamson, of "Stono," the ancestor of the South Carolina and Georgia family of that name, settled upon the Stono River towards the end of the 17th century. He seems to have been married twice, but the name of his first wife is unknown. By his second wife, Phoebe, who after his death married William Peter, of Colleton County, S. C., he left the following issue:

I. John Williamson, married Mary Bower.
II. Richard Williamson.
III. Benjamin Williamson, married *Elizabeth Elliott, daughter of Robert Elliott and Elizabeth Screven.
IV. Joseph Williamson.
V. Henry Williamson, married Margaret Rose.
VI. William Williamson, married Martha Emms.
VII. Elizabeth Williamson, married William Smith.
VIII. Margaret Williamson, married Col. John Smith.
IX. Sarah Williamson, married, first, William Harvey; second, Stanyarne.

John Williamson, son of John and Phoebe, married Mary Bower, the daughter of William Bower and Martha Hext, and had issue:

1. William Bower Williamson, married, first (probably), Sarah Chardon, widow of William Simmons, and daughter of Isaac Chardon and Mary Woodward; no issue; second, Mary Flower.
2. John Williamson, married Magdalene Postell.
3. Mary Williamson, married Jonathan Bryan.
4. Elizabeth Williamson, married John Smith.
5. Sarah Williamson, married Isaac Hayne.

William Bower Williamson died in 1762, and was buried at Savannah, in the Colonial Burying Ground, near his mother, Mary Bower Williamson, who after the death of her first husband, John Williamson, married Joseph Bryan, the son of Joseph Bryan, and brother of Hugh and Jonathan Bryan, and

*Daughter of Robert Elliott, whose father, Humphrey, came from the North with the Screvens.

died in 1766. William Bower Williamson left one daughter by his second wife, a posthumous child, Mary Bower Williamson, who was the first wife of Edward Barnwell, of Beaufort, S. C., and the mother of Capt. Edward Barnwell, whose second wife was Eliza Zubly Smith, of Savannah, Ga.

John Williamson, son of John and Mary Bower, married Magdalene Postell on September 11, 1755, and had issue, amongst others:

A. John Garnier Williamson, married Jane Parmenter.
B. William Henry Williamson.
C. Bower Williamson.
D. Margaret Williamson.

John Garnier Williamson, who was born July 30, 1756, and who married Jane Parmenter on February 8, 1776, had the following issue:

a. John Postell Williamson, married Sarah Williamson McQueen.
b. Elizabeth Williamson.
c. William Bower Williamson. d. Henry Williamson. Twins.
e. Mary Ann Williamson.

John Postell Williamson was born September 28, 1778, and was twice married. He married Sarah Williamson McQueen on January 4, 1804, and had issue, among others:

I. John Williamson, married Julia C. Wayne.
II *Jane Williamson, married November 15, 1821, Maj. A. B. Fannin.
III. Sarah Williamson, married Col. Edward C. Anderson.

From this marriage of John Williamson to Julia C. Wayne, which took place on September 8, 1848, the issue are:

1. Nancy Gordon Williamson, died infant.
2. John Williamson, born February 3, 1852.
3. William Wayne Williamson, born September 1, 1854.

*A branch of Fannin, Anderson, Fish, McIntosh, Holst and others descend from this family, as do the Booths, Potter, Williamson, &c. These data were furnished by Hon. Joseph W. Barnwell. (See Dennis.)

BOWER

Mary Bower, daughter of Wm. and Martha (Hext) Bower, married Jno. Williamson, and had:

I. Mary Williamson, married Jonathan Bryan.
II. Elizabeth Williamson, married John Smith.
III. John Williamson, married Magdalene Postell.
IV. Wm. B. Williamson, married (see Williamson).

John Smith, son of Rev. Archibald Smith, of Dalkeith, Scotland, and Jane Wallace, married Elizabeth Williamson, and had:

I. Mary Smith, married Basil Cowper, died without issue.
II. Elizabeth Smith.
III. John Smith.
IV. Anne Smith, married Capt. John McQueen.
V. Jane Smith, married Thomas Bourke.
VI. Sarah Smith, married Sir James Wright, died without issue.
VII. Archibald Smith, married, first, Miss Joyner; second, Helen Zubly, from whom branch of Barnwell, of South Carolina.

John McQueen and Anne Smith had:

I. John McQueen, married Margaret Couper.
II. Elizabeth McQueen, married Robert Mackay.
IV. Sarah McQueen, married Jno. P. Williamson.
V. William McQueen, married Ann Wright.

Alexander McQueen and Elizabeth Fuller had:

I. Harriet McQueen, married Bryan Morel.
II. Maria McQueen, married Sampson Neyle, second wife.
III. Eliza McQueen, married Patrick Houstoun.
IV. Ann McQueen, married J. Lawson.
V. Lydia McQueen.
VI. Sarah McQueen, married Robert J. Houstoun.
VII. Frances McQueen.
VIII. Octavia McQueen.

NOTE ON MCQUEEN.—John McQueen, probably of McQueen, of Corribrough (see Creek Treaty, 1739), had John McQueen, who married Ann Dallas, and had:

I. John McQueen, married Ann Smith.
II. Alex. McQueen, married Elizabeth Fuller, daughter of Col. Thomas Fuller and Lydia Hazzard.

III. Ann McQueen, married Thomas Netherclift, from whom descends a branch of Morel, Box (see Bellinger & DeVeaux pamphlet).

FULLER

Capt. Wm. Fuller married, January 11, 1726, Martha Whitmarsh, and had Richard Fuller, married Mary, daughter of Thomas Drayton, and had:

I. Ann Booth Fuller, married William Ross.

II. Thomas Fuller, married, first, Lydia Hazzard; second, Elizabeth Miles, widow; married, third, Catharine Foley, from whom descend the Potter family, of Georgia, for on August 22, 1791, Mr. John Potter married Catharine Fuller (see Glen for descent of Poullain, Cuyler, Langhorn, Conover, Hodgson, Higginson, &c.).

POTTER

The Potters, of Mount Potter, an Irish family, was represented in America by John Potter, born at Bally Moran, County Down, Ireland, April 2, 1765; went to Charleston, S. C., December 15, 1784; son of James Potter, of Mount Potter, and Catharine, daughter of Sir John Stewart, of Bally Moran, who was descended from the second son of Sir Alexander Stewart, of the Royal House of Stewart. John Potter married Catharine Fuller, of Beaufort, and had three children:

I. James Potter, married Sarah Jones Grimes, daughter of Dr. John Grimes, of Georgia, and Catharine Jones Glen, daughter of Judge John Glen and Sarah, daughter of Dr. Noble W. Jones. From this marriage comes the Poullains, Langhornes, Hodgsons, Cuylers, Higginsons, Potters, and the various lines of intermarriages with Lynah, Graham, Walker, Hayne, Archer, Manning, MacNeil, &c.

II. Harriet Maria Potter, married Commodore Stockton, of New Jersey.

III. Thomas Fuller Potter, married, first, ; second, Sarah Hall, daughter of Charles H. Hall, of Sunbury, member of the bar.

NOTE.—Sarah Jones, daughter of Dr. N. W. Jones, married Judge

John Glen, son of William Glen, of South Carolina, and Ann, his wife, of Glens of Bar. The descendants of this marriage were branches of the families of Bulloch, Burke, Hunter, Bryan, Williams, Winter, Cuyler, Poullain, Langhorne, Conover, Higginson, Hodgson, Bayard, Colburn and others.

John Potter built a beautiful church in Princeton, N. J., and all his family are buried there; also his wife, Catharine Fuller. Dr. John Grimes, possibly of Grymes, of Virginia, died June 24, 1836, aged 35 years. He was one of the founders of Georgia Medical Society, 1804, and delivered the oration on the death of Dr. N. W. Jones, in 1805.

OWENS

This well known family, whose connections embrace a large number of the very best people of Savannah, and which has occupied the highest social position in the city, and which by intermarriage is connected to the Habersham, Wayne, Wallace, Gordon, Anderson, Lewis, Parsons, Haskell, Thomas, Haynes, Daniel and others, is descended from Owen Owens, at one time an Alderman of Savannah, and who owned a place on St. Catharine's Island, in Georgia. His son, George W. Owens, a member of Congress 1835-39, married Miss Wallace, a daughter of the Hon. John Wallace, British Vice Consul for Georgia. Of members of this family who have contributed to the honor of the State we may mention Col. Geo. S. Owens, President of the Oglethorpe Club, member of Georgia Legislature, and a gentleman well and socially known in many ways. His brothers, John Owens, attorney at law, Richard N. Owens, Solicitor General of Georgia, and others now alive who are well known as gentlemen of standing.

Hon. Geo. W. Owens married Sarah Wallace, and had:

I. Mary Owens.
II. Geo. S. Owens, married Elizabeth Wayne.
III. John Owens, married Margaret Footman, daughter of Richard S. Footman and Mary C. Maxwell, daughter of James B. Maxwell and Mary Habersham.
IV. Sarah Owens.
V. Margaret Owens, married Dr. J. G. Thomas, of Kentucky, a well known popular physician, who became President of Georgia State Medical Society and member of Georgia State Legislature. They had, beside others, dead:

I. Maud Thomas.

II. Meta Thomas.

VI. Richard N. Owens, married and had issue:

1. John Owens.
2. Mary Wallace Owens.
3. M. L. Owens, married Anderson Carmichael, son of Wm. P. Carmichael and Eliza, daughter of Rt. Rev. Stephen Elliott, son of Hon. Stephen Elliott and Esther Habersham, and had issue.
4. Benjamin Owens, married Miss DeSaussure, of Charleston.
5. Elizabeth Owens married S. P. Shotter.

Col. Geo. S. Owens, married Elizabeth Wayne, daughter of Gen. Wm. Clifford Wayne and Ann Gordon, daughter of Capt. Ambrose Gordon, of the Revolutionary War, and had:

1. Sally Gordon Owens, married Lewis Haskell, issue.
2. Geo. W. Owens, married Harriet Parsons, issue.
3. Anne Wayne Ownes, married Daniel, issue.
4. Lizzie Wayne Owens, married Munnerlyn, issue.
5. Margaret W. Owens.
6. Julia C. Owens.
7. Virginia S. Owens, married George S. Haines, issue.
8. Wm. C. Owens, M. D., married Miss Forbes, issue.
9. T. Lloyd Owens.
10. Clifford Owens, died.

ANDERSON

Such was the martial spirit of the early Georgians that one can scarcely point to any one family as a military one more than the other; but certain it is that the family of Anderson deserve this title, and its members in all walks of life have ever been to the fore, and its connection to the Waynes, Houstouns, Randolphs, Dennis, Berriens, Lamars, Wraggs, Jones, Wallaces, Owens, Gordons, Lewis and others shows its high social position; and as we lift the veil and see the many scores of this line who have risen to eminence, well may we feel a laudable pride in the purely Savannah family of Anderson. Among the members of this family we may enumerate: Capt. John W. Anderson, of the "Blues," a prominent merchant and Superintendent of Independent Presbyterian Sunday School; his sons, Gen. Robert H. Anderson, a West Pointer, of the Confederate States Army; Major George Anderson, of Fort McAllister fame; Capt. John W. Anderson, of the Savannah Cadets; Col. Clifford A. Anderson, of 1st Georgia Regiment, and Hon. Edward C. Anderson, brother of Capt. Jno. W. Anderson, who for many times was Mayor of Savannah and a Colonel C. S. A., and his son, Edward C. Anderson, midshipman on Alabama, when in the fight with Kersearge off coast of France; and Col. Edward C. Anderson, Jr., C. S. A., nephew of Col. E. C. Anderson, a prominent banker, and others well known of the name. The ancestor of this family was a Scotchman, Capt. George Anderson, of Berwick, and his son, George Anderson, Alderman of Savannah, 1798, and daughter, Mary, who came to Georgia before the Revolutionary War.

The Anderson Family of Savannah, Ga.

Capt. George Anderson, of the city of New York, was, as far as is known, the first member of this family in America. He is supposed to have come to this country prior to the year 1760, and, according to the tradition in the family, is said to have come from the neighborhood of Berwick on the Tweed, in Northumberland County, England. The plantation owned by his son, near Savannah, and still in the possession of some of the family, received the name of "Berwick," it is said, from that circumstance. Capt. George Anderson was married, on February 16th, 1761, by the Rev. Henry Barclay, Rector of Trinity Church in New York City, to Deborah Grant, also of New York City (born 1736). Their marriage certificate is now in the possession of J. Randolph Anderson, Esq., of Savannah. In the latter part of the year 1763 they removed to Savannah, in the Province of Georgia, where George Anderson became the owner and commander of the ship "Georgia Paquet." George Anderson died at sea on board said vessel, in September, 1775, while on a voyage from Savannah to Great Britain, leaving his widow and three children surviving him. His will is of record in the office of the Secretary of State of the State of Georgia, in Book of Wills "B," pages 194-196. His widow, Mrs. Deborah Anderson, continued to reside in Savannah, and died there at the age of 76, on May 5th, 1812. The issue of George Anderson and Deborah Grant were:

I. John Anderson, born June, 1762; married, March 18, 1790, Susanna Wylly, and left issue.

II. Mary Anderson, born July 30, 1766; died December

31, 1852; married, June 12, 1781, John Wallace, and left issue.

III. George Anderson, born 1767; died May, 1847; married, November 4, 1794, Eliza Clifford Wayne, and left issue.

I. Capt. John Anderson, of the Royal Army, eldest child of George Anderson and Deborah Grant, was born June, 1762. He was intended for the church, and at the outbreak of the American Revolution was at school in England, where he was being educated for that end. The war, however, changed his career. In a letter written by him, May 9, 1838, to his son, Major John Grant Anderson, of the Royal Army, he relates that on the recapture of Savannah by the British in 1778, he sailed for Georgia on a man-of-war in the suite of the Governor, Sir James Wright, and that through the influence of the Governor, who was well acquainted with his family, he was entered as a midshipman in the navy on the books of the vessel, which was commanded by Capt. Sir James Wallace. After taking part in several naval battles of fleets and single ships, he was captured by a French fleet, but was immediately exchanged, and landed in Georgia, where he was given a commission in an infantry regiment, and later transferred to the cavalry. Upon the formation of a select corps of light dragoons, composed of sixty picked men each from six separate regiments, he was appointed Lieutenant of the company selected from his regiment. He served in this corps with distinguished gallantry, and during the last year of the war was promoted to the command of a company, though barely twenty years of age. At the conclusion of the Revolutionary War, he settled in the Bahama Islands, where he was granted 500 acres of land by the government for his services, and where, on March 18, 1790, he married Susanna Wylly (born April 17, 1763), a daughter of Alexander Wylly, originally of Coleraine County, Ireland, who had been Speaker of the Colonial Assembly of Georgia and Secretary of the Governor's Council before the Revolution. The issue of Capt. John Anderson and Susanna Wylly were:

1. Susan Wylly Anderson, born August 28, 1791; married Wm. Brook, and left issue.
2. (Major) John Grant Anderson, born January 17, 1793; married Julianna Hield, and left issue.
3. Mary Eliza Anderson, born May 5, 1799.

4. (Sir) George Campbell Anderson, born January 22, 1805; married, 1842, Mary Annie Brown, and left issue.

Of these descendants of Capt. John Anderson and Susanna Wylly, John Grant Anderson became a Major in the English Army. The youngest son, Sir George Campbell Anderson, became Chief Justice and Governor General of the Bahama Islands, and was created a Baronet by Queen Victoria in 1874; and one of the latter's sons, Sir William John Anderson, was Chief Justice of the Colony of British Honduras up to January, 1900, and is at present Chief Justice of the Island of Trinidad.

II. Mary Anderson, second child of George Anderson and Deborah Grant, was born in Savannah, July 30, 1766, and died December 31, 1852. She married, June 12, 1781, John Wallace, of Scotland, who was the first English Consul in Savannah after the American Revolution, a brother of Hon. James Wallace and of Hon. Michael Wallace, who moved to Nova Scotia and rose to high offices of trust in that Colony. The issue of Mary Anderson and John Wallace were:

I. *Mary Anderson Wallace, born June 3, 1782; married, June 12, 1810, Thomas Savage, Esq., of Savannah, and left issue.

II. Jane Wallace, born December 21, 1785; died March 19, 1848; married, February, 1807, Charles Howard, of Savannah, and left issue.

III. Eliza Wallace, born September 21, 1787; married, May, 1817, Thomas Edward Lloyd, of Savannah, and left issue.

IV. Sarah Wallace, born January 16, 1789; died June 17, 1865; married, June 12, 1815, Hon. George W. Owens, of Savannah, member of Congress, and left issue.

V. John Wallace, born January 8, 1792; died May 13, 1816, unmarried.

VI. Margaret Wallace, born August 14, 1796; died November 27, 1827, unmarried.

*This brings in a wide relationship, embracing the Owens, Lloyds, Howards, Andersons, DeRennes, Jones, Haskells, Haynes, Ravenels and others; also through the Savage family, the Clays, Heywards and others. The Wallaces were Lairds of Carsriggan.

VII. Harriet Wallace, born October 6, 1798; died in childhood.

VIII. Robert James Wallace, born May, 1800; died in childhood.

IX. George Anderson Wallace, born 1802; died in infancy.

III. George Anderson, third child of George Anderson and Deborah Grant, was born in Savannah, 1767, and died May, 1847. He became a very successful merchant and a man of much prominence in the early life of Savannah as a city. He married, November 4, 1794, Eliza Clifford Wayne, a sister of Hon. James M. Wayne, Justice of the U. S. Supreme Court, and daughter of Richard Wayne and Elizabeth Clifford (daughter of William Clifford, of South Carolina, and Mary Elliott). Their issue were:

1. George Wayne Anderson, born May 3, 1796; died April 25, 1872; married, May 11, 1820, *Eliza Clifford Stites, and left issue.
2. Richard Wayne Anderson, born 1798; died in childhood.
3. Thomas Grant Anderson, born 1800; died in childhood.
4. Eliza Mary Anderson, born July 6, 1802; died March 21, 1865; married, January 9, 1823, Hon. Jno. C. Nicoll, and left issue.
5. John Wayne Anderson, born 1805; died August 22, 1866; married, October, 1834, Sarah Ann Houstoun, and left issue.
6. James William Anderson, died in infancy.
7. Georgia Ann Cumming Anderson, born 1810; died June 15, 1844, unmarried.
8. Mary Stites Anderson, born 1812; died February 3, 1855; married, February 5, 1833, Gen. Hugh W. Mercer, and left issue.
9. Edward Clifford Anderson, born November 8, 1815; died January 6, 1883; married, February 10, 1841, Sarah Williamson, and left issue.
10. Julia Anderson, born 1818; died 1819, in infancy.

*Sarah Anderson Stites, sister of above, married, 1821, William Washington Gordon, and is ancestor of the Gordons, of Savannah, Ga.; so that we see through Waynes, Stites and Dennis a wide connection is formed. A branch of Owens descend from Wayne.

1. George Wayne Anderson, eldest child of George Anderson and Eliza Clifford Wayne, was born May 3, 1796, in Savannah, and died April 25, 1872. He married, May 11, 1820, his first cousin, Eliza Clifford Stites, daughter of Richard Montgomery Stites and Mary Wayne (and grand-daughter of Richard Wayne and Elizabeth Clifford). In the war of 1812-1815 he was commissioned Major in the service of the United States and subsequently attained great prominence in the financial world. He was for forty years the President of the Planters' Bank in Savannah, and during the administration of President Jackson was tendered, but declined, the important office of Secretary of the Treasury of the United States. The children of George Wayne Anderson and Eliza Clifford Stites were:

A. Mary Eliza Anderson, born 1823; died in childhood.

B. Edward Clifford Anderson (Jr.), born January 7, 1839; died September 27, 1876; married, November 8, 1860, Jane Margaret Randolph, and left issue.

4. Eliza Mary Anderson, fourth child of George Anderson and Eliza Clifford Wayne, was born July 6, 1802, and died March 21, 1865. She married, January 9, 1823, Hon. John Cochran Nicoll, United States District Judge for Georgia, a son of Col. Abimael Y. Nicoll, of New York, and Caroline Agnes Ledbetter. The children of Eliza Mary Anderson and John Cochran Nicoll were:

I. Eliza Anderson Nicoll, born October 14, 1823; died in infancy.

II. Caroline Agnes Nicoll, born December 17, 1825; married, February 12, 1846, Charles Augustus Lafayette Lamar, and has issue.

III. Georgia Clifford Nicoll, born June 29, 1828; died August 2, 1863; married, November 25, 1856, Dr. James Skelton Gilliam, U. S. N., and left issue.

IV. George Anderson Nicoll, born October 26, 1830; died May 26, 1879; married, January 19, 1858, Sarah Parker Herndon, of Virginia, and left issue.

V. Mary Anderson Nicoll, born April 13, 1833; died October, 1833, in infancy.

VI. Susan Cumming Nicoll, born December 28, 1835; died in infancy.

VII. Ada Clifford Nicoll, born August 28, 1837; died October, 1846, in childhood.

5. John Wayne Anderson, fifth child of George Anderson and Eliza Clifford Wayne, was born in Savannah, 1805, and died August 22, 1866. He married, October, 1834, Sarah Ann Houstoun, only child of Robert Houstoun, of Savannah, and Sarah McQueen, and a grand-daughter of Sir Patrick Houstoun, of the colonial era of Georgia. He held a high office in the business world of Savannah, and in the Civil War became a Captain in the military service of the Confederate States. The children of John Wayne Anderson and Sarah Ann Houstoun were:

A. Robert Houstoun Anderson, born October 1, 1835; died February 8, 1888; married, December 3, 1857, Sarah Clitz, and left issue.

B. Eliza Clifford Anderson, born February 10, 1838; died September 11, 1900; married, January 30, 1861, Hon. Walter S. Chisolm, and left issue.

C. George Wayne Anderson, born August 5, 1839; married, January 9, 1861, Katherine Hunter Berrien, and has issue.

D. John Wayne Anderson, born September 20, 1843; died February 16, 1901; married, October 20, 1865, Jessie Choisie Wragg, and left issue.

E. Clarence Gordon Anderson, born June 13, 1846; married, January 6, 1869, Florida Lamar, and has issue.

F. Clifford Wallace Anderson, born March 19, 1848; died April 3, 1901; married, first, 1872, Clifford Nephew West, and had issue; married, second, 1888, Hannah Townsend Walker, and left issue.

8. Mary Stites Anderson, eighth child of George Anderson and Eliza Clifford Wayne, was born 1812, and died February 3, 1855. She married, February 5, 1833, Hugh Weeden Mercer, who was in the Civil War, became a General in the army of the Confederate States, and who was a son of Col. Hugh Mercer, of Virginia, and Mary Stuart. The children of Mary Stites Anderson and Gen. Hugh W. Mercer were:

I. George Anderson Mercer, born February 9, 1835; married, October 23, 1861, Nannie Herndon, of Petersburg, Va., and has issue.

II. Mary Stuart Mercer, born January 12, 1841; married H. H. Walker, of Sussex County, Va., and has issue.

III. William Gordon Mercer, died, 1844, in infancy.
IV. Robert Lee Mercer, born July 10, 1848.
V. Georgia Anderson Mercer, born September, 1852; died December 6, 1878; married, 187—, Robert Boit, of Boston, Mass., and left issue.
VI. Hugh Weeden Mercer, died in infancy.

NOTE.—A branch of the Clays and Mercers are connected through Herndon to each other and to the Maurys of Virginia, and the Mercers descend from Gen. Hugh Mercer, of Revolution, Cyrus Griffin, President of Continental Congress, and from Lady Stewart (see Virginia Historical Magazine).

9. Edward Clifford Anderson, ninth child of George Anderson and Eliza Clifford Wayne, was born in Savannah, November 8, 1815, and died January 6, 1883. He entered the United States Navy, where he served a number of years and rose to the rank of Lieutenant, but resigned in 18—, and returned to Savannah, where he became a man of much prominence, and was several times elected Mayor of the city. During the Civil War he became a Colonel of artillery in the provisional army of the Confederate States. He married, February 10, 1841, Sarah Williamson, daughter of John Postell Williamson and Sarah McQueen. The children of Edward Clifford Anderson and Sarah Williamson were:

A. Mary Stites Anderson, born April 6, 1842; married, October 1, 1868, Edward Pape, of Baltimore, and had issue.
B. Edward Maffett Anderson, born August 6, 1843.
C. Georgia Anderson, born September 4, 1846; died April 2, 1880; married, February, 1867, Horace A. Crane, of Savannah, and left issue.
D. Hugh Mercer Anderson, died in childhood.
E. Richard Stites Anderson, born August 5, 1852; married, February 3, 1881, Kate Gookin, of New York, and has issue.
F. Sarah Williamson Anderson, born August 5, 1852.

B. Edward Clifford Anderson (Jr.), son of George Wayne Anderson and Eliza Clifford Stites, was born in Savannah, January 7, 1839, and died September 27, 1876, of the dreadful yellow fever epidemic of that year. He was educated at the University of Virginia, where he took the degree of Bachelor of Law in 1860. At the outbreak of the Civil War he raised a troop of cavalry which he equipped at his own expense, and entered the military service of the Confederate States. He became Major of the 24th Georgia Battalion of Cavalry and Lieutenant Colonel and then Colonel of the 7th Georgia Cavalry, and was severely wounded in the battle of Trewillian's Station in Virginia, in 1864. He married, November 8, 1860, Jane Margaret Randolph, of Edgehill, Albemarle County, Va., a daughter of Hon. William Mann Randolph, of Middle Quarter, and Margaret Smith Randolph (daughter of Col. Thomas Jefferson Randolph, and great-grand-daughter of Thomas Jefferson). The children of Edward Clifford Anderson (Jr.) and Jane Margaret Randolph were:

a. Jefferson Randolph Anderson, born September 4, 1861; married, November 27, 1895, Anne Page Wilder, of Savannah, and has issue.
b. George Wayne Anderson, born July 10, 1863; married, December 21, 1889, Estelle Marguerite, daughter of Frederick George Burthe, Esq., of New Orleans, La., and his wife, Mary Adele Nicholas, and has issue.
c. Eliza Clifford Anderson, born October 24, 1864; died September 11, 1876.
d. Margaret Randolph Anderson, born August 21, 1866; married, November, 1893, Abbott Lawrence Rotch, of Boston, and has issue.
e. Sarah Anderson, born May 21, 1872.

A. Robert Houstoun Anderson, eldest child of John Wayne Anderson and Sarah Ann Houstoun, was born in Savannah, October 1, 1835, and died February 8, 1888. He was educated at the United States Military Academy at West Point, where he was graduated in 1857 and entered the U. S. Army as Lieutenant in the 9th Infantry. At the opening of the Civil War he resigned and entered the army of the Confederate States, where he rose to the rank of Brigadier General. He married, December 3, 1857, Sarah Clitz, daughter of Capt. John Clitz, U. S. Army, and Mary Gale Mellen. The children of Robert Houstoun Anderson and Sarah Clitz were:

a. Mary Houstoun Anderson, born September 16, 1859; married, March 12, 1878, Wm. Allen, of Virginia.
b. Robert Houstoun Anderson, born August 27, 1861; died November 7, 1901; married, January 29, 1890, Fannie Taylor, and left issue.
c. Sallie Clitz Anderson, born January 31, 1863; died

March 5, 1883; married, May 6, 1882, Carl Eglinger; left no issue.

B. Eliza Clifford Anderson, second child of John Wayne Anderson and Sarah Ann Houstoun, was born in Savannah, February 10, 1838, and died September 11, 1900. She married, January 30, 1861, Hon. Walter Scott Chisholm, of Savannah, a lawyer of great prominence, who was for many years Judge of the City Court of Savannah. Their children were:

I. John Anderson Chisholm, born December 5, 1861; married, June, 1896, Grace Clarke, of Albemarle County, Va., and has issue.

II. Georgia Barnard Chisholm, born January, 1863; died November, 1895, unmarried.

III. Sarah Houstoun Chisholm, born November 22, 1864; died June 10, 1883, unmarried.

IV. Walter Scott Chisholm, born 1867.

V. Eliza Clifford Chisholm, born 1869; died in infancy.

VI. Edward Clifford Chisholm, born November 27, 1871, married.

VII. Frank Miller Chisholm, born June 12, 1878.

C. George Wayne Anderson, third child of John Wayne Anderson and Sarah Ann Houstoun, was born in Savannah, August 5, 1839. He was educated at the University of Virginia, and at the outbreak of the Civil War entered the military service of the Confederate States and attained the rank of Major. He was in command of Fort McAllister, on the Ogeechee River, in 1864, and greatly distinguished himself by his heroic defence of that post when it was besieged and finally carried by storm by Sherman's army in its advance upon Savannah. He married, January 9, 1861, Katherine Hunter Berrien, a daughter of Hon. John McPherson Berrien and Eliza Cecil Hunter. Their children were:

a. John Berrien Anderson, born October 9, 1861; died March 11, 1865, in infancy.

b. Frank Bartow Anderson, born July 15, 1863; married June 19, 1887, Elizabeth Jadwin, of Brooklyn, and has issue.

c. Kate Berrien Anderson, born April 25, 1867; married, January 7, 1891, Wm. L. Wilson, of Savannah.

d. Lydia McLane Anderson, born January 6, 1875.

D. John Wayne Anderson, fourth child of John Wayne

Anderson and Sarah Ann Houstoun, was born in Savannah, September 20, 1843, and died February 16, 1901. At the beginning of the Civil War he entered the army of the Confederate States and attained the rank of Captain. At the close of the war he engaged in business in Savannah, but afterwards removed to New York, and subsequently entered the government customs service. He married, October 20, 1865, Jessie Choisie Wragg, a daughter of Dr. Thomas Wragg, of Charleston, S. C., and Caroline McDowell. Their children were:

a. Caroline McDowell Anderson, born March 25, 1867; married, April 17, 1890, J. F. C. Myers, of Savannah; has issue.

b. Jessie Anderson, born October 30, 1869.

E. Clarence Gordon Anderson, fifth child of John Wayne Anderson and Sarah Ann Houstoun, was born in Savannah, June 13, 1846. During the Civil War, at the age of 16, he entered the army of the Confederate States, was captured at the fall of Fort McAllister in 1864, and confined as a prisoner of war at Point Lookout, Md., until the close of hostilities. He married, January 6, 1869, Florida Lamar, a daughter of George W. Lamar, of Augusta, Ga., and Sarah Harlow, of Burke County, Ga. Their only child is:

a. Clarence Gordon Anderson, born February 8, 1873.

F. Clifford Wallace Anderson, sixth child of John Wayne Anderson and Sarah Ann Houstoun, was born in Savannah, March 19, 1848, and died April 2, 1901. He was educated at the Virginia Military Institute at Lexington, Va., and took a prominent part in local military matters in Savannah, being for a number of years Colonel of the First Regiment of Volunteers. He married, first, 1872, Clifford Nephew West, of Savannah, a daughter of Dr. Charles West and Eliza Whitehead, and by this marriage had one child:

a. Clifford West Anderson, born April, 1873.

He married, secondly, Hannah Townsend Walker, a daughter of Gen. Wm. H. T. Walker, of Augusta, Ga., and Mary Townsend, of Albany, N. Y. The children of this second marriage were:

a. Mary Walker Anderson.

b. Hannah Townsend Anderson.

A. Mary Stites Anderson, eldest child of Edward Clifford Anderson and Sarah Williamson, was born in Savannah, April 6, 1842. She married, October 1, 1868, Edward Pape, of Baltimore, a son of Dr. Edward Pape of Hanover, Germany. They had one child:

I. Nina Anderson Pape, born August 29, 1869.

B. Edward Maffett Anderson, second child of Edward Clifford Anderson and Sarah Williamson, was born in Savannah, August 6, 1843. During the Civil War he entered the Confederate States Navy and was a Lieutenant on the C. S. S. Alabama at the time of her battle with the U. S. S. Kearsarge off Cherbourg, France, in 1864, and was among the survivors of that battle who were picked up and saved by the English yacht Deerhound. Since the Civil War he has resided in Savannah, and has remained unmarried.

C. Georgia Anderson, third child of Edward Clifford Anderson and Sarah Williamson, was born in Savannah, September 4, 1846, and died April 2, 1880. She married, February, 1867, Horace Averill Crane, of Savannah, a son of Hermon A. Crane and July Underwood, and who has since remarried. Their children were:

I. William Henry Crane, born November 22, 1867.

II. Sarah Williamson Crane, born December 6, 1871; died May, 1872.

III. Horace Averill Crane, born March 27, 1873.

IV. Edward Anderson Crane, born June 16, 1876.

V. Nina Anderson Crane, born April 14, 1879.

E. Richard Stites Anderson, fifth child (and twin with Sarah W.) of Edward Clifford Anderson and Sarah Williamson, was born in Savannah, August 5, 1852. He married, February 3, 1881, Kate Gookin, of New York. Their children are:

a. Helen Fay Anderson, born September 7, 1883; died May 10, 1890, in childhood.

b. Virginia Anderson, born March 13, 1885.

c. Sallie Williamson Anderson, born November 9, 1886.

d. Edward Clifford Anderson, born August 25, 1889; died January 12, 1890.

F. Sarah Williamson Anderson, sixth child (and twin with Richard S.) of Edward Clifford Anderson and Sarah Williamson, was born in Savannah, August 5, 1852.

a. Jefferson Randolph Anderson, eldest child of Edward Clifford Anderson, Jr., and Jane Margaret Randolph, was born in Savannah, September 4, 1861. He was educated at the University of Virginia and at the University of Gottingen, in Germany, and was graduated from the University of Virginia in June, 1885, with the degree of Bachelor of Law. He entered the practice of law in Savannah, and is at present of the firm of Mackall & Anderson, of that city. He married, November 27, 1895, Anne Page Wilder, only child of Joseph John Wilder, of Savannah, and Georgia Page King (daughter of Hon. Thomas Butler King of St. Simons Island, Ga.). They have one child:

I. Page Randolph Anderson, born August 27, 1899.

b. George Wayne Anderson, second child of Edward Clifford Anderson, Jr., and Jane Margaret Randolph, was born at Edgehill, in Albemarle County, Va., July 10, 1863. He was educated at the University of Virginia, where he took the degree of Bachelor of Law, in June, 1888. He settled in Richmond, Va., where he entered the practice of law, and taking an active interest in military matters, was appointed Colonel of the 70th Virginia Regiment of Volunteers, and is at present a member of the Virginia State Senate. He married, December 21, 1889, Marguerite Burthe, a daughter of Frederick George Burthe, of New Orleans, and Mary A. Nicholas. Their children are:

1. Edward Clifford Anderson, born November 26, 1893.
2. George Wayne Anderson, born June 20, 1896.

d. Margaret Randolph Anderson, fourth child of Edward Clifford Anderson, Jr., and Jane Margaret Randolph, was born in Savannah, August 21, 1866. She married, November 25, 1893, Abbott Lawrence Rotch, of Boston, Mass., a son of Rotch and . Their children are:

I. Elizabeth Rotch, born June, 1895; died July, 1895,
II. Margaret Randolph Rotch, born June 15, 1896.
III. Arthur Rotch, born February 1, 1899.

e. Sarah Anderson, fifth child of Edward Clifford Anderson, Jr., and Jane Margaret Randolph, was born in Savannah, May 21, 1872.

a. Mary Houstoun Anderson, eldest child of Gen. Robert Houstoun Anderson and Sarah Clitz, was born at Fort Walla Walla, Washington Territory (now Oregon), September 16, 1859, and married, March 12, 1878, William Allen, of Richmond, Va., a son of William Orgain Allen. They have no children.

b. Robert Houstoun Anderson, second child of Gen. Robert Houstoun Anderson and Sarah Clitz, was born in Savannah, August 27, 1861, and died in Manilla, Philippine Islands, November 7, 1901. He entered the United States Army in 1884 as a Second Lieutenant of cavalry, but was afterwards transferred to the infantry, and during the Spanish-American War of 1897 had risen to the rank of Captain in the 9th U. S. Infantry. He served with his regiment in the Philippine Islands, and in the Chinese expedition of 1900, and was recommended to be made brevet Major for distinguished gallantry in the battles on the march of the allied troops to Pekin. He returned with his regiment to the Philippines and was stationed on the Island of Samar, where he contracted the illness which terminated his life. He married, January 29, 1890, Fannie Taylor, a daughter of . Their children are:

1. Sallie Clitz Anderson, born March 1, 1891.
2. Kathleen Anderson, born February 1, 1893.

c. Sallie Clitz Anderson, third child of Gen. Robert Houstoun Anderson and Sarah Clitz, was born in Savannah, January 31, 1863, and died March 5, 1883. She married, May 6, 1882, Carl Eglinger, of Germany; left no issue.

b. Frank Bartow Anderson, second child of Major George Wayne Anderson and Katherine Hunter Berrien, was born in Macon, Ga., July 15, 1863. He removed to New York, and at present is Assistant Cashier of the American Exchange National Bank. He married, June 19, 1887, Elizabeth Jadwin, of Brooklyn, N. Y., and had issue.

c. Kate Berrien Anderson, third child of Major George Wayne Anderson and Katherine Hunter Berrien, was born in Savannah, April 25, 1867. She married, July 7, 1891, William Langhorn Wilson, of Savannah, a son of William Law Wilson, of South Carolina. They have no children.

d. Lydia McLane Anderson, fourth child of Major George Wayne Anderson and Katherine Hunter Berrien, was born in Savannah, January 6, 1875.

a. Caroline McDowell Anderson, eldest child of Capt. John Wayne Anderson and Jessie Choisie Wragg, was born in Savannah, March 25, 1867. She married, April 17, 1890, James Fairlie Cooper Myers, of Savannah, a son of Frank Myers, of Atlanta, and Fairlie Cooper. Their children are:

I. John Anderson Myers, born March 1, 1891.
II. Carolyn Cooper Myers, born August 12, 1893.

b. Jessie Anderson, second child of Capt. John Wayne Anderson and Jessie Choisie Wragg, was born in Savannah, October 31, 1869.

a. Clarence Gordon Anderson, Jr., only child of Clarence Gordon Anderson and Florida Lamar, was born in Savannah, February 8, 1873, and is at present in business there.

a. Clifford West Anderson, only child of Clifford Wallace Anderson and Clifford Nephew West, was born in Savannah, April, 1873.

a. Mary Walker Anderson, first child of Clifford Wallace Anderson, by his second wife, Hannah Townsend Walker.

b. Hannah Townsend Anderson, second child of Clifford Wallace Anderson, by his second wife, Hannah Townsend Walker.

ADDENDA

There being some controversy as to the descent of the Jones family of Carolina, the author thinks it proper to make the following statement: Mr. Dunwody Jones claims descent from the family of Pinckney through the marriage of a Jones to a Pinckney. The Colcocks, who also descend from Jones, say there was no such marriage; that they descend from the Brewtons. Mr. Jones claims his record is correct, and that he does not descend from the Brewtons, but from Pinckney. The records of South Carolina prove that the Jones descend from the Brewton family, and it also would appear that the Brewtons descend from the Pinckneys through the marriage of Col. Miles Brewton, whose first wife (the widow of Mathew Porter) was evidently a Pinckney, and through the Brewtons the family of Jones descend from the Pinckneys, which apparently reconciles the controversy. The Wests came direct from England, as stated in West history. Since writing this, Mr. Dunwody Jones has authorized me to make the Jones history conform to that as proved by records and by the Colcock Version.

INDEX

ERRATA

Page 19, last line, read Gilbert Neyle probably married Miss Neville.

Page 63, in note, read Commodore Josiah, not E. F. Tattnall, and Col. Mullryne, not Mullbryne.

Page 205, read Edward M. Anderson, Midshipman.

Page 193, fourth line, read Geo. W. Owens, not Geo. S., married Harriet Parsons.

Page 10, read Thomas P. Bond and Julia Gallie had:

Some say it was Sarah, some Matilda, Fenwick who married Macartan Campbell.

Page 99, third line, read daughters of James Gignilliat and Charlotte, not Caroline, Pepper.

Page 84, note, read Abraham Gignilliat, not Absalom, married Mary De Villé.

Page 103, put d. Elizabeth Gignilliat married John Cooper, Jr. Benj. Williamson married either Eliza or Elizabeth Elliott.

Pages 165 and 182, Eliza Clifford, not Georgia, Anderson, daughter of John W. Anderson and Sarah Ann Houstoun, married Judge Walter S. Chisholm.

Page 99, Charlotte Pepper, not Caroline, who married James Gignilliat.

Page 31, Ann Habersham was born after March, 1786.

The Habergham Family.

References to, and remarks upon, the historical records, by Matthew Henry Habershon, Greenhead Cottage, Chapeltown, near Sheffield, Yorkshire. Born at Rotherham, August 12, 1821.

> "The fairest ancestry on earth
> Without desert is poor,
> And every deed of former worth
> Is but a claim for more."
>
> —HANNAH MORE.

"The consciousness of descent from a long line that has sometimes done well and never done disgracefully is an incentive to a noble life."

—*Besant and Rice, in "My Little Girl.*

February, 1903.

The place which gave a surname to our family, Habergham, was a village with few inhabitants in the 12th century. In a charter dated 31st Edw. III (1358), it is called "Hamletta de Habrincham in villa de Brunley." Before then it had been called Hambrigham, referable, says Whitaker, to the well-known Han or Ham-bridge. "The Hanbridge Water, a small spring which lies between Burnley and Townley, yields," says Charles Leigh, Doctor of Physick, "a natron or natural alcali," in his "Natural History of Lancashire, Cheshire and the Peak in Derbyshire," published in the year 1700.

After being written Habrincham, the hamlet got to be spelt Habringham, and lastly Habergham. "Habergham Eaves," says Baines in 1824, in his Lancashire Gazetteer, "is a large township about four miles in length, and from one to two in breadth. A respectable family flourished at the Hall for four centuries, but John Habergham, the last of the race, dying without issue in 1725, and having by his excesses dissipated his paternal inheritance, the estate came into the hands of George Halsted of Manchester, the mortgagee, by foreclosure, and is now enjoyed by the Halsteds of Rowley.

The word Eaves, appended to Habergham, is said to be from the Anglo-Saxon and means "a tract of ground surrounding a principal mansion, as in Bnshill Eaves."

Habergham Hall was pulled down about the year 1801 and a farm house erected near to where it stood for centuries, near to an oak tree still existing in a very venerable condition, the trunk hollow to the top.

Much that is interesting is recorded by Lancashire historians of the Habergham family. In Whitaker's "History of the Parish of Whilley," is the pedigree mainly transcribed from Christopher Townley's manuscript, which shows that more than once there was a union by marriage of the Haberghams and the Townleys of Townley Hall, a family whose pedigree begins as far back as the time of "King Alfred the Great."

Baines' "History and Directory of Lancashire," published in 1824, contains valuable information of the Habergham family. Habergham Eaves is there mentioned as "a place in the town of Burnley" which, on the evidence of a charter dated 31 Edward III, "gave name to a family of whom we find as early as 1201 three sisters engaged in litigation respecting their possessions in Habringham." The ancient record states that Alina and Sabina de Habringham owe xxs to the King on account of a petition pending in the county court for four bovates of land in Habringham (spelt Hauringham) in which they pray that the plaint may be heard at Westminster.

It has been surmised that those three sisters were daughters of the Matthew de Hambringham to whom Roger de Laci (who died October 1, 1211) gave oxgangs of land in Hambringham, and that the grant may be accounted for by supposing that he was with Roger de Laci and King Richard I in Palestine, but the evidence is not clear as to how he was related to the first name in the Lancashire pedigree of the Haberghams.

This "Matthew de Hambrigham" may have been our ancestor for he may have had a son as well as daughters supposing they were his daughters.

Dr. Whitaker in his "History of the parish of Whulley," says (page 315) the two oxgangs of land granted by Roger de Lacy to Matthew de Hambringham "are in fact the original demense of Habergham Hall," and that he cannot acoount for the omission, in the great inquisition, after the death of Henry de Lacy in 1311," of any mention whatever of those oxgangs of land granted long before by Roger de Lacy.

Christopher Townley's M. M. S. from which Whitaker transcribes the Habergham Hall pedigree mentions the name Peter in a passage worded thus, "Grants the homage and service or Adam, son of Peter de Habringham, in Wardis Relievis, etc." Adam de Habringham is the first name in the pedigree, as Whitaker gives it, tracing the decent from father to son, although previously, from charters without date, occur the names Peter and Geoffrey not actually in rhe pedigree. Regarding this Peter as the father of the Adam at the head of the pedigree, we may suppose htm to be the son of the Matthew associated by Whitaker with "the original demenseof Habringham Hall," but he may have been a brother. Whitaker is silent as to the three sisters, Alina, Sabina and Eugenta, who had the litigation in 1201, referred to in Blaines' History of Lancashire. Those three sisters interfere with the thought of a direct descent from the Matthew the recipient of Roger de Lacy's grant.

How are we to suppose they came to have Latin names? Was their mother a Roman lady, and if she had a son would she be likely to choose Peter for his baptismal name?

The evidence we have that the name of the father of the Adam de Habringham who is at the head of the pedigree was Peter. is supplied by the note attached by a star to the person of that name thus, Peter* and which note is worded as I have stated, "Grants the homage and service of Adam, son of Peter de Habringham, in Wardis Relievis, etc. Townley MSS to which Whitaker adds the remark, "This seems to have been the first Adam, that is, the one at the head of the pedigree. and next to which is another Matthew de Habringham," and then in the next line, "Adam de Habringham VIX 1310." and two younger brothers, "Henry and William de Habringham" who "held lands here of the gift of Henry de Lacy, 1310."

Whitaker, to the Adam who lived in 1310, attaches a note

thus." It is extraordinary that Christopher Townley, who first compiled the pedigree had actually transcribed charters from which I have given these five descents, and yet has omitted them all even the first grantee from Roger de Lacy."

It is doubtful which of the five descents Whitaker refers to. He leaves the problem unsolved as to who was the father of Peter de Habringham.

I am able to say I am of a family of which the first name recorded lived in the reign of Richard Coeur de Lion, although I cannot affirm that I am descended from the Matthew de Hambringham to whom Roger de Lacy, who died in 1211, granted two oxgangs of land in Hambringham, and was probably a crusader. Before him land may have been owned by Haberghams in "Hambrigham." The evidence of charters is unquestionable, which cannot be said of the inferences of Dr. Whitaker, who appears not to have known of the three sisters, Alina, Sabina and Eugenta and their litigation about four bovates ot land in 1201. If he had known this would he have have inferred that the grant of two oxgangs of land to Matthew by Roger de Lacy between the year 1192 when Roger became owner of estates in Lancashire, and the year 1211, when he died, was the original demesne of Habergham Hall? Matthew, the grantee of the two oxgangs, must have been dead before 1201, if the three sisters who quarrelled over the four bovates were his daughters. With him, it is certain they were contemporary at a date between 1192 and 1211, but they may have been his sisters or his aunts, members of a family of which Matthew de Hambrigham was not the first recipient of grants of land, or the first occupant of a hall in the hamlet.

The will of the first member of our family who became resident in the Hallamshire part of Yorkshire, is dated 1541, the 32nd year of the reign of Henry VIII. He died in that year, bequeathing his copyhold and leasehold land at Treeton, near Sheffield, and his armour, "used in the service" of the lord of the manor, the Earl of Shrewsbury, to his eldest son Thomas, whose will was proved in 1556, and shows that all his children were daughters. But he had a brother William, who was evidently the father of the Edward Habergham (spelt and pronounced Haberjam) whose names stands at the head of the Yorkshire pedigree which the late Dr. Samuel Osborne Habershon, when a youth, helped his father to verify by reference to the Register of births, marriages and burials in the possession of the Rector of Handsworth near Sheffield. That Edward Haberjam was buried, as evidenced by the Handsworth register, November 12, 1584. We have all supposed, until I obtained from the British Museum, extracts from the will of Thomas of Treeton, and the will of his son Thomas, that the Edward Haberjam who died in 1584 was the first of the Lancashire family who settled in the Hallamshire part of

Yorkshire. I have discovered that the house where the Treeton church registers were deposited in the 16th century was destroyed by fire, and thus may be accounted for no evidence as to the birthplace of our ancestor Edward.

The pedigree shows that the Handsworth and Rotherham Habershons descend from the said Edward's third son Francis. We knew that Edward's eldest son's name was Robert, who named his son Thomas; but, not knowing that Thomas was the name of Edward's uncle, and of his grandfather, and seeing that the name Robert occurs in the Lancashire pedigree at a date which seemed to indicate that the Lancashire and Yorkshire pedigrees may be joined, we all believed that Robert Habergham, the brother of William Habergham of Habergham Hall, near Burnley, was the father of our Handsworth ancestor Edward. We know now, that we are not descendants of that Robert, but of the Robert of the line above, the younger brother of Hugh Habergham, of Habergham Hall, who in the year 1533, 24th of the reign of Henry VIII, had to do with the rebuilding of a portion of Burnley church, as evidenced by an indenture of that date.

The Harlean Manuscripts in the British Museum I referred to, on January 29th, 1874, to ascertain exactly what was the armourial bearings of the family at Habergham Hall when it branched into Yorkshire.

I found that at the "visitation of Lancashire, etc.," made in 1567, 9th of, of Elizabeth. "Haberiam de Haberiam" bore "Ar. 3 Crosses couped sa." pictured thus (1) without any crest, the crosses black couped on silver ground.

This positive evidence that at the date of the visitation only "three crosses couped" were on the Habergham shield, is important from the point of view of the Yorkshire branch of the family, the descent of which is not from the Habergham Hall Haberghams *after* they began to have for their shield "Argent three pole axes sable, or, three cross crosslets."

Not applicable to a period previously to reign of Elizabeth when there was that "visitation of Lancashire, etc," are the words of Dr. Whitaker, "At Habergham Hall flourished for several centuries a respectable family who bore 'Argent three pole axes sable, or three cross crosslets.' "

As early as the resign of Henry VIII we know that a Thomas of our name was located at Treeton, near Sheffield, who had coat of armour, and his arms would be "Ar. three crosses couped sa." as evidenced by the Harlean Manuscripts.

The crest which we Yorkshire Habershons have been using for about seventy years representing the word *Habergeon* which Nuttall's dictionary says means "a coat of mail or armour to defend the neck and breast," was adopted with the sanction of the Heralds College by Mr. Matthew Habershon, the architect of Bonner's Hall, London, the eldest son of Mr.

Matthew Habershon of the Holmes, near Rotherham, Yorkshire, and grandson of the Matthew Habershon who came from Handsworth to Rotherham in the early part of the eighteenth century, was baptized at Handsworth church as the son of Mahlon Haberjam, and had his name spelt Habersham as seen in an agreement of which a copy is extant. About the time he lived the Handsworth Haberjams began to spell the name Habershon, and on his grave stone in Rotherham churchyard his name is spelt thus, although on the evidence of the Handsworth register of baptisms, he was the son of Mahlon Haberjam.

A shield with three poles axes, I saw in the Harlean MSS., Vol. 1468, page 96-102, as the arms of Haberiam de Haberiam. We may therefore infer that at some uncertain date after the Lancashire "Visitation" in 1567, there was a union of two branches of the family, and that thus may be accounted for the blending of the three crosses and the pole axes on our shield. Perhaps some descendant of the "Henry" or "William de Habringham who held lands the gift of Henry de Lacy in 1310" may have married one of the persons named in the pedigree as descending from their older brother. "Adam de Habringham, VIX 1310." Except in one or two instances the pedigree is silent as to who were the wives of the men in the line of succession of the oldest branch:

Gregson in his "Historical Fragments of Lancashire" is evidential as to what arms can be used by Habershams of the branch of the family which is known to have settled in Yorkshire in the time of Henry VIII, and had a grant of copyhold land from the Earl of Shrewsbury, lord of the manor of Treeton in Hallamshire, for in Gregson's book is to be seen "The coat of arms of the family of Haberjam."

I should be much pleased to have confirmation of the statement of a descendant of James Habersham, the president of Georgia, that he was of the Yorkshire branch of the Habergham family. I should like also to know whether in the Lancashire of Yorkshire pedigree can be properly placed the Rev. Samuel Habergham, who was one of the two thousand ministers ejected from the Episcopal church by the Act of Uniformity in 1662. Of him there is mention in Palmer's "Nonconformist memorial" (vol. 3 p. 286) quoting what Dr. Calamy says about him as a student at Emanuel College, Cambridge, and Vicar of Seylam in Suffolk, and eminent afterwards as a Nonconformist minister.

In Baines' History, Vol. III, p. 305, of the Townleys and the Haberghams there is the following:—"Hapton Park was formerly abundantly stocked with deer, and there are the remains of pitfalls dug for impounding stray deer when the two families of the Townleys and the Haberghams were upon bad terms with each other.."

"Immediately above the south banks of the Gulder in this township is the family mansion of the Haberghams built upon a beautiful knoll commanding an extensive prospect but now occupied as a farm house." The farm house built near the site of the old mansion, is called Habergham Hall. I was there in 1854, and met with an old man, a neighbour, who told me what the old house was like. He said it was like the sketch I showed him, but "had a wing at the back, built of rubble and tile."

The author is pleased to be able to add to the genealogical account of the family of Habershon and Habersham by Matthew Henry Habershon and the tradition of the family that they descended from the ancient family of Habergham, seems well borne out. We know that Governor James Habersham was baptised in St. Mary's, Beverley, Yorkshire, and that he was the son of James Habersham of same place. We also see from the foregoing account that Matthew Habershon, eldest son of Mahlon Habershon, was baptised and had his name spelt Habersham. There can be no doubt now of the two names Habershon and Habersham being identical and descending from the ancient name of Habergham, and we take pleasure from the foregoing in assigning to the Georgia family the arms at the head of this chapter, and in adding to and correcting certain mistakes in the book on the Habershams of Georgia.

The above arms are only to signify a mark of cadency or to differentiate them from the family of Habershon now considered to be of same line.

Dr. S O. Habershon and his son were famous physicians. The former wrote Rev. Barnard Elliott Habersham in 1883 that from the records he obtained the following: (He also sent the arms to him.)

De Hambrigham, in 1211 de Hambrigham, as de Habringham in 1310 and 1459 Habergham in time of Henry VIII. Haberzame and Haberjame in Elizabeth's time. Habergham in 1673, Habersham in 1673, Haberjam and lastly Habershon.

The motto we now use is one adopted by an uncle of mine, "In Deo Confide."

We see then that this old family is one to take pride in and that the illustrious Habersham family of Georgia can now undoubtedly trace to an ancient period and is without doubt one of those entitled to bear arms.

J. G. B. BULLOCH.

Errata, Corrections and Addenda, for History and Genealogy of the Habersham family (Dr. J. G. B. Bulloch)

Page 5. Read:

Hon. Richard Wylly Habersham married Sarah, daughter of Capt. Barnard Elliott and Katherine Hazzard, and had the following children:

(a) Richard West Habersham, married Martha Mathewes, daughter of John Raven Mathewes, of Charleston and Eliza Jenkins.

(b) Rev. Barnard Elliott Habersham, married Harriet Emma Mathewes, sister of above.

(c) in this list and on page 8, should be, not Alex. W. Habersham, but —— Katherine Esther (not Elliott) Habersham, xxxx.

(f) not (c) should be, (and on page 8), Alexander Wylly Habersham; officer in the U. S. Navy, imprisoned at North after '61; and author, xxx.

(g) Francis Bolton (not Barnard) Habersham, M. D. xx.

There was also a James who died young.

On pages 6 and 8, should reverse, and read:

II. Katherine Elliott Milledge xxx.

III. Richard Habersham Milledge xxx.

On page 7:

(a) previously corrected.

(5) Katherine Habersham, married Lawrence.

Page 8, should read:

(b) Rev. Barnard Elliott Habersham and Harriet Emma, daughter of John Raven Mathews, xxx had issue:

(1.) Robert Habersham, Surveyor-General of Oregon, 1896–1901, married Mariquinha, daughter of Dr. Jao G. dos Reis, of Brazil.

(2.) Eliza Ann (Ella) Habersham.

(3.) Richard Wylly Habersham, died xxxx, in 1868. Was a youthful, brave Confederate soldier.

(4.) Francis Elliott Habersham, C. E , died and buried in Portland, Oregon, 1893; married Emma, daughter of N. B. Keene of New Orleans, cotton-broker and Consul of Arg. Rep. At fifteen years of age, in '65, entered earnestly into Confederate service.

I. John Milledge, Capt. of Artillery, C. S. A., xxx, married second, Mary Gresham.

(d) 1. Margaret Rives Habersham, married Emerson.
2. Richard Pollard Habersham, married Eva Smith.
3. Pauline Rives Habersham, married —— Holland.

The second (c) should be (f) Alexander xxx, married Jessie Steele xxx, and had:
1. Alexander Wylly Habersham, married, first Alice Tillson; second Bertha Dorsey.
2. Harry Steele Habersham, married Bessie Stanton.
3. Ed. Heddon Habersham, married Ellen McConnell.
4. Nellie Habersham.

For note to (b,) p. 8, read:

Robert Habersham married Mariquinha dos Reis, and had:
1. R. Emma Habersham.
2. Francis Elliott Habersham.
3. John Pinckney Habersham.
4. Richard Edgar Habersham.
5. Mariquinha dos Reis Habersham.

Frank Habersham, son of Rev. Barnard Elliott Habersham, married Emma Keene and had:
Lydia Habersham—died young.
Edith Habersham.
Lillian Habersham.

Page 8.

(d) 2. Richard Pollard Habersham married Eva Smith and has:
Stephen Habersham.

(f) 1. Alexander Wylly Habersham, married first Alice Tillson and had:
1. Jessie Key Habersham.
2. Alice Steele Habersham.

2. Harry Steele Habersham, married Bessie Stanton, and has:
1. Stanton Habersham.
2. Dorothy Habersham.
3. Elizabeth Habersham.
4. Eleanor Habersham.
5. Catherine Habersham.

3. Edward Heddon Habersham, married Ellen McConnell.

Elliott Habersham, eldest son of Robert Habersham, and grandson of Rev. Barnard Elliott Habersham, married Bertha, Mrs. Dudley, nee Osborne, and has:
1. James Edgar Habersham.
2. Frances Habersham.

The Hazzards, of whom came Katherine Hazzard (see page 5), received land-grant from King Charles, and lived in princely style.

Eliza Jenkins pedigree as submitted to Colonial Dames shows her to be descended from Landgraves Blake and Morton, Susannah Smith and the Wilkinsons, page 7.

MATHEWES.

The ancestor of a branch of the Habersham family was Captain Anthony Mathewes, born in London 1661. The following from the S. C. Gazette is found in the columns of that paper. "August 30, 1735. On Saturday last, died here, Captain Anthony Mathewes, an eminent merchant and settler in this province, who, by his industry and frugality and improvement in mercantile affairs, acquired one of the greatest estates in the country. He first arrived in this Province about the year 1680—now 55 years since and died lamented in the 73rd year of his age and was decently buried Monday last." He had six sons and four daughters:

I. Anthony Mathewes. (Had a daughter, Mrs. Dr. Graeme.)

II. John Mathewes, married Sarah Gibbes.

III. William Mathewes, married second Miss Stanyarne.

IV. George Mathewes, died 1768.

V. Benjamin Mathewes, first married Anne Holmes about Feb. 11, 1745, Maria second Anne Holmes, second daughter of Isaac Holmes and Elizabeth Peronneau.

VI. James Mathewes.

John Mathewes, son of John and Sarah Gibbes, was chancellor, member of Congress and Governor of S. C. He married first about Dec. 8, 1766, Mary, daughter of Wm. Wragg. He married second, Sarah Rutledge. His line ended before his death.

John Mathewes and Sarah Gibbes had also:

2. Lois Mathewes, married Geo. Abbott Hall.
3. Anne Mathewes, married August 23, 1769, Godin Guerard, son of Hon. John Guerard, member of King's Council.
4. Mrs. Heyward.

William Mathewes had as daughters Mrs. (Gen'l) Coffin, and among many other names allied were those of Fraser, Legare, Herbemont Flud and Peronneau, and the name of Coffin appears several times in branches of this large family. We find elsewhere that Captain Thomas Lloyd married Miss Nancy Mathewes and that a Mr John Mathewes (son of James) married Miss Nancy Harvey, a celebrated beauty, who died about August 24, 1769, married about February 15, 1767.

George Mathewes, fourth son of Bejamin, fifth son of Anthony Mathewes and Anne Holmes, was father of John Raven Mathews, Eliza Mathewes (Mrs. Ebenezer Coffin,) and others.

John Raven Mathewes and Eliza Jenkins were the parents of Mrs. Richard W. Habersham, Jr., and Mrs. Barnard Elliott Habersham.

NOTE.—Hon. Isaac Holmes, son of Francis Holmes and Rebecca, moved from Boston to Charleston, S. C. in 1702. He became one of His Majesty's Council. Sarah Holmes, his third daughter, married John Raven. Another John Raven Mathewes, third son of Benjamin Mathewes, son of Andrew of London, married Elizabeth Stanyarne Holmes, daughter of Isaac Holmes. The Holmes were allied to the Bees and others, and descended, we think, from Rev. Archibald Stobo. John Raven Mathewes had an uncle and cousin by same name. See tombstone of Mathewes in Circular church-yard, Charleston. Pages 5 and 7, and b, page 8. Should be John Raven Mathewes not Edward Mathewes.

1. page 7, note. John Barnwell married "Martha" not "Phoebe" Chaplin.

2. page 9. The "B" in the name of Mary Fuller, wife of Rev. John H. Elliott, should be "Barnwell."

3. page 9. The "E" in the name of Ralph Elliott stands for "Emms."

4. page 9. The Rev. Stephen Elliott did not marry the second time "Miss" Sarah Gibbes DeSaussure but "Mrs. Sarah" the widow of Dr. Alexander Ladson, who was born Sarah Gibbes DeSaussure.

5. page 15. The "G" in the name of Mary Barnwell, wife of Bishop Stephen Elliott, stands for "Gibbes," and the "G" in the name of John Barnwell, husband of Emma Elliott also stands for "Gibbes," and the "H" in the name of Esther Elliott stands for "Hutson."

6. page 16. The name of the wife of W. P. Carmichael was "Elizabeth" not "Eliza" and the son Stephen Carmichael, who married Miss Claghorn, had as his middle name "Elliott" and was always called "Elliott."

7. page 16. The full name of the Bishop of Western Texas was "Robert Woodward Barnwell Elliott" and the wife of Hon. William Elliott was not "Phoebe Wright" nor was it "Weight." It was "Waight" and was so spelled from the earliest times.

8. page 16. The name of Dr. John Elliott is "John Barnwell Elliott."

9. page 17. The Rev. James Habersham Elliott had a son by his first wife Harriett Fuller, who died as a boy and whose name was "Thomas Fuller Elliott."

10. page 18. Harriett Elliott, the daughter of the Rev. James H. Elliott by Harriett Fuller, did not marry "Butolph" and has never married at all, but is still alive.

11. page 18. The children of Rev. James B. Elliott by his second wife, were Elizabeth Barnwell, who married James David Buttolph, Emma, Stephen, and Francis Wharton of whom Emma and Stephen died before maturity.

12. page 18. The first husband of Mrs. James H. Elliott was Rev. "Joseph Augustus Shanklin" and not "James."

13. page 18. The middle name ot John G. Barnwell, who married Emma Elliott was "Gibbes," and his son's middle

name was the same, and the middle name of Rev. Stephen E. Barnwell was "Elliott" and of Robert W. Barnwell, "Woodward." The last was Bishop of Alabama and died several weeks ago. His brother's name was James Elliott Barnwell.

14. page 18. The son of Gen. Stephen Elliott was not "Rev. Stephen Elliott" but instead he died as a boy under six years old. The second son was "Henry Stuart Elliott" and the third son "Charles Pinckney Elliott."

15. page 19. One of the daughters of Rev. William Hutson, whose name by the way was "Elizabeth," married Col. Isaac Hayne, the Martyr, who was hanged during the Revolutionary War. You have mentioned her husband as simply "a Hayne." Another Daughter, Esther, married William Hazzard Wigg, not William Hazzard; and one, Mary, married Arthur Peronneau; the daughter who married Gen. John Barnwell was named "Ann."

16. page 19. The first husband of Mary Woodward was Isaac Chardon.

Page 8. The ancestors of the Maxwell's is said to have gone to Pennsylvania in 1748, and that he was from Maxwellton, River Nith, Dumfries, and went to County Down, in Ireland. His sons were James and Audley Maxwell.

Page 39. Dr. J. P. S. Houstoun and Sarah Gilbert Cumming had only four children, and the names of the sons should be James P. and Claude Edward Houstoun.

Page 45. Robert W. Strong and Caroline Neville had Josephine Neville Strong. Her aunt, II. Josephine C. Strong, never married.

Page 49. Alfred Cuthbert and Sarah Jones had only one son, Alfred Cuthbert, who married Anna Davis, and had:

1. Alfred Cuthbert, married Ella Shebbard.
2. Mary Cuthbert.

Page 54. Thomas Cumming was intendant of Augusta 1796, not 1786.

Page 83. Audley Maxwell King was born 1830, not 1820.

Page 85. Should be Anna Livingston Bayard, not Olivia. Dr. Wm. King married Augusta Clayton. Mrs. Grady was Julia King.

Page 93 read Marie Clemens or Clemmons, read also John R. or P. King and Graham W. King.

Page 104 read Frances married Rev. John W. Baker; died in 1856; read also Isabella Julia Pratt.

Page 106 read James not John Pryor Pratt, died in Savannah.

Page 126 and 128. James Stanyarne married first about November 2, 1767, Mrs. Henrietta Raven, relict of Wm. Raven and daughter of Thomas Smith and had 1. James Stanyarne, who married Elizabeth Mary Wilson, and had besides sons, who died before him, four daughters, two of whom lived.

Sarah Daniel married Thomas Boone, and had:

I. Mrs. Schultz.

II. Mary Stanyarne, married Dr. Philip P. Mazyck, and had: Annie M. Mazyck, who married ——— Manigault and had Eliza S. Manigault. Jane and Mary Stanyarne were by the second marriage to a Scott.

Page 132. Ellis. The arms of the family below are:
Cross and Crescents.
Crest, a nude female.

In the Congressional Library there is a work by Wm. Smith Ellis of the Middle Temple on the Ellis' and their branches in which he deduces their descent from the French Kings, and wherein he gives the ancestor who went to England with Wm. the Conqueror. Among these families is one of Stoneacre, in which he makes them descend from Sir Archibald Ellis. These Ellis' bore the same arms as Sir Henry Ellis, and used them as early as time of Edward II. The family is found in Otham County, Kent.

He gives the descent of Sir Henry Ellis, Governor of Georgia, and though we do not know that the Ellis' of South Carolina are the same, is quite significant that the name of Edmund occurs in the family of Stoneacre several times. In 1663 Edmund Ellis was head of the family. Edmund Ellis of Stoneacre, gent, son and heir of Thomas Ellis was baptised at Otham, Dec. 24, 1559 and buried August 2nd, 1615. He married Anne, daughter of Henry Fryor gent. He had a son, Edmund, of Stroud County, Kent, who made his will, died 1652. He was a large land owner and left issue a son.

Note page 132. Thomas Capers will dated 1761, mentions his daughter, wife of Edmund Ellis. Thomas was son of Richard Capers, and married Mary, daughter of Wm. Sadler.

On pages 138 and 139 the author wishes to make the following correction. It is not known who Colonel Miles Brewton married first, but the children were all by first marriage. His second wife, Susannah, was not a Pinckney. His third wife was Mary Legare.

Colonel Miles Brewton by his first marriage had:

I. Robert Brewton, married Millicent Bullock not Bulloch, and had:

(a) Robert Brewton, who married Eleanor.

(b) Mary Brewton married Joseph Jones.

(c) Elizabeth Brewton married Munford Milner.

Mary Brewton and Joseph Jones had:

I. Joseph Jones died.

II. John Jones married Mary Sharp.

III. Millicent Jones married John Colcock.

The Jones' though related to the Pinckneys, do not descend from them. This is to correct certain errors on pages 138 and 139.

Colonel Miles Brewton had also these given on page 139. Page 51 read Charles not Charles Cotesworth.

BARRINGTON—COOK—WILLIAMS.

The information about the Barringtons, Cooks and Williams families of Georgia seems to be authentic, and it appears that Wm. Cook, an Englishman, had been a clerk with his uncle, Mr. Frazer, and a cousin, Mr. Lane, the firm of Lane, Lord & Frazer, being a large and wealthy one in London, sending out Mr. Cook to act as agent, who took in as partner, Mr. Wm. Scarborough, also related to same firm in same manner as Mr. Cook. Mr. Cook met Miss Barrington at Williamsburg, Va., where she had been staying enjoying the society of that cultivated community. She was a first cousin of Mr. Cooks, and he drove here to her fathers from Virginia to San Savilla Bluff, in Georgia, where her father lived, accompanied by his brother-in-law, Lieutenant-Colonel Jay Williams of the British army. Miss Barrington's father was Lieutenant-Colonel Wm. Barrington of the British army, and John Cook, uncle of Wm. Cook, William Williams, who came with Gen. Oglethorpe to Georgia, not in regular army, but with a regiment of troops and Thomas Liles, a cousin also, as aid to Gen. Oglethorpe, all were cousins to Gen. Oglethorpe and to each other. Wm. Cook owned 70,000 acres of land in Camden County, Georgia, and had a large claim against the Spaniards for property seized by them. He was imprisoned in Moro Castle, Matanzas, Cuba, and there was quite a correspondence in regard to his case. Page 35 and 38. Though there was a Josiah, the ancestor of the Barrington, was said to be Lieutenant-Colonel Wm. Barrington. Page 30 read Edmund not Edward Pendleton Rogers. Page 209 read Elizabeth Clifford, daughter of Thomas Clifford, and Mary, daughter of ——— .

Page 24, Curtis. John Curtis was a large landed proprietor of Kent County, Delaware, then a part of Pennsylvania. He was member of Colonial Assembly and a member of Penn's Council.

Page 178. Dr. Lewis Johnston born 1735, was member of the King's Council and sided with the mother country, and his family went to Jamaica. Several of his sons were in the British army as officers, and thus eventually went to Nova Scotia, where the descendants rose to high distinction. See book by Elizabeth Lichenstein Johnston. A branch of the Savannah family went to Washington, D. C., where they stood high as physicians.

Page 59, "Son of Joseph Bryan and Mrs. Murray," Should be: Son of Joseph Bryan and ———

Page 174. "Dr. Thomas P. Screven and Adelaide V. Moore had: †1. Ellen S. Screven, married W. W. Gordon." Should be: Thomas F. Screven and Adelaide V. D. Moore had: 1. Richard Moore Screven. 2. John Screven married Mary G.

Bond, daughter of Thomas P. Bond and Julia Floyd Gallie.

†Ellen Screven is the daughter of George P. Screven No. IV.

Page 199. "IX. James Bryan married (March 18, 1790,) Elizabeth, the daughter of James Langley and Elizabeth Polhill. James Bryan and Elizabeth Langley had: 1. Ann Bryan, born April 29, 1791, married. 2. Jane Bryan, born February 22, 1802, died June 1, 1881, married." This James Bryan is said to have died December 20, 1832, and his wife, Elizabeth Bryan, died May 5, 1809. A recent examination of the records in the Superior Court and Court of Ordinary in Savannah, Ga., has developed the fact that the above statement is not true when applied to James Bryan, the son of Jonathan Bryan, and the proof is shown by the following references, viz: Superior Court, Chatham Co., Ga., Minute B'k F., May 29, 1790, in regard to "James Bryan of Brampton." Also B'k B., Feb. 12, and Aug. 14, 1795: Minute B'k C, April 6 and 18, 1796, in regard to "Joseph Bryan, nephew of James Bryan," and to "Hannah Houstoun and Mary Wylly, sisters to James Bryan." Court of Ordinary, March 27, 1797, as to appointment of "Joseph Bryan Admr. Est. of James Bryan, of Chatham Co., deceased." Superior Court, Dec. 19, 1800, "Ann Bryan vs. Jos. Bryan, et. al. in equity." Jan. 8, 1807. "David Middleton and Ann, wife of the said David (formerly Ann Bryan, wife of James Bryan, deceased), to Joseph Bryan, Hannah Houstoun and Mary Wylly, both widows," in regard to the settlement of the estate of James Bryan, deceased, and record that Ann Middleton, widow, bought a house and lot in Savannah in 1816. As will be seen by reference to the genealogy, under the head of "Bryan," published in the "History and Genealogy of the Habersham and other Southern Families." James Bryan, the son of Jonathan Bryan, was the only James Bryan, who was descended from Joseph Bryan and Janet Cochran, of South Carolina, and the above records prove that his wife was Ann Bryan (family name unknown) and not Elizabeth Langley. James Bryan, the son of Jonathan Bryan, and Ann, his only wife, left no issue.

Page 174. "4. Maj. Thomas Screven married Bessie Lawton." Should be: Maj. Thomas Screven married Emily A. Lawton.

The above corrections are made by Thomas F. Screven.

SAVANNAH, GA., April 15, 1902.

Page 19, last line, read: son of Gilbert Neyle and Miss Neville. (?)

Page 25, Simkins, not Simpkins.

" 35, John Williams, not William.

Page 56, David Adams was without doubt son of Nathaniel 3d.

Page 63, last line, Commodore Josiah, not E. F. Tatnall.

" 81, Roswell was son of Timothy King the first.

Page 99, line 4, daughters of James Gignilliat and Charlotte Pepper.

Page 132, Richard Ellis must have married first Elizabeth Green, and second Miss Hogg; last, mother of Mrs. de Treville.

Page 172, line 25: and Alice, not Mary, daughter of Col. Richard Bedon.

Page 200, Benj. Williamson married Eliza Elliott.

Page 205, line 5: Edward M., not C., midshipman on Alabama.

Page 63, IV. Called by some, Matilda: by others, Sarah Fenwick. There may have been two of them, tho' the Jones say it was Sarah.

Page 174, Dr. Thomas F. Screven, not P., had also Richard Screven who died.

Page 165, line 25: John Dennis of Brunswide, N. J., not Brunswick. He had I. Col. Richard Dennis and three daughters, Sarah C., Elizabeth, and Margaret Dennis.

James Gignilliat and Charlotte Pepper had also Elizabeth who married Col. John Cooper. See pages 99 and 103.

Page 120, line 2: Lieutenant Pierre, and not St. Pierre Mercier.

Page 97, Note. Ramsay, not Ramsey.

Katherine Elliott Habersham should by sign be g, not c, and be Katherine as on page 8. See pages 5 and 8. Not sure as to marriage of Margaret Lesesne to one mentioned: might be Matthewes.

Page 167, line 3 from bottom: and her nephew.

Page 146, Eliza Screven Hart was daughter of John Hart, and Mary Screven daughter of Gen. James Screven and Mary Odingsell, son of James Screven and Mary Hyrne Smith, etc. See p. 171.

Page 164, line 11, Madeline Dennis married John Postell (not John Posey) Williamson.

Page 165, line 14, Godin Guerard married Anne Mathewes, daughter of John Mathewes and Sarah Gibbes. Peter Guerard married 1st Elizabeth Haist, married 2nd Harriet Dennis.

V. Lois not Louis Guerard.

Page 165, Harriott not Harriett Guerard, page 167, Harriett not Harriott Guerard.

Page 168. Champernowne Elliott is said to have married a Miss Elliott, daughter of Wm. Elliott, and his daughter Elizabeth to have married Benj. Williamson, the latter evidently also married Elizabeth, a daughter of Robert Elliott.

Page 143, John Jones was son of Joseph Jones and Mary Brewton, not Pinckney.

Edward M. Habersham and Emily Miller had:

I. Edward M. Habersham.

II. Annie Righton Habersham.

Margaret Habersham.

Audley Maxwell member of first General Assembly in Georgia had James Maxwell who married and had Audley Maxwell, who married Mary Stevens, and had Julia Maxwell who married James Roswell King.

Lightning Source UK Ltd.
Milton Keynes UK
UKHW021143100820
367992UK00006B/1478